In Praise of Speaking

Copyright © 2017 by Catriona Hanley

All rights reserved. No part of this book may be reproduced or transmitted in any form or by any means, electronic or mechanical, including photocopy, recording, or any information storage and retrieval system, without prior permission from the publisher (except by reviewers who may quote brief passages).

First Edition

Printed in the United States of America

Paperback ISBN: 978-1-934074-79-4

Design: Elizabeth Nirenberg and Apprentice House
Cover photo by Catriona Hanley

Apprentice House Press
Loyola University Maryland
4501 N. Charles Street
Baltimore, MD 21210
410.617.5265 • 410.617.2198 (fax)
www.ApprenticeHouse.com
info@ApprenticeHouse.om

To Adriaan
First with love, and then with gratitude for what you've taught me:
unyielding hope, infinite responsibility, undying trust,
the possibility of faith.

…Now thinking in itself is concerned with that
which is in itself best, and thinking in the highest sense with that
which is in the highest sense best…
— Aristotle *Metaphysics* Lambda

CONTENTS

Acknowledgements 1
Foreword 3

PART ONE: IN PRAISE OF SPEAKING: READING, WRITING, TEACHING, DISCUSSING

Introduction to Baltimore Symposium 9
Preface 11
Introduction of the Speaker 15

Adriaan Peperzak / Teaching as Learning 21
Greg Clark / Phenomenology of Invitation 35
Marjolein Oele / Philosophy and Friendship 45
Corinne M. Painter / The Place of Philosophy: The Importance of Socratic
    Questioning in Education 59
Colin Anderson / Is This D/Desire? 81
Cationa Hanley / Jesus, Republicans, Peperzak and Me:
    Reflections on Hope, Gratitude and Trust 93
Kristi Sweet / Orienting Oneself In Kant: Reflections On Adriaan Peperzak
    as a Philosopher and Teacher 109
Norman Wirzba / The Truth of Soil: Philosophizing in the Garden ...119
Ryan D. Madison / Teaching and the Active Life According to St. Thomas ...133
Brent Adkins / Jacobi's Revenge: Deleuze's Critique of Hegel 154
Adriaan Peperzak / Responses to Symposiasts 169

PART TWO: IN PRAISE OF SPEAKING: LIVING WITH PHILOSOPHY

Adriaan Peperzak / Introduction to Chicago Symposium 187
Catriona Hanley / Speaking (Listening, Hearing, Conversing) 189
Giancarlo Tarantino / The Spirit of Gratitude 191
Adriaan Peperzak / Epistolary 193
Catriona Hanley / Overview: What was Said in Chicago? 199

21 Short Pieces on the Theme: Living with Philosophy
Various Contributors..209

Not the Last Word
Norman Wirzba, Adriaan Peperzak / Concluding Toasts 305
Catriona Hanley, Adriaan Peperzak / Not the Last Word....................307

Contributors 309
Adriaan Peperzak Biography...311

Generating in beauty...
(Plato, *Symposium*, 206 E)

Thank you, Catriona – and all who assisted you – for commemorating these traces of the philosophical events that we enjoyed together from Baltimore to Chicago.
—*Adriaan Peperzak*

ACKNOWLEDGEMENTS

§

Catriona Hanley

Thanks to all the contributors to this volume for your inspiring thoughts and words. A special thanks to those who attended the first Symposium for their endless patience with the process: they waited long but with nary a complaint.

Thanks to Thomas McCreight, who was taxed and yet still brought me perfect cups of tea. To Alec, for his help this summer in keeping me motivated through the clever use of annoyance. To Susan Fishbein: I could not have done it without your calling me out again and again over the course of years, while always making it seem possible to emerge into the light. To Aron Reppman, for sweet support at crucial moments. To many friends and colleagues, unnamed here, who helped along the way.

Many thanks to Angela Peperzak for her friendship and support, for helping these two symposia happen, and for meeting me with Adriaan at the Art Institute whenever I come to Chicago.

Thanks to Lisa Flaherty, for moral and tactical support. Her extraordinary organizational skills, her dedication to the details of a task and her big heart made the initial Symposium in Baltimore a grand success. Thanks to Randy Newman, Peperzak's assistant, who skillfully handled logistics in Chicago, and to the impressive Chicago student organizers, Justin Nordin, Jean Clifford, and especially

Giancarlo Tarantino.

Thanks to Elizabeth Nirenberg, the senior student at Loyola who initially took on the project of editing the book—then based solely on the Baltimore Symposium-- for Apprentice House Press. Her creative imagination was essential to my envisioning the book, even if we didn't quite finish before she graduated.

And oh: a huge thanks to Kevin Atticks, Director of Apprentice House Press at Loyola University Maryland. He maintained belief in and support for this project through many frustrations, complications and iterations. Always encouraging and accommodating, he not only stuck with me, but put up with me, actually agreeing last April (2016) to accept the addition of another of a whole new set of writings based on the Chicago Symposium to the original volume. His creative suggestions and expert editing transformed the manuscript I initially brought to him: from a box of many broken pieces he made it into a coherent finished jigsaw. Thank you.

Many thanks also to Loyola University Maryland, particularly the Center for the Humanities, which provided major funding for the Baltimore Symposium in 2009. Thanks also to the Department of Philosophy, the Center for Community Service and Justice, and the office of the Dean of Arts and Sciences for their support.

Gaps, errors, repetitions, omissions and all other manner of mistakes are sure to come to light as this book enters the world. I take responsibility for all of these, and apologize in advance for any inconsistencies.

FOREWORD

§

Catriona Hanley

This book has been a long time brewing and stewing. In 2009, the year Adriaan Peperzak was to have his 80th birthday, I thought to celebrate him and his thinking. Initially I imagined a *festschrift*, with well-established scholars contributing articles to a volume in his honour. But when I called Adriaan for a few hints on who to include in this prestigious collection, he gently made it clear that a dry book of essays was not at all how he would like to be fêted.

For Adriaan, it was most important to celebrate his pedagogical relationship with his doctoral students, and to somehow trace how his former students had developed their own thinking in subsequent years. He longed to continue the conversations that he had had with us over the years, from when, as our dissertation director and philosophical mentor, he knew the pathways of our thinking very well, to later years as we entered the professional world of academic philosophy, now engaging students of our own.

The more I thought about it, the more it seemed to match the spirit of Peperzak's teachings to do something much more collaborative, much more conversational in character. Instead of a *festschrift* then, I organized a symposium at my home university, Loyola University Maryland. We invited a group of Adriaan's former doctoral students to write a reflection on the theme "In Praise of

Speaking: Reading, Writing, Thinking, Discussing", and they gathered enthusiastically in Baltimore to present, to listen and above all, to discuss. Adriaan presented a more formal talk to the University on the theme "Teaching as Learning", and that gave us an extra edge to our discussions.

My hope was to find a publisher for our written work, and thus to sneak a *festschrift* in the back door. And then I found the most appropriate press possible for our project at my front door, one that was both very selective and focused on pedagogy: Apprentice House press. A note from their website:

> *Apprentice House is the nation's first entirely student-managed book publisher. Students at Loyola University Maryland are responsible for every aspect of the publishing process, from acquisitions to design and publication of every book. Our mission is, first and foremost, to educate students about the book publishing process.*

Apprentice House took up my prospectus, and I was matched with an excellent student, Elizabeth Nirenberg. But things happened in our lives and the world so that the project was endlessly delayed. By the time Adriaan, now 86, reluctantly agreed to retire after the Fall semester of 2015, I'd almost given up.

Meanwhile, Peperzak's doctoral students at Loyola University Chicago wanted to honour him, and mark his retirement. They organized a great discussion-based symposium in April of 2016. Participants were asked to write a short piece offering a few reflections on the theme, "Living with Philosophy", and these were shared in advance. No papers were read during the course of the "free" Symposium discussions: instead discussions were organized around wide themes. It was a risky experiment, and a huge success. Worth noting, all of the participants in the Baltimore sessions were present in Chicago – no small tribute to the dedication this man inspires in his students.

The energy of those student organizers, as well as the intellectual excitement of the Chicago symposium event got me back to work--with a new idea. Kevin Atticks, the endlessly patient director of

Apprentice House, agreed to include these new contributions in the originally planned volume. Each short essay in Part II of this book is written in a raw, open, nontraditionally academic style.

The stark contract between the rather formal papers in Part I and the more spontaneous offerings of Part II is intentional. Adriaan Peperzak always made clear the necessity for students to read texts—original texts, preferably in the original language, and without guidance from "handbooks." But all this he saw as preparatory work to the highest possibility of philosophical study: conversation.

The papers and musings presented here reflect both the serious scholarly foundation that Adriaan demanded of his students, and the delightful and playful possibilities of discourse among philosophical friends and equals.

INTRODUCTORY REMARKS

INTRODUCTION TO BALTIMORE SYMPOSIUM
§

Catriona Hanley

The theme of the gathering in Baltimore is not primarily or directly Peperzak's extensive opus, but rather some of the constantly renewed tropes in his eighty years of thinking. Much of his thought concerns the relationship between reading, writing, speaking, and teaching, and the role of conversation in coming to understand. As former students honoring our beloved teacher, the nature of dialogue and the activity of teaching seem appropriate to emphasize in our conversations, as well as how we have developed our own thinking in the wake of his teaching us.

Peperzak's work is also very much centred on the issue of the meeting of philosophy and faith, or more precisely the confrontation and reconciliation between supposedly presuppositionless rational philosophical thought and the demands of active faith, particularly Christian faith. Plato, Augustine and Levinas are among his greatest philosophical friends, while he continues to admire Hegel and Heidegger as the greatest challengers.

Some of the contributors to the symposium chose to write directly on one or another of these philosophers, others addressed the theme more directly, still others wrote about the influence of Peperzak's thinking on their own, and about the dialogue they have somehow maintained with him through their intellectual flowering. In the spirit of dialogue, Peperzak suggested he formally respond to each of the symposiasts after the event; I then asked each person to respond to that response, and also to add a short preface in which a general reflection on the symposium would be offered. The form of each paper then is preface, formal paper, and response to Peperzak's remarks. For the sake of cohesion, Peperzak's responses are altogether in a separate section. His first contribution, "Teaching as Learning" was delivered as a lecture to the entire university.

Collected here then, are papers delivered in Adriaan's honour and for his enjoyment, as well as for ours. But I hope also… through all the essays gathered here, an interesting and challenging pathway, and one that reveals something of Peperzak's wisdom.

Finally, I hope that these writings might serve to enflame conversation among the small but dedicated circle gathered here to celebrate Peperzak's life and works, on the occasion of his eightieth birthday. Addressing to… directing towards: Adriaan taught his students that all meaningful text is address. We write to someone, talk to someone; we send a text or a link to someone. And we express love and gratitude to someone. In this case, to our beloved mentor, Adriaan Peperzak. Happy Birthday.

PREFACE
§

Catriona Hanley

Hope, trust and gratitude: this trio of virtues are at the centre of Adriaan Peperzak's thought. For him, they are the concrete expression of faith, where faith is understood not as doxa, but as orientation to the Good, to the Infinite. Faith expresses itself concretely in love for all others, and intellectually in the adequate orientation of philosophical thought to that which lies beyond its thematizable scope. Genuine thought, oriented by the Good, requires commitment to truth, and engagement in personalized participation in communication with others. A genuine search for wisdom takes place as conversation: it addresses the universally human in each individual or group, it questions assumptions common to the group, it is dialogical, and it respects the unicity of the individuals listening. Philosophical thinking, Peperzak holds, requires that you be attuned to the uniqueness of your human life, oriented to the good, open to the other before you. It requires faith: hope, trust and gratitude.

Adriaan Peperzak committed to Loyola University Chicago the same year I did, and with similar culture shock. He had spent some time in Chicago already, but was now faced with the reality that he and his wife Angela were actually going to live in the States, probably for years. Of course he was happy to have found a good position at a supportive institution where he could continue his work, his teaching, his writing, his conversations.

Meanwhile, I came to ground in Chicago with an MA in hand, set to do my doctoral studies after spending seven or eight months of wandering. A couple of months before getting to Chicago, I'd been meandering around and about East and Central Africa, from Kenya to Zimbabwe, from Zambia to Rwanda and Burundi, mostly just by myself, taking local transport or hitchhiking.

Gratitude was foremost in my mind as I arrived in Chicago on scholarship, not, I confess, so much to the University, but rather to the path I'd trodden the previous year that had made my mind free and my spirit ready to study. I wanted to express gratitude to those among the lovely people I met in so many countries who, though they had almost nothing material, were both insistent upon sharing and tremendously grateful at the opportunity to share. It was hard to accept food from people who did not have enough for themselves or their children; hard to accept shelter from those who offered me a place on the floor under the thatched straw roof of a mud hut, from those who crowded curious children together in sleep so as to give me a small space of my own in the corner. But I came to learn that saying "yes" to an offer of hospitality is to grant dignity and respect to the one who offers, and that dignity and respect weigh more than physical need.

Loyola University Chicago offered me hospitality in the form of scholarships and funding, and welcomed me very nicely. I arrived in Chicago nearly broke, and stayed for the first couple of weeks of the semester in a rather seedy "transients welcome" hotel. It took me a while to realize what the main business of the hotel was (don't ask), beyond the obvious raising of a cockroach farm and shelter, with itinerant mice invited. After a conversation or two, the Dean's office advanced me money to help me cover my first month's rent in a real apartment, where I was able to farm cockroaches all on my own. The real problem was that I was not prepared for a housing system that would require the tenant to come up with two months rent in advance. Tough on those who live month to month: and I am grateful to Loyola Chicago for providing the loan.

It seemed easy then to be grateful for concrete things, for love, for health, for having a good mind and a strong body, for the leisure of doing philosophy. Even more, it was easy to be grateful for being born into privilege in a world of hunger and deprivation, grateful for my existence. But what of those others who were not so lucky? Doesn't their misery make a mockery out of my gratitude? And if I am grateful, who is there to thank? If there is such a thing as existential gratitude, to whom is it addressed? In joyful moments, I called it the universe.

Similarly, trusting in the goodness of the local folk on the African continent, or in any of the other places I'd travelled was not hard. Trusting in the universe, having faith that things would turn out all right was quite easy most of the time—at least for my own self. But it is so much harder to trust on a larger scale. There is so much blind and deliberate betrayal of the wealthy towards the poor. The powerful spread the lie that nothing is wrong with our disastrous current economic, social, political, environmental models. Can the millions of people born to injustice, to excruciating poverty, to war, terror and torment be expected to trust in goodness? Can they be existentially trusting, trusting in the universe to unfold as it should?

Again, it is one thing to hope for change when change seems likely, or even possible. Easy to hope, until the situation is hopeless. For so many, there is little reason to hope. And if I hope despite, what does that entail? If I express this hope in cries or in prayer, who might be listening? The universe?

It is a struggle to have faith. It is hard to find an answer to Ivan Karamazov. While I try to be kind and even grateful to all the Alyoshas that I meet, like Ivan, I want to challenge them. How can they not see how stuck we are, how corrupt the world is? Like so many of us looking at the world situation, I struggle with despair.

In Adriaan, I found a soul who shared/shares my worries about the world, but who nonetheless has hope and trust and gratitude. Though I cannot pretend to have absorbed all his lessons about the net of trust, and though I cannot seem to "let go" to the promise of hope, still, the special light that surrounds my Doktorvater keeps me trying even now. Adriaan is more Zossima than Alyosha, though it seems to me that he has, quite delightfully, preserved the wonder and innocence of the young novice (along with a much better sense of humour). But mixed in with all the slugs and snails and puppy dog tails is a rather larger share of Ivan than would seem appropriate for a man in his position. Thank God for the inappropriate. I'm grateful for that.

INTRODUCTION TO THE SPEAKER

§

Catriona Hanley

I am, I confess, still rather intimidated by Adriaan Peperzak. I phrase this as a confession, since I know he would not want this to be so. From our first encounter at Loyola University Chicago 18 years ago, Adriaan treated me as he did all his students who showed interest in and excitement about philosophy—a philosophical partner, a co-seeker, a fellow traveler on the path. I realize now that this was a conscious or unconscious enactment of the Levinasian dictum, to understand the indebtedness each individual has to every other, to see the stranger's needs as superior to one's own, to encounter the Other as always above you.

Adriaan Peperzak is, for those of us gathered in his honour today, a teacher. He is a real teacher, not just one in name, not just someone who fits the descriptor, not as some little "add-on" to his role as professor. No. Adriaan *teaches*. He is a wonderful teacher, who has inspired (and this is no mere hyperbole) generations of students. Only a few of the hundreds of students he has mentored over the decade-long career as are able to be present here today to help celebrate a rather important birthday for Adriaan on July third of this year. But it is worth mentioning that every single former student of Adriaan's who I invited to come today—at his or her own expense, I might add-- responded immediately, pretty much within a few hours of getting the invitational email. The two or three who were unable to come sent genuine regrets: Steve Werlin, engaged in humanitarian aid in Haiti, Tom Bowen, caught up in his many teaching and professorial duties, Cynthia Brincat, now an obstetrician and medical researcher.

But let's back up from that. "Peperzakian" is the wrong term for those of us inspired by his thinking, since Adriaan was not interested in converting us to his way of thinking, as if he had an edge on truth. Rather, he patiently showed us how to think, how to interpret texts, how to see the correlation between our own individual human struggles both existential and spiritual, and the difficult works and thoughts of those humans who, before our time, had struggled with the same human problems.

Peperzak taught us that there was a right and a wrong way to interpret texts, but that the right way was precisely not simply to engage in an effort to "get it right", as if there were one fixed definitive meaning, a secret code or entry point for written words, one that needed to be uncovered. Instead, he showed us how to enter into dialogue with a text, how to listen to what those before us have written, and how to begin to respond adequately to what we heard. We all, his former PhD students, remember staggering out of Adrian's lectures feeling a kind of intellectual elation. I would emerge from class uplifted, awakened and filled with a certain peace—and then rush home to read more. Adriaan never insisted that we read (that was taken for granted), but he propelled us to enjoy a text, to revel in the wonderful intellectual and spiritual exercise of entering a conversation with an author.

As Adriaan taught us to converse with a text, so also he showed us how to dialogue with each other. Adriaan and his wife Angela invited us often to their home for "musical afternoons", where those of us who played instruments or sang would share their efforts with each other. I remember many afternoons of putting books aside to practice my poor neglected flute, readying for a musical afternoon. I remember my brother, a clarinet player of particular sensitivity, visiting me in Chicago, and being invited up to the Peperzaks along with my good friend Anya, a Russian pianist/accompanist. It was a veritable *salon* there in Wilmette! Those unschooled in music would present poetry they had written, or present poems that inspired them. Adriaan, an accomplished pianist, would fill us with his musical interpretations.

And then Angela would sing, Angela, who, with her beautiful operatic voice would take us soaring, accompanied by Adriaan on the piano. Finally we would eat together the banquet Angela had prepared, and we would converse. And then it all made sense: this was the practice of philosophy

Adriaan Peperzak famously starts to teach his students to embrace the practice of philosophy on the first day of class. This is when he hands out file cards, and asks students to list the languages they speak, read and write, the courses they have taken, their philosophical formation, their mentors, philosophers they know "well", musical instruments they play, and so forth. He imbues the students with the sense that philosophy is not just parroting dead ideas, but living in the light of ideas, ever-renewing the human conversation, always orienting oneself, one's thinking, one's life to the Good.

When I wrote out my file card on the first day of the first class with Adriaan, I spoke of my wise and beloved thesis director, M. Bertrand Rioux, who guided me through my master's degree at the Université de Montréal. Not only did he help me in my efforts to understand Aristotle, Aquinas and contemporary French philosophy, but he was patient and kind as I grappled with the turbulence of life in my twenties.

After the next class, Adriaan took me aside. How wonderful to learn that he and M. Rioux and he had been at the Sorbonne together as students! Both did PhD's under Paul Ricoeur; they had been contemporaries and friends, and, from what I understood, sparring partners. That was it... somehow, I was suddenly switched in my assignment of TA from Frank Yartz to Adriaan Peperzak.

I have always felt grateful for the strange set of coincidences that led me to work with Adriaan—our shared initiation into the ways of the Big City, American style, and our shared fond relationship with Bertrand Rioux. And Gratitude is really the biggest theme of this gathering, the gratitude of Peperzak's students for what he has given us in our development as thinkers and as human beings.

PART ONE
In Praise of Speaking: Reading, Writing, Teaching, Discussing

TEACHING AS LEARNING

§

Adriaan Peperzak

My first appointment as full professor in philosophy at the University of Utrecht burdened me with the task of teaching not only the history of modern and contemporary philosophy, but also several thematic disciplines, such as philosophical anthropology, social philosophy, and metaphysics. An enormous task, which, of course, I could not fulfill in any satisfactory way. It forced me, however, to think about the question of how I could take responsibility for making our students familiar with the world of philosophy. My own philosophical education in a Franciscan friary and the Universities of Leuven and Paris had emphasized the history of philosophy from the pre-Socratics through Plotinus and Medieval philosophy, to Husserl, Scheler, Heidegger, Marcel, Sartre, Merleau-Ponty and Ricoeur. Since, in Utrecht, other professors took care of Ancient and Medieval philosophy, I decided to make modern philosophy the first pillar of the program I would offer, to begin with Descartes, Kant, and Hegel. While intensely studying again Kant's *Critique of Pure Reason*, now for the third time, and the secondary literature on that monument of thought, I realized more sharply than before how little I really knew about Kant, the 18th century context from which his revolution emerged, and the ramifications that sprang from it. Already during the preparation of my doctoral dissertation on Hegel, I had been aware that I knew only a few fragments of philosophy's history, but I promised myself that during each following year

I would study another classic of modern philosophy, such as Hobbes, Spinoza, Leibniz, Hume, and so on. The various appointments I have had the fortune to receive have given me the opportunity to combine my teaching with year-long scrutinizing of great classics, and especially of Plato, Aristotle, Plotinus, Aquinas, Descartes, Kant, Fichte, Hegel, Marx, Nietzsche, and Heidegger, but it quickly became apparent that one year of acquaintance is far too short to absorb and think through what each of the great thinkers offers, while also relating them to one another and to the questions we need to ask in our own time and situation. I have always found this fact more sad than the other impossibility of not being able to read the current streams of thematic literature about epistemology, anthropology, social philosophy, metaphysics, and the philosophy of history. Parts of this literature bored me because I found it endlessly repetitious; part of it pales when compared to the excitement that issues from reading the classics; and part of it emerges from presuppositions that seem improbable or false to someone who, in Leuven and Paris, has been trained in phenomenology.

Is my philosophical upbringing responsible for my emphasis on the classics (which, is not exactly the same as an emphasis on history) or can a preference for the history of philosophy over thematic studies be justified on philosophical grounds?

To tell the truth, it is not primarily the academic and typically European education I have received, which has marked my personal bent. It was the study of Plato's dialogues, and foremost of all, of his *Symposium*, parts of which we had to translate in high school, that made me fall in love with Diotima's hymn to *Eros*, as reported and explained by Socrates and our teacher, O. Damsté, to both of whom I will remain eternally grateful. I believe that this, together with another, markedly religious, experience that befell me around the same time, have determined my main orientation to this day, including the orientation of my thinking, which, even earlier, had been touched by another teacher's speaking to us about philosophy in relation to music and literature.

Why do I tell you this? Do such personal experiences have anything to do with teaching philosophy? They certainly have a lot to do with the practice of philosophy, if this practice cannot be separated from the way in which a philosopher's life is, inspired, oriented, and conducted. If philosophy is an integral element of the existential experiment or adventure we call a human life, it is indubitable that life's most serious concerns – including, in the first place, its "care of itself"[1] – cannot be ignored in any analysis of the philosophy it issues. However, a philosopher must have enough reflexive distance to be aware of the difference between an individual's own existentially and historically triggered experiences, on the one hand, and the universality (or the potentially universal validity) of intuitions that can express themselves in a variety of existential manifestations, on the other.[2] What Diotima, the priestess of Zeus's temple in Dodona, reveals about the human heart can be experienced by anyone, I trust, but others may remain unimpressed in reading her hymn on the ascent of love, because they are already inspired and affected or caught by other revelations that mark their universe differently. Perhaps *Eros* plays a subordinate, dormant, or sidelined role in their life, or their thought is more fascinated by honor, fame, might, money, or holiness.

Much could and should be said, described, discussed about the central inspiration and the basic orientation of each singular philosopher's thinking. As basic and central, they are not only inexhaustible but also deep and deeply hidden, which demands extra efforts, or even a conversion, to become aware of them. Their hiddenness easily causes misunderstandings and contradictions on more superficial levels of awareness and discussion (as is shown, for example, in the first five discourses of the *Banquet* and the behavior of Alcibiades towards its end) and such misunderstandings cannot be solved directly, by comparison or confrontation of *eros* with other deep orientations, because of its originary, i.e., archi-archaic, character, which inevitably withdraws into darkness, when sought by direct perception, insight, or fully enlightened description.

Before we pursue our reflection about inspiration and orientation, however, let's focus on the teacher, who, notwithstanding personal pref-

---

1 *Meletē heautou,* cf. Plato, *Alcibiades I,* 127b ff.
2 Such as a decisive *epoptia,* revelation, shock, illumination, inspiration, or emotion.

erences, is responsible for a variety of students who either have already found, or are still searching for their own most profound passion. To simplify the questions that arise from encounters between various teachers and their various students, I will provisionally bracket the fact that no one, old or young, can stop searching for the adequate and best orientation that perfectly corresponds to each one's unique destiny or vocation. Provisionally, I will also neglect the very real possibility of fundamental changes and conversions in orientation on both sides, in order to first ask whether a teacher's basic orientation is not an impediment for the loyal guidance of students who depend on their guide's initiation in, for example, metaphysics or ethics. Will their introduction not take the form of an ideological training in, e.g., a Platonic worship of the erotic Good-and-Beautiful?

If it is not possible to practice and teach philosophy while completely hiding the basic inspiration of one's specific philosophy and, at the same time, being concerned about the intelligent freedom of one's students, an aporia seems inevitable: how can a Platonist, a Kantian, or a Nietzschean unfold the history of philosophy without interpreting the various figures and epochs and the network of relations between them in a more or less Platonic – or Kantian or Nietzschean – way? We are familiar with Kantian, Hegelian, Heideggerian, and Russelian histories of philosophy, but we also observe the partisan fights in which they result. It would contradict the very idea of introducing people to philosophy by unfolding its history, if their teacher interpreted each highlight as a preparation, shadow, distortion, or failed attempt at producing the "true system" of, for example, Thomas (which Thomas?), Kant (which Kant?), Hegel (which Hegel?) or Heidegger (which one?). On the other hand, however, we cannot teach any philosophy if we are not allowed to have a determinate philosophical perspective, distinct criteria for selection, and a method of our own. Is it possible to tone down the typically Kantian, Nietzschean, or one's own character and perspective in order to show what the thoughts of representative thinkers have in common? Can't we at least begin by bracketing the question of a basic, central, or final orientation, in order to focus instead on the not so deep but still substantial questions suggested by the various works that offer us facts, experiences, descriptions, analyses, arguments, and theses? Whatever the ultimate orientation of a philosophy may be, we always must begin by a close reading of the surfaces that are immediately available to us. Later we can delve into the soil from which the studied texts emerge, in order to examine the inaugural breath that propels and animates them.

If we follow this device, we suspend our concern about the existential and philosophical sources of the students' basic stance and search for meaning; but is it not the only way of avoiding shameless indoctrination? Shouldn't we leave the most relevant and ultimate questions and answers of life and philosophy to the private preference of our students themselves? In other words, shouldn't we withdraw from any attempt to guide or influence their struggle for discovering the basic and ultimate meaning of their existence and thought?

Our relation with the students will thus be restricted to distant and limited, but professional and still caring information about and explication of the philosophical highlights of all times, including their contexts and the pre- or extra-philosophical conditions and suppositions on which they are based. What we will not do is to get our audience or ourselves involved in personal confrontations with the fundamental engagements, existential decisions, religious or pre-philosophical sources from which they, we, and the authors we study receive and draw their basic inspiration. Our courses will thus resemble more a guided tour through the museum of philosophy than a workshop in which, together with apprentices and colleagues, we already practice philosophy. Perhaps such tours are useful and necessary in all introductions but they seem to lose their attraction after the first acquaintances are made. A more interesting way of organizing guided tours is, of course, to group authors and topics around great works of different epochs and to show, with the help of the best research, how these works bring together thematic and historical lines of thought and transform them into new sources for further developments. But in both options the question of which philosophies we present as worthy to be studied remains unresolved. We just tell the students that our "classics" are exemplary. But don't tell them then that authority is not a philosophical principle because a modern philosopher thinks autonomously!

A possible schema of the questions and themes that could be taught in a "neutral" and uncommitted introduction to philosophy would follow something like the outline sketched below.

1. Close reading of methodological works that are typical of different schools or styles generally recognized as respectable, such as Aristotle's *Analytics*, Descartes's *Discourse on Method*, Kant's *Critique of Pure Reason*, Hegel's *Logic*, Husserl's *Ideas*, Heidegger's *Being and Time*.

2. Close reading and explications of selections of all the representative oeuvres that are considered to be classics.

3. In commentaries that need to be offered on all these difficult works, the teacher must give much information and explicitation that cannot easily be found in the studied texts themselves. For example, about the *context* of the author's life and genesis, the historical context of the culture in which the author was educated, his or her relations to other philosophers and the non-philosophical writers and works quoted or referred to.

4. Since nothing in the studied works means anything unless it is reactualized by a new audience, ruminated upon, and personally re-thought, teachers and students must engage in a retrieval of selections from the philosophical heritage. Re-thinking as emergence of new beginnings keeps the history of philosophy alive. Teaching is the enlivening *transmission* of a heritage that thereby fulfils a part of its promises, and its re-appropriation by learners generates a surprising future. Newness and originality are not opposed to transmission and tradition of the past, but belong to it if it is not dead.

Further reflection on the temporality of teaching philosophy would have to show to what extent the teacher symbolizes the past as a lively present and how students incorporate the future as *transformation of the present past into their learned future*. While the teacher must *learn* what the beginning future *already* is, (s)he equips her students for their future from the perspective of a cordial "Farewell!"

If a teacher decides to realize over time a program like the one outlined here, she will probably find out that only a well-accorded *team* of philosophers may hope to do something similar. This condition could then trigger the question of how a department should be constituted, which kind of professors should be hired, and which credits should be taken. Even a partial fulfillment of the listed demands would presuppose that the teachers, however learned they are, *remain learners as much as their students*, or even more so, but from the perspective of another responsibility. Not only must they continue to learn from the past and present literature, but also from the present and future needs and shared desires of their ever different, unique, and changing students. Besides passing on what from the tradition(s), through own and others' retrievals, remains inspiring, they must prepare a future in which, thanks to their exchange and cooperation with their students, philosophy remains as exciting as ever, but differently from yesterday and today.

The measure of excitement that philosophy in learners and teachers awakens greatly depends on the relevance of the questions asked. While laboring on the many layers of philosophizing, most teachers and students are longing for a personal engagement in the ongoing practice that makes them also responsible for the continual renovation of authentic philosophy. Is it possible at all to distinguish a good professor in philosophy from a creative philosopher?

Some philosophers complain that some of their colleagues replace real philosophy with its history. They miss "arguments" in their colleagues' historical studies and think of them as a certain type of reporters who are not able or willing to think for themselves. If these reporters do not adequately represent the arguments of the presented authors, such as Aristotle, Cusanus, or Kant, their critics might have a point, because such historians do not fairly reproduce the old documents. If, however, the critics claim that old arguments must be corrected, changed, refuted, or updated *before* they can be taught or that the arguments produced in the last ten years "of course" are better than the classical ones, their hypothesis is completely arbitrary until they themselves produce (or quote!) better arguments. It is also possible, however, that they use the word "argument" in a shortsighted or arbitrary way. They might, for example, be ignorant about the power of phenomenological descriptions or blind and naïve with regard to the incorrect prejudices that condition their own points of departure or favorite style of demonstration.

Presupposing that we indeed have learned how appropriate descriptions and argumentations are structured and practiced, and how skillful critique of philosophical failures must operate, we also want to scrutinize the soil, the situation, the tonality, the suppositions, the intuitions, and the hidden or half-hidden roots and perspectives from which others' *and our own* philosophies emerge and bloom or die. And this leads us back to the question of the basic stance, the inspiration and the orientation, which we bracketed for awhile in order to focus on a more sober, but also more superficial, though still rather thorough, examination of the normal philosophical business, briefly evoked above.

In fact, while executing such a program, we discover that our own teaching and the students' responses to it, emerge from a longing for more than well-observed and well-reasoned answers to the traditional questions of modern philosophy. The really relevant and most serious questions have more to do with wisdom than with the kind of superscience offered in most academic philosophy; and fragments or seeds of wisdom are present, albeit in rudimentary or dated forms, in the deepest convictions which function as unproved but resistant prejudices that hide, while forcefully influencing our formally correct discussions. However much both sides of the seminar room try hard to silence their deep, pre- and post-philosophical convictions, the philosophical positions they promote are unmistakably connected to these convictions and the various kinds of inspiration expressed in them. If we accept the predicate "religious" in its widest possible meaning (instead of "deep," "profound," "rooted," or "radical") to characterize the basic and primordial dimension of our mindset, we might say that we, modern Westerners, are reticent (or prudish or perhaps ashamed?) to unveil our "religious" convictions in public, and especially in philosophy, because we are proud of its autonomy. Has this reticence to do with the separation of public life and privacy, education and intimacy, or perhaps with a particular kind of "enlightened" intimidation? In any case, the repression or systematic concealment of the most fundamental sympathies does not facilitate a frank discussion of the most decisive questions. True, it is not easy to even know which intuitions, guesses, wagers, feelings, or desires compose the soil from which each one's thinking emerges, but should philosophy not include a method of fundamental analysis and deciphering? Or must we abstain from digging into existential depths and leave such kind of scrutiny to mythic or psychoanalytic imagination?

Even when teachers and students in dialogue do not thematize the various interpretations and self-interpretations of their basic stance, trust, or faith, they discover fundamental affinities or contrasts among the perspectives that determine their positions. Before and during our participation in the philosophical practice, each of us has already espoused a particular orientation with regard to the meaning and the most desirable course of one's own life and the role that philosophy should play in it. When we meet, we bring our deepest convictions with us, although we seldom explicitly confront them with one another. They may conform, confirm, contrast, or contradict one another, but in any case, they play a role in the less profound dimensions of our discussions, but it is not clear and not easy to formulate how exactly they do or should, for instance, determine our philosophical or common sensical arguments.

However, we share at least large parts of a *cultural* agreement. Our pre-philosophical education has provided us with generally accepted opinions, customs, postulates, behavioral automatisms or rituals, and theoretical dogmas. We share in the ethos and the doxa of "the many," but "the many" represent the multitude of a limited region, e.g., a nation or a historical epoch. Of course, such opinions do not constitute a philosophical justification, but it is difficult to ignore or contradict them, especially if they concern certain shibolleths of our time, such as autonomy, free choice, human rights, and democracy. Once we are involved and advanced in philosophizing itself, however, we discover that the dominant ethos of a national or epochal culture by itself is not a solid basis for a philosophically valid position or critique.

However, there is no other way of entering the realm of philosophy than to be already educated in some pre-philosophical manner of living, trusting, and believing, which is always shaped and structured by a particular, locally and epochally limited culture. As Heidegger has tried to show, we cannot *begin* to think unless we initially agree with the ethos of *das Man* or *hoi polloi*, while globally accepting the dominant code of mores and convictions. We can neither jump from this powerful platform onto a totally different culture, nor radically change our entire life style and mindset. What we can do, however, is to correct, amend, bend, or transform the manners and expectations we have inherited from the education and the society that have formed us. To do this in a philosophical way demands that our critique of the existing ethos can appeal to a standard or principle that is independent from the characteristically American ethos of the 21st century. Can such a standard or principle be discovered?

To answer this question seriously, it is not enough to compare our ethos to that of other cultures in space or time, because none of those can by itself claim to possess a better standard than ours. Some meta-cultural measure or ideal of humanness must be found that allows for a thorough evaluation of all ethoses that are proposed to new-born humans.

At this point we might be tempted by a philosophical intuition that has been nicknamed "essentialism" by its enemies. As is often the case, even among philosophers, the nickname is mainly due to a misunderstanding of what, during millennia, has been called "essence" (*ousia*), or "nature" (*physis*): that (e.g., being human) which, in all its abstraction, is the (mode and way of) being of a certain kind of beings insofar as it characterizes all the instances of that kind, even when we bracket all that is responsible for the possible variations and varieties in which the ess-ence may realize and express itself. The "essence" of a culture, for example, is the same in all cultures, but none of the various cultures is equal to any other, although their – often widely differing – similarities are obvious, thus testifying to the affinities that link them together and their essential sameness. The same is true of language and all other phenomena, even leaves, as Leibniz noticed. Nobody speaks "language," but "language" is what "makes" all languages at the same time identical and irreducibly different.

However, if all the varieties of a kind express an identical essence, which constitutes them as phenomenally similar-though-different, how then can we determine, observe, describe, or imaginatively capture that essence?

Some philosophers and scientists have pretended that they could give a description or definition of the essence in its nakedness, without touching any of the differences that are responsible for the phenomenal varieties. This seems improbable, because the essence cannot be seen, touched, heard, or described if it is stripped of all its variegated expressions. It can only be thought as the hidden identity of that toward which all its varieties point as their common, but as such invisible, insensible, unimaginable, and conceptually non-isolatable being or ess-ence.

Other philosophers have thought that the naked or "abstract" thought of an essence, as stripped from all the variations in which it is realized, could be reduced to a core that is determined through "induction": all instances could be reduced to an abstract-universal that is found in each one of them and we would be able describe it as a thing. They forget then that the essence of, e.g., a culture, a language, or a plant cannot be separated from the rest, because it is also responsible for its endlessly varied concretizations, and that no plant or culture can exist as plant, language or culture without *including* the characteristic variety it displays as this or that instance of its kind. Each essence includes the necessity of its instantiation, which is singularly different each time it occurs.

What has been said is also true of the essences of a philosophy, a fundamental intuition, a basic stance, an ultimate orientation or an originary conviction. If a singular philosophy includes the essence of philosophy as the source of its particular emergence and ramification, we cannot fully understand that philosophy, and certainly not appropriate any philosophy – even in the form of a tentative or distantly didactic identification only – without being confronted with that source, to which it owes its liveliness and attraction.

Much has been written about the essential origin, core, structure, method, conditions, and properties of philosophy, but here I would like to emphasize that its essence includes its being rooted in the most profound and radically primary – and thus absolutely initial – impulse or pathos of the life that speaks in it. Each philosophy grows out of an original thrust from which it draws its inspiration. Mustn't we dig deeper than is usual in modern or postmodern philosophies in order to discover their deepest – prephilosophical – source which gives that trust its urgency?

Whatever answer the elaboration of this question may yield, it seems clear to me that, as a teacher in philosophy, in conversation with my students, I cannot entirely abstain from a dialogue about the deepest conviction, trust, faith, or stance of an oeuvre that we are studying, even if it shows only obliquely or through hardly perceptible hints. Such a stance or faith elicits in us an – albeit vague – affinity, sympathy, antipathy, or disagreement; but it also evokes and challenges our own established or provisional, still seeking or experimentally attempted, stance and orientation. On this – the original – level, the basic positions or faiths confront one another. A common unity of our faiths is not given; sharp clashes have even caused ideological and civil wars. May we hope instead that, despite considerable differences, our fundamental positions converge somehow somewhere, even if no one is able to capture a common source or future union in the form of unified conceptual, verbal, poetic, or musical language or practice?

The source is deep and hidden, not readily available for inspection or straightforward delving. If a philosophy is not only an expression of the roots from which it stems, but also a translation into understandable language of the inspiration that comes from the deepest depth – in other words, if philosophy includes a search for intelligence of the faith from which it emerges, our philosophical dialogue cannot exclude those faiths from its orbit, even if philosophy itself might need to recognize its incompetence, lack of power, or indignity to play the judge by proclaiming itself the supreme standard for a final evaluation of those primordial ways of having found soil and rootedness.

The source of primordial inspiration contains a promise of decisive meaning: the meaning of a life, and thus – if all authentic philosophy is rooted in existence – also the decisive meaning of philosophy. But then the inspiration and the meaning to which it points imply a final orientation. An authentic life and true philosophy imply the meaning of a destiny and its destination.

What does all this mean for the dialogue between teachers and students, once they have reached the point where they can no longer avoid the question of a meaning that, in the end and from the beginning, all their philosophies and philosophers try to express? If philosophy involves us not only in its own practice, but also directs our questioning to the *pathos* that propels and motivates human existence in each of them and ourselves, we cannot avoid a *philosophical* kind of research about the types of faith that make sense because they seem well-inspired and well-oriented. Their sense will then have to show in meaningful expressions of mood, attunement, taste, tonality, intelligent selectivity, justice, peaceful community, and wise cordiality.

A second consequence is that neither students nor teachers in philosophy will ever be able to terminate their learning. For who could ever reach complete wisdom about existential needs and desires? Who would be able to wisely discuss all the varieties of decisive meaning that guide the various philosophers, including one's students or teachers? And who would already have reached the depth where one's own and others' originary source becomes entirely transparent?

A successful dialogue between persons who are no longer afraid of descending into the primordial dimension of thought will familiarize the participants not only with themselves, but also with one another. Since they show the highest respect for each one's intimacy, they are ready to engage at least in one kind of what Aristotle calls virtuous friendship, perfect *filia*.

The dialogue between teachers and students of philosophy reaches its most serious form, when the interlocutors are able to combine an appropriate distance toward their own stance with a strong mutual trust and great respect regarding their differences. The conviction that their discussion is meaningful, is motivated by the hope that, in the end – and that end is now – the most authentic elements of their positions converge somewhere in an as yet hidden, but enigmatically common truth.

PHENOMENOLOGY OF INVITATION

§

Greg Clark

A Preface

    I hope that a poor imitation remains an acceptable form of flattery, because I lack the gifts and the background to pull-off a good imitation of Adriaan. Nevertheless, in the following essay, I try in my limited way (further limited by constraints of space) to honor through imitation. At the most superficial level, there is a repetition of some vocabulary, of a few characteristic moves, of engagement with some favorite philosophers, and, I hope, a sometimes playful tone. At a more significant level, the essay departs from what I know of Adriaan's emphases. Plato's analogy between philosophy and hunting connects philosophy to a practice central in many rural cultures world wide and to a powerful current in American culture. The analogy opens the question of how less urbane life experiences might inform our philosophizing. But, finally and most fundamentally, the essay reflects on the life that can call forth and sustain philosophical thought. I take this life, modeled by Adriaan in the classroom and with Angela in their home, as a model to imitate with my own students in our classrooms and with my own family our home. This essay tries to think certain aspects of this life while allowing it to also remain a mystery.

Introduction: Philosophy as Hunting

Philosophers are hunters after true concepts. Socrates employs this image of himself and Glaucon while tracking the concept of justice in *The Politea*.[3]

> S: Now then Gaucon, we must post ourselves like a ring of hunters around a thicket, with very alert minds, so that justice does not escape us by evaporating before us. It is evident that it must be there somewhere. Look out then and do your best to get a glimpse of it before me and drive it toward me.
>
> G: I only wish I could! It will be enough if I can see what you point out as you guide me.
>
> S: Come on, then, I'll encourage you!
>
> G: That I will, provided that you lead me.
>
> S: Very well, but, by heaven! Look how obstructed and overgrown the woods are. What a dark and hard-to-see place! But there's nothing to do but go forward.
>
> G: Let's go then!
>
> S: By the devil! I think we have a track, and I don't think it will escape us now.

Here we have hunting as a communal activity in search of quick, elusive game probably with the use of nets. And so the analogy to philosophy works. It works if philosophizing is a communal activity pursued among friends chasing close-by concepts.

Does the analogy of hunting to philosophy still hold?

Plato's image of hunting strikes us as strange today. Our methods have changed. And natural selection would work against hunters who tote guns and form a tight ring around a thicket. So, we don't run deer off cliffs or into an ambush; we sit in tree-stands drinking coffee and hope for one to walk by. We don't shoot at moving targets; we devise ways to get deer to stop so that we can get our gadgets set and line up our sights. And for all intents and purposes, we hunt, or rather, each one hunts alone.

---

[3] *Politea*, 432 b. Translation from Jose Ortega y Gasset, *Meditations on Hunting*. Wilderness Adventures Press, 2007, p. 139.

Our practices are determined more by our technologies than by the nature and habitat of our quarry or by our own skills. Those with means can even purchase a "hunt," that is, pay to have themselves inserted in a locale where they have spent no time, to harvest game whose patterns they have not studied, with equipment built and adjusted by people they do not know.

By many measures our practices appear to be progress. Have you ever tried to chase a deer through a thicket while carrying a bow in one hand and a quiver full or arrows strapped to your back? But perhaps the activities have become so dissimilar that the change marks not progress but an equivocation in the word "hunt."

This image of hunting, so dissimilar from the one employed by Socrates, may, nevertheless, still provide an analogue for the activity of philosophizing. For most of us in modern universities it is all we have ever known. We sit alone in offices drinking coffee and hope for a concept to float by, one which will stop for us and submit itself to our techniques, phenomenological or analytic, so that we can turn it into a trophy.

For now, however, let us stick with Plato's vision of hunting and its implications for philosophy. That is, let us take philosophizing as a communal activity pursued among friends chasing close-by concepts. We will chase not this first animal, "philosophy," but another, "invitation." I am about to jump into the thicket. I hope to scare something out. I need you all to take up positions on the other side, and, if something comes running out, grab it, hang on for all you are worth, and tell us what you caught in about twenty minutes.

Hunting Invitation

We have all been invited guests around Angela and Adriaan's table. We each received an invitation to this gathering. Billy Graham once issued invitations at his crusades. I've recently been invited to apply for a very prestigious credit card. "Invitation" is said in many ways. Sometimes, however, we extend invitations without saying the word. Asking someone on a date is an invitation, as is a proposal of marriage. Saul seems to have received an invitation of sorts on the road to Damascus. Even more strongly, sometimes we invite and don't speak any words at all. A home can be inviting, as can a meal. Eyes or lips may extend an invitation precisely through the lack of words. Invitation can appear in many forms.

Where, then, ought we look for the idea by virtue of which we call these many appearances by the same word, "invitation"? Here a certain kind of phenomenologist may come rushing in with the following account:

To invite is to extend an offer to, or to ask another to join the inviter. Most simply, the inviter takes the initiative and acts. She throws a graduation party, for example. The invitee is passive simply receiving the invitation. Whether the invitation is accepted is immaterial to whether the invitation was extended and received. The graduation party will go on whether or not the invitation is accepted.

On this account, an invitation refers to three elements, and these elements are purely functional, not ontological. That is, the inviter, the invitee, and the party all have an identity and an existence independently of the invitation. The invitation is a functional relationship between the three subsisting entities.

Put differently, on this account, invitation is not an ultimate reality. At best it supervenes on an ontology of substances. But this functional account of invitation means that we have not thought the nature of invitation according to itself but rather according to some other preconception of what is real. We have allowed words and previous phenomenological descriptions to cloud our vision.

We will have to try again. This time, we will need to consider invitation according to its own standards. If we hope to catch invitation, we will need to attend to the features that make for a "good" invitation – both well-executed and successful. The poverty of the description of an invitation "to a graduation party," simply can't carry any philosophical weight. We will not understand any phenomenon by focusing in privative cases or, by failing to distinguish between exemplary and non-exemplary cases, or by short-changing our descriptions. Those who study wines don't refine their pallets or sharpen their pens with Wild Irish Rose.

Invitation

What, then, makes for a good invitation? Here, we must fall back on our own exemplary experiences. Over the holidays my family formally, though not legally, adopted one of my former students into our family. That is, we have explicitly said that we will be as family to each other. In truth, the adoption was more a recognition of the relationship that had grown over several years than a declaration of a project that still existed only in our desires.

In coming to that declaration she and I retraced how we had come to this place. I said, "It feels to me as if you chose us." She was, I think, a little puzzled by this observation, and she replied, "Yes, and you were extending invitations all along." I confess that I was somewhat shocked. I had not set out to extend invitations. No cards were dropped in the mailbox, and I don't think I ever said to myself "Let's invite Karima to join our family." And yet, she was clearly right. We were able to recount how we continued to extend invitations and she continued to accept. The process was much like a dance. At this moment in our conversation I first caught a glimpse of this swift and elusive concept out of the corner of my eye.

But this model of invitation leads to a completely different analysis than our first one. In this case, while I extended many invitations, with each new one shaped by the previous ones, I did not experience myself as the only or even the primary agent. I acted, but my entire family also acted before, in, and after the invitation. Likewise, the agents have been affected by the invitations given and received. The life my family shares has grown and been reordered by the giving of the series of invitations. Further, the invitee did not passively receive an invitation. She was an active participant as my sense that she chose us indicates. The invitations were not "things" extended from one entity to another; they were openings in the family, each successive one a little wider than the previous, each taken up, until the "our" of our family has a new identity and existence. The reception of the invitation too was made possible by an openness to the invitation in Karima.

To invite is to open oneself to another, to risk being changed,

> to welcome being changed by the other who joins with you. To be invited is to have a door opened through which you can join yourself to others, and with them form a new unity, to become "one spirit," a "I that is We and a We that is I." Invitation is the condition for the possibility of "a life lived together."

<u>Objection and Reply</u>

The other hunters in my group may object that this analysis required a retrospective vantage point, and perhaps the game I have scared out of the thicket is not what I think it is. We seemed to not fully know what we were doing; we reconstructed it after the event. Isn't something amiss? Put in more direct terms: Why does my analysis require the retrospective vantage point? Does this belong to the ontology of invitation? Or is this a feature of my example which might make it less than exemplary?

Recall that in my first, inadequate, phenomenological analysis, I described the invitation primarily in terms of what it was an invitation *to* ... "a graduation party." The verb "to invite" requires an indirect object. In my second, more adequate, analysis, any specifiable indirect object seemed to recede from view. In reality, however, the indirect object takes over the entire analysis. Invitation is the condition for the possibility of "a life lived together." The inviter and the invitee participate in that life. This allows us to specify the exemplary forms of invitation: In the first rank are invitations to share life: proposals of marriage, invitations to join a religious order, and adoptions into families. In the second rank stand invitations to shared activities: meals, concerts, gatherings, graduation parties. We can safely classify invitations to apply for credit cards as the simulacra of invitation. To classify invitation into levels, a phenomenology of invitation does not require a retrospective view.

However, this analysis remains abstract. Invitation presupposes a context; only within the particular context can we determine whether we have preformed an invitation well, poorly, or not at all. An invitation to apply for a credit card assumes nothing more than a mailing address. The inviter can come straight to the point. Both parties know what is afoot.

By contrast, invitations to activities presuppose some prior relationship or at least a shared context, and they point toward a possible future whose boundaries remain open.

A marriage proposal can go awry in at least three ways. The first two ways view the marriage proposal as on par with one of the other levels of invitation. If one person simply walks up to another in the grocery store and proposes marriage, then the proposal amounts to an invitation to apply for a credit card. No common life can emerge from such a proposal. Second, the proposal may come too early in a relationship. Obsessing on the question, "Is this the person I will marry?" on a first date will scuttle any new romantic interest. The possible future has taken on definite boundaries too soon. We can entertain proposals of marriage only *after* many invitations to meals, gatherings, and other activities.

But the marriage proposal can also go wrong on its own proper level; I may perform it artlessly by moving too directly toward the goal. I ought not blurt out "Let's get married!" during a television commercial break. Rather, I should plan a dinner, engage in discussion, lead my beloved back into our shared life, perhaps spend time recollecting that life that has already built together. There should be enough distraction to make the proposal a surprise, and enough of a common life to make it the most obvious an natural next step.

I can propose, but I cannot declare by an act of my will, that we share a life, for our shared life, by definition, exceeds my own. Facing into the proposal means taking stock of possible rejection and failure. Making the proposal explicit could undermine not only the proposal, but also the shape of my own life and a building pattern of activities which I already share with you. So we court one another, sometimes with our eyes open, sometimes with our eyes closed.

This explains the essential place of retrospective viewpoint. The relationship in review allows us to open our eyes to all that happened when our eyes were shut. Put differently, a shared life is an indirect object, once removed. We don't start by inviting others to a shared life. We start with a drink, with a meal, asking for help, offering assistance – with invitations to activities that can lead to other activities and then to patterns of activities. That is what we can allow ourselves to see. Eventually those activities take on a coherence and a shared life emerges. We can look back and see how we came to live within that pattern, see how each opened to the other and came to depend on the other and (what is quite different but intertwined with dependency) came to love one another. The shared life was not there at the beginning, but it came to be there. Only looking back can we tell the story of how it came to be.

A Life Lived Together

In the famous passage from the seventh letter, Plato explains how philosophy is taught, or, rather, caught: "after much converse about the matter itself and a life lived together, suddenly a light, as it were, is kindled in one soul by a flame that leaps to it from another, and thereafter sustains itself."

So, here we are, souls aflame, gathered to philosophize. And because of that flame, we cannot help but ask about the necessary conditions for the possibility of that flame. Plato tells us of two conditions: "much converse about the matter itself" and "a life lived together." Each of these conditions could fascinate a community of philosopher friends. I have taken "the matter itself" to be the emergence out of invitation of a life lived together.

I have argued that the condition for the condition of philosophy is the invitation to a shared life. We began that life not just in classrooms around desks (though that was also essential), but with a call from Angela, with a gathering in Angela and Adriaan's home around a piano, a psalm offered for grace, and purple yam ice cream. The ice cream was no less necessary than Heidegger's "On the Essence of Truth," and it was certainly harder to find. Both contained the seeds of something more.

My companions in the hunt, as you can see, I have emerged from the undergrowth. I believe I have at least a line on my game. But I am in need of your help, both to test the nature of what I've snared and to report on what you also have caught.

<u>*Greg Clark, Response to Adriaan Peperzak*</u>

"Philosophy does not live in fleeting words or muted texts, but only in thinking lives."

I had not met most of my colleagues prior to this conference, and yet between us I recognized "that I know not what." While we have all lived in or near Chicago, while we all share an *alma mater*, these did not suffice to bring us together. We knew only that we shared a teacher whom we wished to honor more than our biological progenitors. But we also discovered a fondness for certain texts, a familiarity with certain approaches, and surprise to find congruous thoughts emerging from others. I still find myself wanting to talk with Norman about attention, with Marjolein about belonging together of teacher and student, with Aron's account of finding voice, and with the rest of you. As Adriaan recognizes there was "a kind of belonging together that came by itself." It came by itself, but the ground was prepared, the seeds were planted, watered, and tended by Adriaan. Catriona gathered what Adriaan had sown.

Adriaan offers me and my essay a helping hand. He points out that the purpose to which we are invited must be "sufficiently desirable" and that the process of accepting can be described as a joining of desires. I hesitate here only because I would like to hear Adriaan's and Colin's discussion play out further. In particular, I would like an account of what it means to "join desires." But clearly a phenomenology of invitation does need not only an ontology, but an account of its goodness and its being seen or felt as good. An invitation to something evil and/or something seen as evil would not be experienced as an invitation. We should develop an account of how the desire for the good precedes and creates both the ontology and the community. But perhaps the lines of dependence don't run in straight or direct routes. Should our hunt develop along these trails, surely many good surprises would await us.

PHILOSOPHY
AND FRIENDSHIP
§

Marjolein Oele

Preface: Lost in Translation

    Lost in Translation is the title of Sophia Coppola's 2003 movie about two strangers, a young woman with a degree in philosophy from Yale and a middle-aged movie actor, who happen to meet in a hotel in Tokyo. Far removed from the cultural and linguistic routines of their American lives, they feel lost and help each other explore existential questions. Despite this interesting premise, the movie itself does not move beyond the usual platitudes. Yet, the title *Lost in Translation* resonates with me. For what better description could there be to explain my own experience as a Dutch student coming to Chicago to take my first course at an American university – a course on Plato's *Republic*, taught in English-with-lots-of-Greek by Adriaan Peperzak? Far away from my own familiar world, Adriaan Peperzak opened up an entire Greek world, excavating Plato's magnum opus layer by layer, while simultaneously relating Plato's critique on Athenian society to contemporary American society. I literally felt lost in translation and experienced – to a heightened degree – the "liquidity"[4] of modern life that Zygmunt Bauman has associated with our current precarious and uncertain form of living and which he has contrasted with the "solidity" of

---
4 Z. Bauman, *Liquid Modernity*, Cambridge: Polity Press, 2000.

previous eras.

Yet, what I experienced that first semester was not only a distinctively modern phenomenon, but also an age-old phenomenon closely tied to the practice of philosophy: the stance of being "in-between."[5] When caught within this state of "in-between," one is immersed in experience yet reflecting on it, speaking a common language yet not identifying with it, sharing common practices yet being estranged from them. Newly initiated students of philosophy may not express it in this exact way, but they sometimes describe this experience of the "philosophical in-between" as "confusing," "frustrating," or simply "weird" –akin to the Attic Greek word for "strange," *atopos*, which Socrates' interlocutors attributed to him[6] to denote a similar kind of confusion or displacement associated with philosophy.

However, despite the overwhelming uncertainty and strangeness of that very first semester, I also felt oddly "at home" – at home with an intellectual community that was equally excited by a close reading of the classics as I was, and at home with a teacher who shared my Dutch background (not to mention love of Dutch cookies!) and who viewed teaching as "the enlivening *transmission* of a heritage that thereby fulfills a part of its promises."[7] Notwithstanding the learnedness of this teacher, never did I doubt that we were in pursuit of anything else than "wisdom" as opposed to "superscience,"[8] and that our philosophical questioning was directed nowhere but to "the *pathos* that propels and motivates human existence."[9] Unsurprisingly, and largely because of this inspiration, my dissertation was focused on the meaning of *pathos* in Aristotle.

I feel deep gratitude to the teacher, friend, and community I have found, and I share in the hope that some of the most authentic elements of my essay *Philosophy and Friendship* will converge with those of my teacher and fellow students – "somewhere in an as yet hidden, but enigmatically

---

5 Famously, Diotima's speech as recounted by Socrates in the *Symposium* addresses the "in-between"(*metaxu*) when discussing *eros* as mediating between beauty and ugliness, ignorance and knowledge, etc. (*Symposium*, 202a ff.)
6 For example, Plato, *Gorgias*, 473a1, 480e1.
7 A. Peperzak, "Teaching as Learning," p.7 of the submitted manuscript [**reference?**]
8 A. Peperzak, "Teaching as Learning," p.9 of the submitted manuscript [**reference?**]
9 A. Peperzak, "Teaching as Learning," p.15 of the submitted manuscript [**reference?**]

common truth."[10]

But as for those among whom no agreement has been made for services rendered, it was said that those who give freely to one another for their own sake are free of complaints (for friendship in accord with virtue (*aretē*) is of this sort), and one ought to make a return in accord with one's choice (*proairesis*) since this is characteristic of a friend as well as of virtue. And it seems to be this way too with those who have shared in philosophy (*philosophias koinōnēsasin*), for its worth is not measured in money and no honor could be of equal weight with it, but perhaps it is enough, as with gods and one's parents, to give what is possible.

(Aristotle, *Nicomachean Ethics*, IX.1, 1164a34-1164b6)[11]

Introduction

In this gathering in honor of Adriaan Peperzak's 80th birthday, we celebrate philosophy and friendship, and specifically their intertwinement. Although our gathering confirms the possibility and viability of this intertwinement, its philosophical underpinning remains far from clear. In his article *Friendship and Philosophy*, Adriaan Peperzak writes about the various aspects of the philosophical republic, its institutions, and how one becomes a philosopher and member of this particular kind of republic.[12] In his words, the process of becoming a philosopher depends upon initiation: "Nobody is born a philosopher; everyone is taught before becoming a partner in the tradition whose heirs we are."[13] It is at this point that the central question of this paper emerges: how does teaching contribute to becoming a philosopher, and how are teaching, philosophy, and friendship related to one another? More specifically, how can we characterize the relationship between teacher and student in philosophy – can friendship and philosophy merely be the *result* of this teacher-student relationship, or

10 A. Peperzak, "Teaching as Learning," p.16 of the submitted manuscript [**reference?**]
11 Translation Sachs slightly adjusted. Aristotle, *Nicomachean Ethics*, translated by J. Sachs, Newburyport: Focus Publishing, 2002.
12 A.T. Peperzak. *Philosophy: Wise About Friendship*? Version Nov. 7, 2001, p.3; published in Dutch under the title "Vriendschap en filosofie (*Friendship and Philosophy*) in: A.T. Peperzak, *Aanspraak en Bezinning*, Kampen: Klement, 2007, pp. 159-181. The English version was published in D.J. Martino (ed.), *Phenomenology Today. The Schuwer SPEP Lectures* 1998-2002, Pittsburgh: Duquesne University, 2003, pp. 54-70.
13 Ibid.

is friendship and partnership, from the beginning, the very *foundation* on the basis of which philosophical teaching takes place? This last suggestion may strike the listener as odd, since the teacher-student relationship seems, at least on the surface, to start off with teacher and student being strangers, marked by difference and inequality in knowledge. Only when knowledge is transferred and a common ground is established, can friendship grow and take root. But despite the appearance of initial difference and inequality between student and teacher in philosophy – with friendship only resulting later in the process – it is my thesis that the relationship between teacher and student in philosophy *presupposes* a rudimentary friendship embodying both kinship and difference. It is the task of this paper to explain this foundation of friendship in more detail, and I will do so by first turning to Plato's *Lysis* and *Symposium*.

Part One. Identity and Difference: Friendship in the Lysis *and* Symposium

In the *Symposium*, Socrates arrives late at the house of his friend Agathon. Agathon urges Socrates to sit next to him, as he hopes to catch some of Socrates' wisdom (*Symp.* 175c8). In response, Socrates says: "How wonderful it would be, dear Agathon, if the foolish were filled with wisdom simply by touching the wise. If only wisdom were like water, which always flows from a full cup into an empty one when we connect them with a piece of yarn…" (*Symp.* 175d3-7). Socrates' remark emphasizes the puzzling nature of acquiring philosophical wisdom: the process is not that of simply filling empty heads with knowledge by connecting them to "full heads." Knowledge can never be a simple "item" to be exchanged for something else, such as physical beauty. Even though particular social practices such as Greek pederasty are founded on this exchange model (as we see particularly strongly defended in the speech of Pausanias and embodied in Alcibiades' behavior, e.g. 217a), Socrates' refusal of Alcibiades' seductions (*Symp.* 217-219) demonstrates his rejection of the idea that knowledge and virtue can simply be taught and exchanged for something else.

For our understanding of the relationship between teacher and student this means that their relationship cannot just be understood in mechanistic terms as a mere vacuous connection – comparable to the yarn that connects the full cup to the empty cup. Similarly, their relationship cannot simply be that of unequals, with one person possessing knowledge and the other person lacking it. Further, neither can their relationship be assessed as one between equals, since pure equality cannot explain what both seek from one another. In other words, it seems that neither absolute difference nor identity can underlie the relationship between teacher and student.

Here, the *aporia's* concerning friendship as raised by the *Lysis* may be helpful, and in particular the ones that focus on the identity or difference underlying friendship. The issue of affinity that we feel for those who share particular ideals or styles of life with us becomes the reason for Socrates' suggestion that friendship is based on identity or similarity – where like is drawn to like. For this view, Socrates cites Homer's *Odyssey*, where it is stated that "God always draws the like onto the like" (*Odyssey* 17.128; *Lysis* 214a6). Yet, as Socrates argues, friendship cannot be based on mere similarity for the following reasons. First, with regard to bad people, this would imply that they would have friendships with themselves and with other people. However, since bad people are not even consistent with themselves,[14] they could not have friendships with themselves and certainly not with others (*Lysis* 214c8-214d2). Secondly, there is no sufficient reason for those alike to be drawn to each other. As Socrates argues: "When something, anything at all, is like something else, how can it benefit or harm its like in a way in which it could not benefit or harm itself?" (*Lysis* 214e5-7). In other words, why would we prize and seek friendship with someone who is similar to us, since we already have all the qualities the other person has? More specifically, a good person would not seek friendship with another good person, since goodness implies self-sufficiency, thus excluding the need for good friends (*Lysis* 214e2-215b). Thirdly, people who are most alike often quarrel or are jealous of each other. In Socrates' words, things that are most alike "are filled with envy, contentiousness, and hatred

---

[14] Aristotle takes up a similar position in his *Nicomachean Ethics*, arguing that wicked people lack constancy and accordingly can only become friends for a short time, "as long as they continue to provide each other wish pleasures or material advantages" (*EN* VIII.8, 1159b11-12).

for each other...." (*Lysis* 215d3).

Based on the above reasoning, identity or similarity between two people cannot be the basis for their friendship. Thus, Socrates seeks to argue for the exact inverse in his subsequent argument, which posits that it is opposites who are each other's friends (*Lysis* 216a3). Argued in a Heraclitean vein, Socrates claims that it is opposites that attract, for example "dry desires wet, cold hot, bitter sweet, sharp blunt, empty full, full empty" (*Lysis* 215d6). By grounding friendship on opposition, Socrates implies that it is based on lack and deficiency – as one desires the other on the foundation of one's own lack.

This suggestion that friendship is grounded in radical opposition is also refuted, since it includes a fundamental contradiction: since friend and enemy are complete opposites of each other, the reasoning that opposites attract would mean that friend and enemy are friends. Since this is contradictory, the proposal that friendship is based on absolute difference must also be set aside (*Lysis* 216a6-b6).

Overlooking both rejected possibilities it appears that neither absolute similarity nor absolute difference can account for the friendship between two people. Regarding our analysis of philosophical knowledge in the teacher-student relationship, this implies that, if friendship underlies this relationship, the knowledge sought is neither something that one "has" and the other "lacks" nor that both are completely equal to one another qua knowledge. Yet, we may ask: can the answer to the problem of friendship not be found by *mediating* between the two radically opposed views just rejected? In other words, is it not possible to reconcile the view that friendship is based on identity and self-sufficiency with the view that friendship is based on difference and deficiency? And what does this imply for the student-teacher relationship? The next section will discuss this third option on the basis of Plato's *Lysis* and Aristotle's *Physics*.

Part Two. Belonging Together: Friendship in the *Lysis* and Teaching and Learning in Aristotle's *Physics* III.3

In the *Lysis*, the third option that negotiates between the two positions of identity and difference finds expression in Socrates' view that friendship, similar to passionate love (*erōs*) and desire (*epithumia*) is directed towards that which belongs (*oikeios*) to oneself (*Lysis* 221e3). We desire out of lack that which originally belongs to us but that has been taken away from us (*Lysis* 221e3). To explain this meaning of "belonging" further, we need to look closely at the Greek term *oikeios* – derived from the Greek term for house or household: "*oikos*." With regard to things, the term *oikeios* means that which belongs "to one's house or family," and with regard to people it refers to that person who is "of the same household, family, or kin."[15] Thus, Socrates' argument that friendship is aimed at that which is *oikeios*, i.e. that which belongs to us, indicates that friendship aims at being at home, at being akin, at retrieving one's original home. In other words, we find here the friend as the one in whom one finds one's home – one's home that has originally been lost. If we find in the other our home, this means that we become *ourselves* through and in the other. Our home is with the other – and as long as that home is there, the other will not cease to be dear to us, as Gadamer writes in his reaction to this passage.[16]

Yet, in addition to homecoming, the concept of *oikeios* also includes a distinct negativity: friendship is based on what belongs to us, but also on that of which we are deprived. Thus, true friendship operates within the tension between what is our own, i.e. what belongs to us, and that of which we are deprived, that which we lack.[17] Ultimately the true friend is someone to whom we belong, i.e. someone with whom we are unified, but also someone who is ultimately different – someone whom we cannot possess, someone who transcends our all-encompassing grasp.

Although belonging (as the basis for friendship) is ultimately rejected in the *Lysis* (but revived in the *Symposium*)[18] our own quest to grasp the

---

15 H. Liddell and R. Scott, *A Greek-English Lexicon*, Oxford: Oxford University Press, 1996, p. 1202.
16 H.-G. Gadamer, *Dialogue and Dialectic: Eight Hermeneutical Studies on Plato*, New Haven: Yale University Press, 1980, p.19.
17 Cf. F.J. Gonzalez, "Plato's *Lysis*: An Enactment of Philosophical Kinship," in: *Ancient Philosophy* 15 (1995), pp. 69-90, p. 83.
18 It is rejected because belonging, according to Socrates, can ultimately be reduced to likeness, and, by implication, has to be rejected on the same grounds on which the argument that friendship is based on likeness has to be refuted (*Lysis* 222b). Importantly, belonging returns in the *Symposium* in Aristophanes' speech (191a7; 192b8) and later, in a more poignant form, in Diotima's speech about *erōs* as recounted by Socrates. Diotima emphasizes that true belonging only applies to the good

interconnection between friendship and philosophy has nonetheless made progress based on the preceding. First of all, the analysis of *oikeios* shows us that friendship, and by that definition also philosophical friendship, depends upon a sense of belonging that implies both difference and identity. Friendship includes difference, but this difference is not radical since it is based on what belongs to oneself, and thus implies similarity. Likewise, friendship is based on similarity, but not radical similarity, since it is based on a lack and thus implies difference. With regard to the friendship underlying the relationship between student and teacher, we may need to ask how it is that this concept of "similarity in difference" or "difference in similarity" applies to it.

Here, Plato's student and friend Aristotle provides further elaboration. In particular, Aristotle's analysis of teaching and learning in *Physics* III.3 offers an interesting continuation of Plato's insights concerning difference and identity in the context of the teacher-student relationship. Aristotle argues that the two processes of teaching and learning are distinct. They are so both in terms of their being (*to einai*) and in terms of their meaning or principle (*logos*) (*Physics* III.3 202b16-22). Importantly, the difference between the *action* of teaching and the *passion* of learning is not just an issue of linguistics, as Thomas points out: compared to linguistic synonyms such as "raiment' and "dress" whose names are different but who share the same *logos* or *ratio*, teaching and learning are similar in subject, while differing in terms of *ratio*.[19]

In support of this claim we could argue that teaching is indeed very particular in its use of pedagogy and teaching style, while learning has its own particulars in the form of preparation, attentiveness, memorization, etc. Although the processes of teaching and learning are distinct in meaning or principle, according to Aristotle they belong to the same movement, the actualization of the potency of the student to acquire knowledge. The activity of teaching, although originating in the teacher (the agent), finds

---

(*Symposium* 205e2-206a11).
19 St. Thomas Aquinas, *Commentary on Aristotle's* Physics, trl. by R.J. Blackwell, R.J. Spath and W.E. Thirlkel, Notre Dame: Dumb Ox Books, 1999, Lecture 5: 317, p. 159. I am grateful to Ryan Madison for drawing my attention to this particular passage.

its actualization, according to Aristotle, in the student (the patient), since the goal of teaching consists in a student acquiring knowledge. Thus, in Philoponus' words, should a teacher speak "in the presence of the learner, but does not work upon the learner, he is not said to be teaching; teaching, therefore, is not simply the application of the theorems, but the persuasion which the words of the teacher bring about in the learner."[20]

Although the two processes of teaching and learning are different in being and meaning, they are identical in that they *belong* (*hyparchei*) to the same "thing" or movement (*kinēsis*): that of the student going from a potential state of knowledge to an actual state of knowledge. In other words, teaching and learning are identical in that they both inhere in the same substratum.[21] It is ultimately this sense of belonging together to one underlying phenomenon that binds these two processes together into one, just as climbing a ladder ties together ascent and descent.[22]

The actualization of knowledge is the motion upon which both teaching and learning hinge. This actualization is not in the possession of either student or teacher. Rather, both student and teacher participate in this event – they belong to this event, yet cannot be reduced to it. For the student-teacher relationship this means that student and teacher *belong* together, but are also utterly different qua student and teacher.

Concluding words

As shown in Plato's account of the *Lysis*, neither absolute difference nor absolute identity can underlie friendship; rather, a tension between belonging and being apart grounds friendship. In *Physics* III.3, Aristotle clarifies the specific kinship that underlies the relationship between teacher and student. As shown in Aristotle's account, teacher and student are always tied to the process of actualizing knowledge, which both unifies and separates them. Without this process or without each other they cannot be properly called teacher or student; they cannot be reduced to each other or to this process either. Thus, actualizing knowledge holds a spell over both

---

20 Philoponus, *On Aristotle's* Physics, Ithaca, Cornell University Press, 1994, 381, 15-16
21 Ibid., 383, 23.
22 Ibid., 383, 24-27.

student and teacher: from the beginning, it gathers them together, ties them together, yet also keeps them apart. While this applies to all forms of teaching and learning, this dependence upon the actualization of knowledge is most prominently present in philosophy, as philosophy thematizes this process explicitly and always questions whether it has truly taken place or what kind of knowledge has been actualized. As philosophers, our belonging to the process and the dynamics of philosophy holds us together and divides us. Our belonging to this event is not possessed by anyone, but instead, to reiterate Aristotle's opening words with which I began this paper, student and teacher "share in philosophy" (*philosophias koinōnēsasin*) (*EN*, IX.1, 1164b3-4).[23]

Philosophy and Friendship II: A Response to Adriaan Peperzak

In his response to "Philosophy and Friendship," Adriaan Peperzak elaborates on the mutual dependency of teachers and students and insightfully formulates how teacher and student are drawn to each other and their discipline through a convergent desire – a "desire for *eudaimonia*, enlightened by the knowledge that *eudaimonia* without (*philo-*)*sophia* is impossible." Indeed, it is through reflection on this convergent desire that Plato and Aristotle gave new meanings to words such as *eudaimonia* and *philosophia* by showing the existential and conceptual interdependence of these two concepts.

Yet, both Plato and his student Aristotle have struggled with the tension between the practical and theoretical life that arises when *eudaimonia* and *philosophia* are brought so closely together. This tension is made especially palpable through the *Republic*'s haunting image of the ethereal philosopher-king – lonesome even while living together with fellow "kings" in barracks, whose only family is constituted by the anonymous faces of the *polis*, and who is forced to rule a city at the risk of his own life. This is, at the very least, an uneasy compromise between a practical life and a theoretical life that is divine but lonesome, and at most, pure torture for those involved. Aristotle's analyses of the theoretical and the practical life in the *Nicomachean Ethics* are not less problematic than Plato's. Having

---
23 I am grateful to my students Kristin Drake and Heather Fox for their editorial assistance and the insights they provided on earlier versions of this paper, its preface, and the ensuing response.

devoted the majority of this work to explaining the importance of virtue of character and practical wisdom (*phronēsis*) for *eudaimonia*, the happy practical "bubble" implodes when contemplation (*theoria*) enters the stage and stakes a claim to *eudaimonia*. Gone is the active political leader with his flourishing family, surrounded by friends, sponsoring a great festival and exhibiting courage on the battlefield. A pale, lonesome, self-sufficient (*autarkēs*) philosopher takes his place, with a scroll in hand, far removed from the busy activities of the market-place.

But: isn't this a caricature? Perhaps – but even when we admit this and disregard the exaggerations, we are still confronted with the same problem: how to integrate *eudaimonia* and *philosophia* while easing the tension between the *practically* and the *theoretically* virtuous way of life. This issue is also at the core of any inquiry into the role of teaching in the philosophical life. For insofar as teaching is practical and philosophizing is theoretical, it seems that Plato's and Aristotle's answers to this question will invariably suffer from the same kind of tension as described above. Is then the only way out indeed through Thomas's appeal to charity, as Ryan describes it? Can only charity synthesize *praxis* and *theoria* in didactic communication?

Perhaps not: for another, more "Greek" solution presents itself when we take a closer look at what it means to share philosophy with others – specifically when we consider how the teacher-student relationship can acquire meaning in the context of Aristotle's accounts of friendship (*philia*) and philosophy in his *Nicomachean Ethics* and in his *Eudemian Ethics*. To reveal the correlation between teaching, *philia*, and philosophy we must explain how Aristotle defines *philia* and how this definition applies to teaching philosophy. As we will see, the pivotal axis around which this conceptual affiliation turns is the concept of the friend as "another self."

First, in his ethical works, Aristotle famously distinguishes three "motivations"[24] behind friendship, and argues that only friendship based on virtue (*aretē*) is friendship proper, whereas friendships based on utility and

---

[24] Notably, as Adriaan Peperzak explains in "Vriendschap en Filosofie" (*Friendship and Philosophy*), the distinction between these three forms of friendship is to be understood as "a distinction between three motivations which can possibly occur simultaneously" (Adriaan Peperzak, 2007, p.173).

pleasure are only derivatively so (*EN* VIII.4, 1157a29-34). In the latter two cases, people are friends based on an incidental quality of the friend (*EN* VIII.4, 1157b3) and they do not love the friend as himself *qua* himself (*EE* VII.2, 1237b1-4). Moreover, complete (*teleios*) friendship or friendship proper implies virtuous equality between two friends. Finally, Aristotle defines the true friend as "another self" (*heteron authos*, *EN* IX.4, 1166a31, IX.9, 1169b6, 1170b7).

It is exactly by understanding the concept of "self" and "other self" that more of the connections between friendship, teaching, and philosophy can be clarified. To comprehend the Greek "self," we first need to take a step back from our own (post)modern conceptions, since for the Greeks the self was "differently organized from our own."[25] Vernant argues that for the Greeks "[t]he subject does not constitute a closed internal world, which he must enter in order to find or, rather, to discover himself. The subject is turned to the outside. In the same way as the eye does not see itself, the individual looks elsewhere, outwards, before apprehending himself."[26] A passage such as the following seems to underscore this relational and secondary character of the self: "In perception, we perceive that we perceive, and in thinking we perceive that we think. But to perceive that we are perceiving or thinking means that we exist (*hoti esmen*)" (*EN* IX.9, 1170a31-35). This passage implies that self-awareness is only secondary to performing activities such as perceiving and thinking. Secondly, it shows that this "entity" that possesses awareness has no conceptual name. Stern-Gillet keenly notes: "to denote what later philosophers will call the self Aristotle has to resort to a subordinate clause 'that we are.'"[27]

But about what kind of self are we talking here? Aristotle's self has to be understood as an "achievement word,"[28] as it represents the ideal balance between the various parts of the soul[29] ruled by reason. The

---

25 J.-P. Vernant, *L'Individu, la Mort, l'Amour: Soi-Même et Autre en Grèce Ancienne* (Paris: Gallimard) 1989, p. 224.
26 Vernant, 1989, p. 225.
27 S. Stern-Gillet, *Aristotle's Philosophy of Friendship* (Albarny, NY: SUNY Press) 1995, p.21.
28 Stern-Gillet 1995, p.29.
29 As Stern-Gillet writes, it is for this reason that "akratic and vicious people are not 'selves'; not only do their passions and appetites pull in different directions, but they rebel against and weaken the part that ought to direct them." Stern-Gillet,1995, p.29.

ideal is one of harmony and balance, whereas a wicked soul is one that is divided against itself: "one part pulls in one direction and the other in another as if to tear the individual to pieces" (*NE* IX.4, 1166b21-22). Thus, "wicked people run away from life and do away with themselves" (*NE* IX.4, 1166b11-12). The ideal self is a self that is under the mastery of intelligence (*nous*). In fact, Aristotle argues that "it is the thinking part (*to nouon*) of each individual that constitutes what he really is or constitutes it in a greater degree than anything else" (*EN* IX.4, 1166a22).

Since intellectual activity proves to be the ultimate definition of the self, complete friendship necessarily entails "intellectual symbiosis."[30] Due to the fact that life for humans is characterized primarily by perceiving (*aisthanometha*) and thinking (*noōmen*) as well as perceiving *that* we perceive and think (*EN* IX.9, 1170a30), to regard a friend as another self means to share this very perception (*sunaisthanesthai*; *EN* IX.9, 1170b11). As Aristotle writes, sharing in this meta-perception can be accomplished by living together and "by sharing each other's words and thoughts" (*koinōnein logōn kai dianoias*, *EN* IX.9, 1170b11-12).

After clarifying how the Greek self has an essential outward character that is mostly defined by intelligence, and after having defined true friendship as intellectual symbiosis, it is easier to grasp how teaching philosophy is to be assessed from an Aristotelian perspective. On the one hand, Aristotle seems to argue that teaching and learning (of any subject, so also philosophy) seem to exclude perfect friendship, since they imply an inequality between teacher and student: one (the student) lacks what the other (the teacher) has (*EE* VII.12, 1245a17-18), while true friendship is defined on the basis of similarity. On the other hand, on the basis of the definition of true friendship as intellectual symbiosis, it could easily be argued that teaching philosophy operates within the context of complete friendship, as teaching philosophy is less defined by "deficiencies" that need to be filled than by *sharing* (*EE* VII.1245a15, *EN* IX.1, 1164b6) in philosophy and par excellence in philosophical thought-experiments about "the end (*telos*) one is capable of attaining" (*EE* VII.12, 1245b7-8). In other words, when

---

30 Stern-Gillet, 1995, p. 54.

we bracket the formal terms in which two people engage in philosophical dialogues – the one *qua* teacher and the other one *qua* student – and focus instead on the process or dialogue that takes place, namely the actualization of the divine activity of thinking, then teaching-and-learning philosophy is part of the life lived-together-with-friends-in-*eudaimonia*. It is in this vein that Aristotle can be seen to approximate Peperzak's words in his essay *Friendship and Philosophy*: "philosophers can become friends, insofar as they enjoy sharing a tradition, a selection of favorite texts, a specific affinity with exemplary thinkers, and a focus on essential problems. Their conversations are oriented toward a common goal – the discovery of truth which cannot be privatized but which is important to all – while they, by considering each other's statements, will ameliorate their own thinking skills."[31]

If Aristotle expresses this idea only hesitantly and cursorily – "But a wise man is able to study even by himself… perhaps he could do it better if he had colleagues (*sunergous*) to work with him…" (*EN* X.7, 1177a35-1177b1) – we need to underline that his theory of friendship and his understanding of philosophizing or contemplation as a divine activity warrants a far more explicit recognition of the rich conceptual connection between friendship, teaching, philosophy and *eudaimonia*.

The above analysis adds force to Adriaan Peperzak's point that Aristotle's understanding of teaching and learning in *Physics* III.3 needs to be amended, since the image it evokes "of one ladder on which teacher and learner walk in different directions" is too static and needs to instead allow for "an intermittent movement up-and-down on both sides." Indeed, as long as teaching and learning philosophy are considered as different – though complementary – movements, Aristotle's argument in *Physics* III.3 holds little promise for understanding the truly dialogical nature of philosophy. However, if we focus less on the divergence of the two movements but focus more on "the ladder that joins heaven and earth" along which those movements take place, teaching and learning again become part of one process – as "teaching-and-learning" in the hyphenation suggested by Adriaan Peperzak, or as "sharing philosophy" in true intellectual symbiosis, as Aristotle envisioned it.

---

31 Adriaan Peperzak, 2007, p. 173.

THE PLACE OF PHILOSOPHY: THE IMPORTANCE OF SOCRATIC QUESTIONING IN EDUCATION
§

Corinne M. Painter

<u>Preface</u>

The May 2009 gathering in honor of Adriaan Peperzak, held at Loyola University Maryland and graciously hosted by Catriona Hanley, as well as this volume, which is filled with our conversations both during and inspired by that beautiful meeting of souls, may – nay, should – be characterized as a truly fine display of genuine philosophical dialogue, insofar as it exhibits our shared, humble and cautious pursuit of truth and wisdom, which is both *informed by* our experience of the world, of our place in that world, and of each other, as well as *directed toward* gaining ever greater – albeit always inadequate – insight into this same human experience. Though much philosophizing (both historical and contemporary) follows what might be referred to as a "Parmenidean model," which emphasizes logic and certainty, and, thus, completeness and finality, the most honest philosophizing is, in my view, characterized by the philosopher's commitment to live an examined life that, recognizing its own finitude, pursues a life that manifests in the most authentic ways what it means to be human, to live mortally in the light – and indeed the partial hiddenness – of that which orients all thinking and living: that most primordial dimension of our being that calls us forth to become what we "should be," namely, humble and cautious pursuers of truth, wisdom and justice, indeed erotic imitators of all that is excellent. Rather obviously, philosophy conceived in this Platonic-Socratic manner is a dynamic, continuous, flowing and fluid life-project that, unlike other expressions of philosophical praxis, will not see a proper end during our mortal lives. On this view, the philosophical life demands the recognition of the essential *mimetic* connection between that which is pure and good and that which falls short of these ideals, together with the commitment to live in accord with the wisdom and character that such a recognition affords.

I believe that unlike most philosophical meetings and many philosophical texts, which seek to *end philosophical debate or discussion by pronouncing the final truth on a particular matter,* our philosophical dialogue, which is so splendidly captured within this volume, bespeaks *authentic philosophical friendship amongst its contributors,* and thereby reveals not only our shared concern for each other and for our ceaseless collective pursuits of wisdom and excellence, but also our shared appreciation for the provisional, tentative, inspiring, dialogical, and yet transcendentally-oriented nature of our pursuits, which are necessarily bathed in our beautiful, albeit incomplete, humanness. Indeed, I believe that in this conversation, *"In Praise of Speaking, Reading, Writing, Teaching, Discussion: A Gathering in Honor of Adriaan Peperzak,"* just as each of has been transformed by the others, each has also transformed the others, and moreover, I believe that each of our contributions to this unfinished conversation represent exactly what they should, namely, in the words of Dr. Peperzak, "first episodes of a discussion between participants who do not offer their last thoughts, but rather support one another in developing their questions, experiments, descriptions, thoughts, and provisional conclusions, as stages on the way [of our] philosophically nourished and co-oriented journey."

As for my own written contributions to this project, I hope that my focus on the place of philosophy and the importance of Socratic questioning in education inspires us to reflect further on our role as educators, particularly of those who are not amongst the philosophically anointed. For it may be the case that the promise of humanity depends on whether the many come to recognize and appreciate that a truly meaningful and excellent human life, which acknowledges the inability of material goods to offer genuine or appropriate fulfillment, is not only possible but is loudly – and proudly – calling forth to us.

I. Introductory Remarks: A Tribute to Adriaan Peperzak

Nearly twelve years after I began my doctoral studies with Dr. Peperzak, I still find myself in awe of Adriaan's work and his person. Nearly ten years ago, as I began to prepare for work on my dissertation, and in celebration of his 70th birthday, I wrote a letter to Adriaan in which I expressed my deepest gratitude and appreciation for his work and his teaching, as well as for his personal guidance and support; for there is no doubt that all of these treasured gifts shaped me into the thinker, scholar, and teacher I am today. In that letter, I noted how fortunate I and his other students were to be *his* students, how we were all benefiting in tremendously significant ways as a result of his generous wisdom, which he shared with us in so many different venues, including in the classroom, in his public lectures, in his private meetings with us, and in his writings. In addition, I expressed my hope that our connection would remain strong, long after I finished my studies, and that we would continue to be engaged in critical dialogue and discussion as long as life would allow. Participating in this meeting in honour of Adriaan this weekend surely demonstrates his lasting influence on me, and on all of us gathered here, and it shows that my hope for a continuing connection, dialogue, and discussion has not been disappointed. I do not exaggerate in saying how truly honoured and excited I am to be here, indeed how proud I am to be celebrating Adriaan Peperzak as a philosopher, as a teacher, and as a person, on (or very near) his 80th birthday.

Having settled, a few years ago, into a permanent position at a Community College in Ann Arbor, I have become – at least professionally

– much more of a teacher of philosophy than a scholar or researcher, as most of my time is spent preparing and offering undergraduate philosophy courses (to the tune of 5 per semester, in fact). As such, I primarily identify myself with my work for and in the undergraduate classroom, and it is this work, that is, the task of doing philosophy with undergraduate students, and the responsibility that is associated with this extremely important project, that I want to discuss in the brief set of reflections that follow. After briefly discussing how studying Plato with Adriaan helped shape me into the responsible teacher of philosophy that I hope I am, I will attempt to outline how essential I think Socratic philosophy is to the project of educating students.

II. Philosophy as a Teaching Vocation: Socratic Education of the Soul

A. Everyone knows that a good teacher can be one of the greatest influences in a person's life. As I mentioned in my opening, Adriaan certainly played that role for me. But not just in the obvious way of teaching me how to read Plato or Heidegger or Levinas or Gadamer, which he did beautifully, not to mention skillfully. And not just by gently guiding me towards more appropriate or thoughtful interpretations of these and other thinkers. In addition to this, Adriaan demonstrated through his writing, his teaching, and his very person, what it means *to be a philosopher*, i.e., what it means to live a philosophical life. Indeed, save for Adriaan and very few others, "the look" of the philosopher is something I had primarily been exposed to only through the figure of Socrates, who comes to life for us in the challenging dialogues of Plato. In fact, it was my love for Socrates, which took hold of me when I studied Plato as an undergraduate, that motivated me to become a philosopher myself. Thankfully, while a doctoral student, Adriaan fostered my love for Socrates and Plato, by demonstrating his own appreciation for the wisdom, truth, love, and goodness that the dialogues give us, and by showing how that appreciation informed his whole character and not just his thinking.

Of course, such claims require some discussion of how I am conceiving of the philosophical life, and more specifically, of how I take it to be expressed within Plato's dialogues as well as why I think Socratic philosophizing should govern our praxis as teachers. In this vein, I submit that for Plato philosophy is quite certainly intimately bound up with the human attempt to understand ourselves, each other, our world, and our place within that world, and that he conceives this attempt to be not merely theoretical in nature but fundamentally practical and thus ethical in nature as well.[32] This understanding of philosophy, which rather conspicuously identifies philosophy with *Socratic philosophy*, rejects the notion that philosophy is understood by Plato as a mere theoretical activity, which is unconcerned with or in some way removed from social, practical and ethical interests. And it suggests, rather, that Plato conceives of philosophy as a *vocation*, perhaps even – as I will advance – a vocation of teaching within which the philosopher devotes herself, as Socrates did, to the never-ending project of attempting to understand not only "what reality is and why it is so" (Peperzak, 32),[33] but also how we are to act towards and within this reality, the latter of which requires one to be concerned with what I like to call "the problem of how to live." While this understanding of philosophy as a vocation, and more specifically, as a *Socratic way of life that is decisively chosen and to which one remains committed*, is in some measure simply assumed in this discussion[34] (as I will not offer an argument against those who would advance another conception of philosophy), in the remarks that follow, I will nevertheless attempt to show how Plato seems to endorse, through his dialogues, and especially through his *positive* depiction of the figure of

---

[32] I recognize that to speak of "Plato's conception of philosophy" could be problematic, especially given that, with the exception of the *Seventh Letter*, Plato does not speak of philosophy within his dialogues in his own voice. Nevertheless, I take it that there are certain "themes" that are so central in Plato's work that they deserve to be viewed as those thoughts concerning the nature of philosophy about which Plato is strongly convicted and to which he is, thus, at least somewhat committed. This is most easily seen when we acknowledge the way in which Plato offers these thoughts to us through the mouth of his own "teacher" Socrates.

[33] Peperzak Adriaan. *System and History in Philosophy: On the Unity of Thought and Time, Text and Explanation, Solitude and Dialogue, Rhetoric and Truth in the Practice of Philosophy and its History* (New York: State University of New York Press, 1986). All further references to this author will refer to this text and shall be cited by author's last name, followed by the appropriate page number(s).

[34] I fully appreciate that some have a different conception of philosophy, and do not see an essential connection between the philosophical enterprise and ethical or practical life. And although this is not the understanding of philosophy with which I am sympathetic, I will not attempt to *directly* argue against such a conception of philosophy here; rather, I simply wish to articulate the conception of philosophy that is in play in this discussion.

Socrates, a Socratic conception of philosophy that supposes an intimate connection between what may be called the "academic" or "theoretical" pursuit of philosophy and the practical pursuit of an ethical and good life. And related to this, I intend to show how the merging of the academic and the social-practical-ethical aspects of philosophy should inform our role as teachers. Thankfully, Adriaan showed that such a merging is possible, through his own constant and steadfast theoretical and ethical pursuit of truth, wisdom, and goodness, which was exhibited quite clearly and consistently to his students.

B. Here, it is important to highlight that because I am operating with a conception of philosophy that identifies it as a *teaching vocation*, not only should we resist the temptation to wholly identify philosophy with abstract theoretical activity, but we should also resist the temptation to conceive philosophy as able to access the *final* truth of the matters that it is most interested in pursuing. Accordingly, we should recognize that the Socratic philosopher's pursuit of truth and knowledge is decisively different than non-philosophical (or anti-Socratic-Platonic) pursuits of truth and knowledge, insofar as – and somewhat paradoxically – it is both more cautious and fuller. For, it is, I submit, the Socratic philosopher who is most fully oriented towards a wisdom that, following Socrates – and as Plato expresses in the *Apologia* – we might want to refer to as "human,"[35] and it is this pursuit that the Socratic philosopher is poised both to demonstrate to and to inspire within our students. In this connection, we would do well to admit that it is likely the Socratic philosopher alone who acknowledges the limitations of her attempts to discover truth, and admits that her ignorance as well as her finitude are fundamental pre-conditions of her desire and thus of her attempts to know. And it is perhaps she who relishes in the relation between admitted ignorance, finitude, love of wisdom and ethical life, which she, in turn, presents to her students. Indeed, as Socrates remarks in his defense, "it is *better* to be as [he is]" (*Apologia*, 22e8, emphasis mine), precisely because he recognizes that his knowledge is limited (23b5), and that he does not and cannot know everything. For it is this recognition

---

35 *Apologia*, 20d9-13.

that allows him to respond to his "condition" by remaining committed to "practicing philosophy" (29d8), since he does not presume to know what he does not know, an admission that is a prerequisite for philosophy and is opposed to the condition of blameworthy ignorance, which is cloaked in hubris and arrogance. As is well known, practicing philosophy in this Socratic sense involves exhorting everyone, including oneself, by questioning whether we "are not ashamed of our eagerness to possess as much wealth, reputation and honors as possible, while not caring for nor giving thought to wisdom or truth, or to the best possible state of the soul" (29e1-6).

Indeed, I take over Socrates' view (which I suggest is Plato's view) that the genuine philosopher tries to live a *life of human excellence*, which is nothing else than *a life that cares for knowing and doing excellent things in an excellent way*, and that she takes it to be her responsibility to inspire in her students the same sort of concern for living an ethical and good life. Furthermore, I think that it is our responsibility as teachers of philosophy not only to expose our students to the claims and theories of those thinkers who have framed our views and our thinking, but to instill in them the proper sense of awe for the philosophically inquisitive life, and, thus, for the proper and the good. Just think: if there were more Socratic models teaching our students as they prepared for their professional careers, perhaps we would have fewer Bernie Madoffs, and fewer AIG corporate executives who feel no shame taking for themselves what is surely not theirs to take, all while unabashedly deceiving and harming others..... Sadly, many more examples could be given, but I shall move on for fear that our moral disgust might take over!

I suppose that part of what I am emphasizing as essential to our vocation as teachers is the recognition that our pursuits of wisdom necessarily bear the stamp of the practical and the ethical, i.e., of what matters – or of what should matter – to us as living beings who speak, think, and act within a world inhabited by others. To put this in the words of Adriaan, all genuine philosophical questions touch upon the central questions of human life in the world and in history, directly or indirectly, [and as such], being absorbed by such problems is one of the characteristics of philosophy: it is always related to what truly and ultimately matters (13).

As I suggested a moment ago, this is, to put it plainly, a life of ethical excellence, that is, a life of virtue, which is dedicated to truth, justice, and goodness.

On this view, as Joe Sachs writes,[36] "Parmenides, for example, had it exactly backwards when he told Socrates that philosophy requires a studied indifference to its topics" (44), and he was therefore wrong when he claimed that Socrates was "not yet completely philosophic, because he wanted to inquire not about dirt but about the just and the beautiful" (ibid., 40).[37] For, ultimately, "philosophy can only be about what matters to us..." (ibid., 44), and thus Plato would want us to reject conceptions of philosophy that describe the philosophical enterprise as one in which disconnected, "a-ethical," entirely indifferent investigations of its matters are in order. In fact, when reading a Platonic dialogue, one gets the impression that "indifference seems to be the only reaction one cannot have to a [genuinely] philosophical question, if one is aware of it at all" (ibid.). This, I think, is the conception of philosophy that we ought to display to and engage in with our students, and thus it should replace the much more practically removed and abstract sort of philosophizing that has given philosophers a bad name outside our very insular community, and which often causes students' eyes to become heavy as they fight succumbing completely to the comfort of dreaming while sitting in our classrooms.

We may put this differently by acknowledging that because philosophical inquiry (just as every inquiry) takes place within what we may call the "space" of human life, our truth-seeking endeavors, no matter how abstract they may seem to be, are linked, ultimately, to practical and ethical interests. For without recourse to such an interest, namely one that is grounded – whether admitted or not – in the thought that it is useful, helpful, worthwhile, appropriate, interesting and/or better, to discover the truth about something, one cannot explain the initial motivation to engage in

---

[36] Sachs, Joe. "What is a What-is Question?" in *The St. John's Review*, Vol. XLII (1993). All further references to this author will refer to this essay and shall be cited by author's last name, followed by the appropriate page number(s).

[37] See *Parmenides* 130e.

the project of coming to know about that something. This can perhaps be seen most clearly when we recognize, as Socrates routinely does, that engagement in the project of coming to know about something requires one to suspend any earlier claims to know the matter(s) at issue. This might best be explained by acknowledging that "there has to be some issue that matters enough to us to make it worthwhile to call into question all the safe opinions on which we base our lives, [since] someone who does not care about the thing in question cannot see the point of suspending his prejudices,..." (Sachs, 44). Certainly, to maintain this is to argue against the "Parmenidean line... that topics of philosophy do not count for philosophy while only logical structures do, [such that] the philosophic discipline requires purging ourselves of any motive to care about any one thing more than another" (ibid., 41), and it is to argue for the Socratic position that philosophical inquiry admits its origin in a desire to know about what is at stake in our lives, which is to say, about that which touches us in the most intimate way. To attribute this view of the connection between philosophy and what is at stake in our lives to Plato makes good sense if we but take notice of how Plato typically only has "Socrates ask 'the what-is question' about certain kinds of things" (ibid., 44), namely, about virtue, knowledge, justice, beauty, love, the good, and so on.

Consequently, since it is Socrates – or, more generally, the Socratic philosopher – whom Plato depicts throughout the dialogues as the one who acknowledges and embraces both [a] her own finitude, her inescapable lack, indeed her limitation in the face of her pursuits of knowledge and her associated commitment to continue these pursuits nevertheless, as well as [b] the way in which her pursuits of knowledge bear an intimate relation to practical and ethical concerns, i.e., to what matters most in life, it is the Socratic philosopher whom Plato offers as the one who is most fully in touch with the nature of her pursuits of truth and wisdom, and who I argue is in the proper position to genuinely educate students, not just in the academic discipline of philosophy, but also as ethical persons who routinely question their claims to know and their characters, and who call others to do this as well.

Given the contentious and rather bold tenor of these claims, both about the nature of philosophy as Plato conceives it, as well as about the proper approach to teaching, we may be compelled to raise several questions, including the question of how the prospective teacher of philosophy should be described. To be sure, the attitude of such a (prospective) teacher would be characterized by a certain radicality, as it were, since her understanding of the project of philosophy presupposes a break with more "traditional" pursuits of truth and knowledge, including Parmenidean pursuits that attempt to distance themselves from the ethical and the practical. In this way it would appreciate that "the fear that the presence of desire will destroy our 'objectivity' is misplaced" (Sachs, 44, emphasis mine) and it would replace this fear with a commitment to follow out our desires to know what is true and best and right and good precisely within the "intersubjective reality" (Peperzak, 26) that seems to provide the necessary foundation of philosophy (ibid.), not to mention defines the situation of our classrooms. In addition, it would e not only the limitations inherent in one's attempts to gain knowledge, but also the related need to subject to critical examination those claims of knowledge that are widely accepted as true, which we often hear our students (not to mention our colleagues!) offering both within and outside of our classrooms. Indeed, our challenge as teachers of philosophy requires us to subject every knowledge claim to radical critique, and to abide by the demand that all knowledge be examined and legitimized, if it is to count as knowledge. What could be a better project in which to engage with one's students?! Just imagine the new world of possibilities for thinking and living that would be opened up to them, if they were to be educated in such a manner! This, I submit, is a view of education that is wholly Socratic, which genuinely expresses the desire to live a true and good life by way of engaging, continuously and with the utmost of dedication, in self-critically reflective examinations, both of our own claims and of our own characters, as well as the associated desire to present the possibility of such a life to others, most especially to our students. I contend that it is precisely this that displays the height of our vocation as teacher, insofar as it is through argumentation, dialogue, and example that we can demonstrate that the philosophical life is the life of human responsibility and excellence, i.e., that it is what we are called to be.

III. The Classroom as the Philosophical Space for Considering the Problem of How to Live

Though we might be tempted to think that in connecting responsibility and philosophy in such an intimate way we must understand this rather heightened understanding of responsibility as "absolute," in the sense that it is not subject to the "peculiarities" – if you will – that frame human experience, precisely the contrary is the case. For it is rather the case that the responsibility that belongs to the philosopher depends upon the philosopher's humanity in such a way that if the philosopher had no "place" she would in turn have no "responsibility." Though there are probably many ways to defend this claim, perhaps it is most instructive to consider the distinctive importance of the dramatic, context-specific settings that frame the Platonic dialogues, which, not incidentally, also frame our classrooms, giving our teaching its own dramatic context. Drew Hyland forcefully addresses this when, in one of his central texts on Plato,[38] he discusses the significance that "place" is given in the Platonic dialogues. In this connection, Hyland claims that perhaps the single most distinguishing feature of the Platonic dialogue compared to other formats of philosophic writing is that the dialogue always begins in a specific place, a specific situation, within which the limitations as well as the possibility of each dialogue arise (Hyland, 14).

In this way, he says, "the Platonic dialogue is realistic in a manner matched by no other philosophic writing, quite especially the dominant one, the philosophic essay or treatise" (ibid.). Hyland boldly states that though most philosophical texts and discussions present themselves as if the place and circumstances within which the philosophical text is written, or within which the discussion occurs, are irrelevant to the philosophical content, this presentation is only "pretense" (ibid.), and I contend that we

---

38 Hyland, Drew. *Finitude and Transcendence in the Platonic Dialogues* (New York: State University of New York Press, 1995): p. 10-11. All further references to this text will be cited by author's last name, followed by the appropriate page number(s).

would do well to emphasize this to our students in every discussion we have in the classroom.

Characterizing philosophy in this way may seem dangerous, though, given that philosophy is supposed to be that practice which is removed from the subjectively determined factors of human experience; for otherwise philosophy warrants no special status. In this case, philosophy, or so some scholars might argue, could not be considered a "science" – not to mention the ground of science – since its discoveries would be affected by the various conditions and limitations of human experience – e.g., time, circumstance, historical situatedness, the psyches of those participating in the philosophizing, just to name a few – all of which are subject to change, thus calling into question the so-called immutable truthfulness that is meant to characterize the discoveries that are won on the basis of philosophical work. Accordingly, there is no temptation on the part of many scholars to take into serious account these "conditions" of human experience when attempting to understand a philosopher's claims or a philosophical text. In fact, the temptation is precisely the opposite, namely, to discount such factors in the name of "saving" philosophy from a fate worse than death: its determination as a non-scientific, tentative praxis that commands no reasonable person's assent to its claims, and which understands itself as subject to some limitation, allowing its claims to be repeatedly subjected to critical examination and modification.[39]

There are of course many ways in which "place" seems to be significant to the praxis of philosophy for Plato, which (in the interest of time and space) I will forego discussing explicitly. Instead, because I think it is especially important in a discussion of teaching, I shall simply highlight the significance that Plato seems to place on the peculiarity of the particular characters (psyches, souls) of Socrates' interlocutors. For rather than having Socrates' logos be directed to "just anyone," Plato always depicts him speaking to particular interlocutors, who display distinct characters. According to Hyland, "Socrates … always says what he says to specific people, to particular character types" (20), which suggests that Plato's depiction of Socrates' attempts to discuss whatever is at issue in a way that could attract and hold the attention of his individual interlocutors was intentional, probably rooted in his hope to show that even at the beginning stages of genuine discourse, that is, within Socratic dialogue, those with whom one is speaking must be taken into account if one has any hope of being philosophically responsible. This point cannot be emphasized enough when discussing our roles as teachers, given that our interlocutors are our students, who have placed themselves in our hands, entrusting us with the responsibility of attending to them – of holding their attention – by educating them. This responsibility is all the more important, given that many of our students may not understand all that is at stake in their own education, and thus we must be ever so careful and cautious with them, just as Socrates was, for example, with Theaetetus.

However, even while we admit that the motivation to do philosophy after the manner of Socrates, which involves becoming a teacher of philosophy and living a philosophical life, is rooted in our uniquely human wonder about how to understand and account for what is beautiful, best, and true about ourselves and our world, we should also be careful to acknowledge that this does not lead to the conclusion that philosophy must be understood as an entirely "subjective" endeavor, according to which only "relative truths" may be discovered. Instead, the difficult "truth" of the matter is that although philosophy cannot occur outside of the "place of human life," which is always concretely situated, particular, dynamic and fluid, it is precisely the project of the philosopher to attempt to transcend these bounding parameters in order to understand their origin and meaning.

We could also put this in the following way: we could say, following Adriaan, that

> *philosophy is a way of becoming true that does not stand on its own, independent of how the philosopher exists and is related to other persons and things. Truth does not deliver itself to an abstract, uprooted thought; it rather makes way for itself at the most genuine and truest "level," where the meaning of life is realized* (55).

On this view, that is to say, on Plato's view, what is at issue for the philosopher is nothing less than the truth about life, which, as such, involves the search for "the meaning" of everything we say, think, and do in the context and happening of our lives. This means that the philosophical search takes place while we live as human beings in the world of our experience, which is a dynamic and fluctuating world. However, this dynamic world always-already points beyond itself to its own conditions of possibility, indeed to its intelligibility, and it is in large measure precisely this project of attempting to follow out this "pointing" in one's thinking, speaking and acting – i.e., to transcend the limitations of the human condition – that commands the attention of the philosopher, and not just as she writes books or presents papers at professional, academic conferences, but as she engages in philosophizing with her students.

Importantly, acknowledging the precarious nature of the project in which the genuine, Socratic philosopher is engaged, should lead us to surmise that the philosopher's attempts to transcend the boundaries of the particular human situation within which philosophical concerns arise and which take the form of our attempts to discover and imitate what is best, beautiful, and true about ourselves and our world, are not short lived, and that they are, rather, never-ending, characterized by struggle and strife, quite complicated and difficult, and yet still compelling beyond all else. In addition, it should lead us to surmise, moreover, that given philosophy's "place," namely the dynamic and fluid space of human life, "complete knowledge is not possible in philosophy, and that this is an unattainable ideal" (Peperzak, 71). For, as Adriaan tells us, "the questions philosophy asks are just too difficult ... [as] they go beyond the boundaries of our capacity for insight" (ibid., 71), even as "the idea of a pure and complete truth continues to rule all authentic thinking, so that the discoveries of thoughtful – truly philosophical – activity do not abolish, but rather enrich, its limited perspective" (ibid., 73).

Thus, finally, insofar as Plato's dialogues "suggest that we must always begin within [the human] situation, and transcend it only with the greatest of caution and thoughtfulness, and always with the recognition of the finitude or partiality of all human transcendence" (Hyland, 8), it certainly seems clear that Plato, perhaps more than anyone, appreciates how the desire to know that which commands our most considered attention marks not only the beginning of philosophy but remains present throughout the philosophical life. This certainly reflects the intimate connection between the "human place" of the philosopher and her care and quest for truth and justice, which, I suspect, she may engage in most distinctively and influentially with her students, whose souls have been entrusted to her (often without them knowing it), and whose souls she is preparing for "conversion," whilst she shows them the way of philosophy. I am compelled to end this set of reflections on the intimate connection between Socratic philosophy and education by once again thanking Adriaan for taking such good care of his students' souls; he certainly prepared my soul for conversion!

> In this connection, one need only think of Descartes, and the many who follow his thought that philosophy must not make claims that are subject to the vagaries of human – contingent – experience. See Descartes, Rene, Discourse on Method and Meditations on First Philosophy; any French edition or any translation should do.

The Place of Philosophy: The Importance of Socratic Questioning in Education: Response to Adriaan's Comments and Questions

I am compelled to thank Adriaan for his concise and yet extremely thoughtful and accurate explication of my claims regarding the intimate connection between Socratic philosophizing and education. It is certainly true that, as he writes, I view "the Socratic ideal as a personal vocation that calls for responsibility and growing wisdom" and that I "emphasize the student's spiritual needs and the union of theory and practice as a primary condition of all education, without forgetting the limits of the human condition." In addition, more eloquently than I, Adriaan underlines the importance with which I view the "relevance of a philosopher's singularity for her exchange with her students" as well as the worry I have about the dangerous "philosophical vices that threaten the virtuous 'procreation in beauty' (as Plato refers to it)" of the philosophical transformation that genuine education of the soul makes possible.

I am also grateful for Adriaan's gentle and insightful question about how we can, and why we should, "be authentically Socratic or Platonic in word and manners," particularly given the post-medieval and post-modern world that we currently inhabit. His question stems, at least in part, from the astute acknowledgment that although my claims about "vocation, responsibility, and wisdom are not entirely exempt from religious connotation," my analysis, perhaps in true post-medieval and post-modern fashion, does not does explicitly admit of any religious origin, inspiration or goal for its reflections. Adriaan's question, quite nicely, mirrors questions that arose in our communal discussion of these claims during our May meeting, during which it was asked what conditions and realities characterize our philosophical situation in the 21st Century, and whether there is something peculiar about our present position that calls for a specific kind of philosophical praxis that may be different from those practices that have come before. In response to these important questions, which represent an "unfinished, first episode of a discussion" about how "a philosophical life may only realize itself in concrete manners and exercises," although my reflections remain fairly general, I should like to ever so briefly discuss in what way I think there both are and are not religious underpinnings and goals providing the ground and aim of the Socratic-Platonic conception of philosophical education I defend, and why I think this is important in the 21st Century. In my response, I shall attempt to show how this calls for a return to – indeed a retrieval of – Socratic-Platonic philosophy rather than a move towards a praxis of philosophy that associates itself with particular conceptions or prescribed paradigms of the Divine that are closely associated with many of today's most prominent organized religions. In any case, my brief remarks should be taken as "a promise rather than as a last word" about our current position and the philosophical praxis for which I think it beckons.

It would seem that if we are unwilling to employ a broad notion of religion, which (for example) does not rely upon personified conceptions of a Divine reality that is defined by characteristics or qualities of perfection that fly in the face of our sensibilities, philosophical and otherwise, and which, in turn, motivate us to become philosophically unreflective insofar as we are asked to cease attempts to try to *understand* the mysteries of life and existence by appealing to a God who denies us access to the very truths that we naturally seek, then philosophical praxis and education should not be associated with religion. For such a narrow understanding of religion, typical of many main-stream, organized religious traditions, denies the necessity of a never-ending, dynamic, fluid, and flawed, but yet sophisticated philosophical reflection, which, while certainly pointing towards a transcendent, non-material, ultimate condition for the possibility of meaningfulness (and perhaps for reality itself), does not and cannot issue in a claim to "know" or to adequately capture within our logos, nor within a set of exclusive dogmatic beliefs or practices of worship, this "ultimate original" that religion typically refers to as "God." Instead, the human, provisional, humble, always inadequate and yet necessary character of Socratic philosophy rightly struggles against such unsophisticated and yet arrogantly dogmatic answers to those questions with which humans find themselves most troubled, at least when they bother to engage in the practice of reflection at all. And although this sort of reflection has steadily declined over the centuries, as we have seen the rise (especially in the developed nations) of conceptions of human success and meaningfulness that emphasize material wealth at the expense of virtuous character and ethical excellence, this is not because people have become less religious, but it is consistent with becoming less philosophically engaged with the world.

While it is certainly appropriate to argue that the very notions of virtuous character and ethical excellence, insofar as they are not entirely relativistic or merely rooted in social convention, presuppose a Divine reality of some sort, this does not require us to suppose a "personal" reality who commands our obedience and dispenses upon us specific rules and regulations that we must follow in order to live according to a divinely-determined purpose. To believe this, commits us, in fact, to an *unphilosoph-*

ical life, just as surely as a sophistic life does, inasmuch as it stops us from being co-responsible for ourselves and for each other as we live in accord with our shared, common pursuits of truth and justice. Just as a sophistic life is mired in deception and blameworthy ignorance, the dogmatically religious life is also mired in deception and blameworthy ignorance, though for different reasons. Whereas at least some sophistic programs are characterized by a rejection of objective notions of truth and justice and goodness that is replaced by a relativism such as that which is famously proposed by Protagoras in his proclamation that "man is the measure of all things" (*Theaetetus*, 152a), the dogmatically religious life is undialogical and hubristic in its claims to know the final and complete truth about life and human purpose.

Alternatively, religion understood more broadly (for example) as a way and manner of life that appreciates the transcendence and ultimacy of the Good, which may only ever be partially uncovered through philosophical reflection and examination but which may never be captured in a set of dogmatic proclamations about the Divine or in a set of exclusive rules to be followed once and for all, must, it seems, provide both the *condition for the possibility of philosophical praxis, as well as the goal of philosophy*. As I offered, quoting Adriaan himself, in my initial essay, I believe that

philosophy is a way of becoming true that does not stand on its own, independent of how the philosopher exists and is related to other persons and things. Truth does not deliver itself to an abstract, uprooted thought; it rather makes way for itself at the most genuine and truest "level," where the meaning of life is realized.

Here, I mean to suggest – though admittedly without explicitly stating as much – *that philosophy is and must be religious, and conversely, that authentic religion is and must be philosophical,* given that both deal with the meaning and fulfillment of human life. So, while I do not want to completely identify the genuinely philosophical life with the authentically religious life (as I have characterized it just above), I do want to suggest that they complement one another.

The return to Socratic-Platonic philosophy for which I argue, then, is borne both (1) from my acknowledgment that I view the Divine condition, inspiration, and goal of philosophy in much the same way as I believe Socrates and Plato do, as well as (2) from my view that our present condition (which has been taking shape probably (at least) since the Enlightenment), with its dangerous emphasis on material and monetary success at all costs – which Capitalism especially promotes – and its associated disvaluing of virtue and ethical excellence, can best be overcome by recognizing that the human excellence to which we are all called by virtue of our membership in the human community, may only be achieved by engaging in continued and shared examination of our claims to know and of our characters. In this way, Socrates' centuries-old exhortation to the Athenians (offered in his defense reported on in the *Apologia*) that the "unexamined life is not worth living for man" (38a), which is prefaced by his explicit admonition of the Athenians, during which he questions whether they are "not ashamed of their eagerness to possess as much wealth, reputation, and honours as possible, *while they do not care for nor give thought to wisdom or truth, or the best possible state of their soul?*" (29d-e), proudly admitting that he will never cease trying to "persuade [everyone] ... not to care for their bodies or their wealth in preference to or as strongly as they care for the best possible state of their souls..." (30a), is precisely, in my view, what is required if we are to have hope for a future within which we flourish as a human community, not just materially, but emotionally and spiritually.

It is my contention that such a program is indeed religious in the most demanding and appropriate way, insofar as it speaks to an underlying bond of communion that binds humans together on their shared path to meaningfulness and excellence, which is a path that must be cautiously, humbly, and graciously lived, even as it is bathed in the light that shines forth – but only partially – from the Good. However, religious beliefs, rules, or practices that through their prescribed dogmas and hurtful, arbitrary exclusions constrain this most human endeavor to walk together on this fragile path to the Good do not provide appropriate models for human excellence and thus they must be challenged and eliminated, and they must be replaced by social-political-economic programs, policies, and practices that engage our natural empathetic and sympathetic imaginations. I dare say that these "programs" (as I have called them) are made possible and encouraged by a philosophical education that takes as its main project the transformation of the whole person such that she is oriented toward the Good, both in logos and in deed. Whether the Good must be identified or even associated with "God" (understood in the typical way) remains unclear, but what is, at least in my view, rather plainly transparent is that genuinely philosophical education may not forbid critical challenges to its tentative knowledge claims, just as it should not presume to know the full and final truth about ourselves or about our world.

To end this admittedly inadequate response to the thoughtful provocations of Adriaan regarding whether we can still be Socratic or Platonic in our world, with its 21st Century problems and threats, I should like to briefly appeal to the notion of "critical pedagogy" advanced and persuasively defended by Paolo Freire, who is well-known for his seminal work, *Pedagogy of the Oppressed*. Although the Socratic-Platonic conception of philosophical education I have defended here should certainly not be identified with the critical pedagogy of Freire, it is nevertheless the case that both paradigms (would) argue that the main goal of genuine and proper education should not be reduced to satisfying corporate and market-driven demands to produce workers who are skilled enough to allow companies or even entire nations to maintain their superior (global) economic positions, particularly at the expense of, to use contemporary jargon, social justice. Nowadays, there is little interest, as Henry Giroux writes, in understanding education "as a deeply civic, political, and moral practice… [since it is] increasingly subordinated to a corporate order… and replaced by training and the promise of economic security." I believe that both the Ancient and the contemporary critical view of education supposes, instead, that pedagogy is, or at least should be, "a political and a moral practice that provides the knowledge, skills, and social relations…. [that enable people to] "realize what it means to be a member of the community" (ibid.), and, more concretely, what their critically crucial role is as a responsible citizen of that polis. Just as Freire rejected educational systems that are "organized around the demands of the market, instrumentalized knowledge, and the priority of training over the pursuit of the imagination, critical thinking, and the teaching of freedom and social responsibility" (ibid.), in like fashion, Socrates and Plato recommend that our task as educators is not to "place sight into the blind" by teaching them to believe what our current political, religious, or economic interests dictate, which is akin to indoctrination; rather, our task – indeed our responsibility – is to "transform" those with whom we come into contact by redirecting the "eyes of their souls" such that they can awaken from "only dreaming about reality" (see *Republic*, 533c-d), since such dreaming thwarts our pursuits of truth, justice, and the Good, replacing them with dangerously deceptive ideologies. We might put this differently by stating that it is our duty to show out students the way and importance of freely and responsibly and critically thinking for themselves about those things that really matter; defending this notion of his life's work is, arguably, why Socrates was sentenced and put to death: he was simply too threatening to the status quo.

    I am convinced that as long as we allow powerful ideologies, whether they are political, economic, or dogmatically religious, to govern our educational paradigms, we will not overcome the personal and social problems that threaten our humanity in the Twenty-First Century, including those that involve our insatiable demand for and worship of money, as well as our unreflective worship of a God that forbids, punishes, excludes, and commands obedience to rules that do not seem to be grounded in care, compassion, justice, or love, but in something quite opposed to this. Instead, a return to a Platonic-Socratic program of education, with its fierce commitment to educating the whole person such that she can be guided by truth, justice, and the Good, even while she remains utterly and completely gracious, thankful, and humble in her attempts to be so guided, may offer us the best hope for a humanity that lives up to its potential of ethical excellence. For such a pedagogy, quoting Giroux again, "attempts not only to provide the conditions under which students can come to understand particular texts and different modes of intelligibility, but also opens up new avenues for them to make better *moral* judgments that will enable them to assume some sense of responsibility to the other (and to the world) in light of these judgments" (ibid., 3, quotation slightly altered). Perhaps such a program of education is *both* Socratic-Platonic *and* profoundly religious, in the most authentic way.

Philosophical education might be undertaken as a part of religious training, but often it is not.

Sadly, owing to time and space restrictions, I will not defend this claim here, but will save it for a future philosophical conversation, promised for another time.

Adriaan Peperzak. System System and History in Philosophy: On the Unity of Thought and Time, Text and Explanation, Solitude and Dialogue, Rhetoric and Truth in the Practice of Philosophy and its History (New York: State University of New York Press, 1986), p. 55.

Paolo Freire. Pedagogy of the Oppressed (New York: Continuum Publishing, 2000).

Political and military positions could also be discussed in this context.

Henry Giroux. "Rethinking Education as the Practice of Freedom: Paolo Freire and the Promise of Critical Pedagogy" in Truthout (3 January, 2010). All further references to this author have this on-line OpEd as their source.

IS THIS D/DESIRE?

§

Colin Anderson

Preface

What follows differs substantially from an inchoate and preliminary version of the same essay that I shared in Baltimore last spring. I intended to start from questions that puzzle me about Platonic philosophy, questions about desire and its relationship to knowledge, about whether, and how, we can be ignorant of our desires, and then to examine several Platonic texts before indicating how Adriaan's "phenomenological Platonism," if I may call it that, could be seen as both a recognition of the importance of these questions for philosophy and an indication of the presuppositions any possible answers. The essay was not successful: Here I offer a new version, which I hope is more successful than the first.

Plato indicates in a number of central texts that philosophia is not merely conditioned or caused by desire, but that there is a convergence towards the identity of knowledge and desire for the philosopher. This convergence strikes many, under the sway of the Aristotelian and modern conceptions of desire, as confusing and, perhaps, confused. The possibility of knowledge seems to require a clear distinction between cognition and connation. Knowledge is an attainment, and, even if specifying its conditions and nature, as we learn in Theaetetus, presents singular difficulties for Platonism, that it has conditions for its attainment, which differentiate it from mere belief, seems sure. We can coherently ask questions such as: "What is knowledge?" and "Is this (really) knowledge?" For the Platonist, the nature of knowledge, it seems, remains mysterious and undetermined, but the ability to answer the second question constitutes Socrates' maieutic art, is a condition of the Socratic elenkhos, and therefore constitutes (at least) a condition for the possibility of philosophia.[40] But if knowledge and desire converge for the philosopher, the same questions should be coherent for connation as for cognition and their answers should be connected: we must be able to ask "What is desire?" and "Is this (really) desire?" Oddly, in this latter case, the first question seems coherent and perhaps even answerable, as the Phaedrus and Symposium would seem to attest, while the second raises difficulties, which I intend to explore in the following essay.

These questions about the relationship between desire and knowledge, the nature of philosophy, in general, and especially in Plato, first became θαυμάσια for me in Adriaan's seminars at Loyola University, and then in reading groups on key texts of Plato, Plotinus, and Augustine, with Adriaan and many of the friends who gathered in Baltimore last spring. There are many reasons that philosophers return to Plato. Some perhaps relish the challenge of making Plato clearer and more rigorous through philosophically careful exegesis. Others return, it seems, to find in Plato a conception of philosophy which confirms or bolsters their views of the contemporary decadence or at least decline of thinking. Many of us, I think, return at least in part because the role of friendship and desire, which is centrally present in the life that we recognize as philosophical, was first, and, perhaps even uniquely, made explicit in Plato's texts. This would be the philosophia that we learned and learn with Adriaan, which Catriona made possible again for many of us with her invitation and hospitality, and which we shared in our conversations and essays.

---

40 That knowledge remains mysterious for Plato seems to be a reasonable inference from (a) the mysterious advent of knowledge in the analogy with ἀνάμνησις, (b) the vision metaphor throughout the dialogues, (c) the *aporetic* conclusion of the only dialogue that aims at an "epistemology," the *Theaetetus*, (d) the infamous descriptive epistemology of the *7th Letter* (344b). These texts suggest that knowledge occurs as "insight" and without a clear causal story, its advent retains something "mysterious."

Desire and Philosophy

The commonplace among introductions to the discipline that explicates philosophy through etymology as a love of wisdom avoids too easily the difficulties of thinking philosophy as essentially a form of desire. Since the origins of the word are shrouded in obscurity, and thus it is difficult to know how far this thinking was explicit prior to the classical age, Plato is of necessity the author to whom we must turn to understand the curious and distinctive relationship between desire and knowledge, which he saw and then made manifest in his portraits of Socrates' philosophical practice.

For the Platonic understanding of Socratic philosophizing, desire is not merely a cause, nor merely an external condition of philosophizing. Rather, in the fullest sense, desire is philosophy. Although this thought may seem paradoxical at first glance, the relationship in Plato is an identity. That is, philosophy is, first of all, a condition of desire, and, then, conversely, desire, properly "purified" and oriented, is philosophy. Both sides of the identity present difficulties for later philosophers. For example, it is tempting to translate the first claim by saying that philosophy is an interest, understanding "interest" here as a sort of intellectual desire. Then we might understand the claim as nothing more than the assertion that philosophical interests are a necessary condition of being a philosopher. Setting aside the question of whether such an attenuated notion of desire captures Platonic ἔρως, even this attenuated conception of interest presents significant difficulty for post-Platonic psychology. In Aristotle's de Anima, the faculty of ὄρεξις is the cause motion and action. Any voluntary action of the human being originates in and depends upon an actualization of the faculty of ὄρεξις. Thought, as Aristotle argues in III. 9-10, moves nothing. The closest thing to "intellectual interest" in Aristotle seems to be βούλησις, though this seems to be a desire that is expressed intellectually, rather than an "intellecting" that is, at the same time, a desire.41 This account, and its derivatives, continues to dominate modernity from Hume to much con-

---

41 Βούλησις would more typically be rendered a "wish" in Aristotle. See NE III. 4,5. In dA III.9, Aristotle argues that if the soul is tripartite, then ὄρεξις will be found in all parts, βούλησις will be found in the calculative. But, he argues that the calculative part of the soul (τὸ λογιστικὸν καὶ ὁ καλούμενος νοῦς) moves nothing. This seems to suggest that the calculative at most "mediates" ὄρεξις.

temporary philosophy of action, which sees desire as one of two elements in the explanation of action, with the other being belief. Although there are some who hold that moral judgments have internal relations to desires (so called internalists), even for most of these philosophers it seems that beliefs themselves are not connative, motivational, or directive. One very interesting exception, worth noting, are those internalists who argue that moral judgments are not merely beliefs, but rather besires—curious hybrids of cognitive and connative states.42 There is considerable controversy as to whether (a) positing such states is necessary and (b) whether such states are coherent.43

A second strand of thought about the relationship between desire and knowledge is detectable in two prominent texts, Nicomachean Ethics X and Metaphysics Λ. Here we find descriptions of wisdom that seem to incorporate desire within cognition in a way reminiscent of Platonic views of knowledge. The details of these texts would demand careful elaboration, but in brief, it seems that the object of thought (truth, god, or the totality of species-forms) elicits both motion throughout the cosmos and mind. Insofar as it moves the intellect to contemplation and understanding (νοῦς), it seems to excite thought's desires. Aristotle is not explicit about these seemingly cognitive desires in these passages and whether these views are consistent with the psychology of de Anima is unclear. If they are, then it would seem that the faculty of ὄρεξις can be moved by an object of thought and insofar as the cosmos is moved by the same object, it would appear that νοῦς, contra de Anima, III.9, does in fact "move" (ὁ κίνων, d. A., 432b27). Some, however, would advert to the expedient of chronologizing to find in these latter texts the residue of an early theological and Platonic view that Aristotle struggled to overcome in his more mature and scientific works. But, however, that might turn out, we can at least note that such

---

42The name is owed to J. Altham, in "The Legacy of Emotivism," in G. Macdonald, C. Wright (eds.), *Fact,Science and Morality*, Blackwell, Oxford, 1986, 275-288.) *Besires* are cognitive states that are both descriptive and directive.

43See, for example, Michael Smith *The Moral Problem*, Blackwell, Oxford, 1994, pp. 118-125, who defends Humean moral psychology and theory of motivation against criticisms from McDowell's criticisms (found in "Are Moral Requirements Hypothetical Imperatives? (in *Mind, Value, and Reality* (Harvard University Press, 1998, pp. 77-94)).

a strand seems to virtually disappear in later thinkers such as Hume and most modern philosophers of action.

The second part of the identity between knowledge and desire, however, is the distinctive and controversial element in the Platonic conception of philosophy. In asserting that all desire is really desire for knowledge, the Platonic view finds in desire a cognitive or intellectual essence or telos that for most post-Platonic psychologies seems unsustainable. The closest we can find in Aristotle, for example, is the singular first sentence of the Metaphysics, (Πάντες ἄνθρωποι τοῦ εἰδέναι ὀρέγονται φύσει. σημεῖον δ'ἡ τῶν αἰσθήσεων ἀγάπησις·) in which the desire to know (ὄρεξις εἰδέναι), curiosity, is evidenced by our enjoyment of perceiving. This seemingly lone passage suggests that curiosity is an expression of ὄρεξις, just as action and locomotion is. But, even if we interpret this sentence broadly, we get no hint that the other desires are somehow deficient, attenuated, or misdirected forms of intellectual desire. And, this Platonic view suffers an even worse fate than the first in post-Aristotelian thought. An echo of it might be found in some psychologists and some pragmatists like Dewey, who see in play and infant behavior rudimentary forms of curiosity and intellectual engagement with the world--as though through action an infant comes to understand the world.[44] The Platonic conception of philosophy would see all desire as having this aim and fulfillment.[45]

"Is this desire?"

καὶ ἐάν τις ὑμῶν ἀμφισβητήσῃ καὶ φῇ ἐπιμελεῖσθαι, οὐκ εὐθὺς ἀφήσω αὐτὸν οὐδ' ἄπειμι, ἀλλ' ἐρήσομαι αὐτὸν καὶ ἐξετάσω καὶ ἐλέγξω, καὶ ἐάν μοι μὴ δοκῇ κεκτῆσθαι ἀρετήν, φάναι δέ, ὀνειδιῶ ὅτι τὰ πλείστου ἄξια περὶ ἐλαχίστου ποιεῖται τὰ δὲ φαυλότερα περὶ πλείονος.

Then if one of you disputes this and says that he does care [*viz.*, about virtue], I shall not let him go at once or leave him, but I shall question

---

[44] Dewey, *How We Think*. (Dover Publications, 1997).
[45] This might be most clearly seen in *Phaedrus* where the ultimate fulfillment of ἔρως, of the attraction to the beauty of another, lies in "nourishing of the soul" through intellection of reality.

him, examine him, and test him, and if I do not think he has attained virtue but says he has, I will reproach him because he attaches little importance to the most important things and greater importance to inferior things. (*Apol.* 29e3-30a2 Cooper, translation altered).

The Socratic art of maieutics is shown in the Theaetetus to be a mysterious and anomalous art.[46] Without knowledge of knowledge, Socrates is able, perhaps with a certain assistance from the god, to deliver and examine his companions' intellectual offspring.[47] Mysteriously Socrates is able to answer the question, "Is this knowledge?" without, it seems, being able to say what knowledge is.[48] But, if philosophy is desire, if knowledge ultimately is desire, then to test knowledge is also to test desire. Socratic elenkhos not only shows whether the interlocutor knows what he thinks he knows, but also whether he desires or cares about what he says that he desires and cares about. Thus, we might say, the elenkhos asks "Does this person know?" in order to ascertain, "Does this person desire [knowledge]?"

And yet it seems difficult to say that these questions are, in some sense, the same. Socrates' argument in the Apology presupposes only that someone who believes that they know something cannot desire the truth because they cannot seek what they believe that they know. Thus, false beliefs about knowledge prevent desires for the most important things. To put it another way, in order to desire the truth we must first recognize that we do not know the truth. Whether a person who knows the truth would be said to care about (desire) the truth is unclear from this passage alone. Though in Symposium Diotima argues that a desire for something is not just for its attainment, but for its continued, indeed eternal, attainment (Symp. 207ff.). But to answer negatively the question concerning knowledge would allow us still to answer positively the question concerning desire (which means this person would be a philosopher), but it leaves the question still open. Whether

---

[46]"The god and I are responsible for the midwifing." (τῆς μέντοι μαιείας ὁ θεός τε καὶ ἐγὼ αἴτιος. *Theaetetus* 150d10-e1).

[47]The differences between *maieutics* as it is described and practiced in the *Theaetetus* and the Socratic *elenkhos* and practice that is described in *Apology*, must be left to the side here, even with introducing a bit of imprecision at times.

[48]Thus, if it is the case that he holds that in order to know whether something is x, one must know what x is--the so called "Socratic Fallacy"--his very philosophical practice would seem to fail by his own lights.

someone who does not know the truth is a philosopher or a non-philosopher remains an open question after the elenkhos.

And so the elenkhos would need to be followed by further examination that seeks to ascertain not whether there is knowledge, but whether there is desire. This question can be helpfully examined by considering the difference the difference between Theodorus, the mathematician, Protagoras, the sophist, and Socrates, the philosopher. Both Theodorus and Protagoras know that they do not know the most important things. Theodorus' interest in the refutation of Protagoras, and the conversation in general seems to extend as far as necessary to secure his science from threat. He has an interest in philosophy to the extent that it can assist "science" in protecting its boundaries from sophistical, skeptical, and relativist incursion.

Protagoras' teaching that man is the measure of all things--of what is, that it is, and of what is not, that it is not--is almost Socratic in its consequences, since it would entail that Protagoras "does not think that he knows what he does not know" and "that he is aware that he knows nothing of importance." Protagoras, disavowing knowledge with Socratic single-mindedness, it seems, should never fall victim to Socrates' elenctic examinations. Further, from the perspective of the city, Protagoras and Socrates will ultimately be indistinguishable.

And yet, the Theaetetus reveals the reason that Protagoras is not a philosopher, but remains merely a sophist. Protagoras' disavowals of knowledge, his "relativism,"[49] does not result in the philosophical adventure that starts with the πάθος distinctive of the philosopher, τὸ θαυμάζειν (155d1-3), Protagoras, without thinking he knows what he does not know, lacks the desire of wonder, and so is not a philosopher. We can see a difference, then between Socrates, and Theodorus or Protagoras. We know, somehow, that Socrates desires the truth he does not possess, whereas neither Theodorus nor Protagoras does. Yet, how do we see or know this? How do we distinguish the philosopher from the sophist? How can we ascertain whether someone desires the

---

[49] There is considerable question as to how best to characterize Protagoras' view in the *Theaetetus*. At the risk of imprecision, I'll characterize it only crudely.

truth? If the possibility of Socrates' maieutic art, of ascertaining whether someone knows--remains mysterious, is it any less mysterious how we ascertain whether someone desires the truth?

Not knowing that we desire

ἐρᾷ μὲν οὖν, ὅτου δὲ ἀπορεῖ· καὶ οὔθ' ὅτι πέπονθεν οἶδεν οὐδ' ἔχει φράσαι, ἀλλ' οἷον ἀπ' ἄλλου ὀφθαλμίας ἀπολελαυκὼς πρόφασιν εἰπεῖν οὐκ ἔχει, ὥσπερ δὲ ἐν κατόπτρῳ ἐν τῷ ἐρῶντι ἑαυτὸν ὁρῶν λέληθεν.

And then the boy is in love, but with what, he is at a loss. He neither knows what has happened to him nor is he able to explain. But as if he caught an eye disease from someone else, and could not identify the cause, he does not realize that he is seeing himself in the lover as in a mirror. (*Phaedrus*, 255d)

Answering these questions requires further consideration of how desire can be known or unknown. Clearly there are many ways in which I might be ignorant of, or with regards to my desires. First, I might be unclear about what it is that I desire. At least, I sometimes say such things as "I don't know what I want," which could mean at least one of two things. Perhaps I know that I'm hungry, but I can't determine what would satisfy my hunger, or what, while satisfying my hunger, would give me enjoyment and pleasure. We might describe this by saying that my desire for food is a desire for a certain sort of food that I cannot yet determine. In this case, the desire would be read de dicto, rather than de re. If in the latter sense, it would be impossible not to know what I desire. But de dicto, I am not ignorant that I desire, only of what it is that would satisfy this desire.

Another form of this experience of "I don't know what I want" might occur when I feel discomfit and don't know what will bring satisfaction or peace. This restlessness appears as a sort of indeterminate formless desire that will not be quelled until I discover what I desire. Perhaps in this case I know that I desire something other than this, or other than the status quo. In this case, the obscurity of the object of my desire is only its (temporary) indeterminacy. This seems to come close the beloved's condition described in the Phaedrus: the beloved neither seems to know that he desires--that is, he does not know "what has happened to him" (ὅτι πέπονθεν)--nor what he desires. Having suffered something like an illness, he is at a loss to know from whence it came, and without knowing its cause, he doesn't know what has happened to him, and hence is ignorant even that he desires as well as what he desires. The cause of love and the object of love are both obscured, leaving the boy at a loss to know where to turn.

This aporetic condition of the beloved, his unsettling experience of some indeterminate desire like condition without a clear and determinate object would seem to echo that distinctive πάθος of philosophia, the wonder (τὸ θαυμάζειν) that is open to the truth without yet knowing the truth or even perhaps knowing the cause of the wonder. Theaetetus first expressed his perplexity at some problems concerning relations among multitudes and magnitudes. His perplexity is expressed as an inability to explain these phenomena, or to answer what seem to be simple questions about the phenomena. Socrates points to this perplexity of the fundamental mood of philosophia--an inarticulate perplexity which manifests the desire to know without an awareness even of what one wants to know or needs to know.[50] A wonder that is experienced as indeterminate perplexity rather than the desire to know some determinate thing or solve a problem.

Deceptive Desire

Οὕτω τοίνυν καὶ περὶ τὸν ἔρωτα. τὸ μὲν κεφάλαιόν ἐστι πᾶσα ἡ τῶν ἀγαθῶν ἐπιθυμία καὶ τοῦ εὐδαιμονεῖν ὁ μέγιστός τε καὶ δολερὸς ἔρως παντί· ἀλλ' οἱ μὲν ἄλλῃ τρεπόμενοι πολλαχῇ ἐπ' αὐτόν, ἢ κατὰ χρηματισμὸν ἢ κατὰ φιλογυμναστίαν ἢ κατὰ φιλοσοφίαν, οὔτε ἐρᾶν καλοῦνται οὔτε ἐρασταί, οἱ δὲ κατὰ ἕν τι εἶδος ἰόντες τε καὶ ἐσπουδακότες τὸ τοῦ ὅλου ὄνομα ἴσχουσιν, ἔρωτά τε καὶ ἐρᾶν καὶ ἐρασταί.

---

[50] Theaetetus 155d. The phenomena of relative magnitudes and multitudes make two other similar appearances. First, in the *Phaedo,* Socrates points to similar phenomena, *viz.* the cause of addition and division, as the origin of a recognition of the inadequacy of "material" causes during his autobiography (96-97). In the *Republic,* these phenomena are identified as "summoners" (παρακλητικὰ) which first reveal the inadequacy of sense-perception and effect initally the *periagoge* towards being (523-525).

That's also how it is with desire. The chief point is: For anyone, every urge for good things or for happiness is "the great and cunningly deceptive desire" itself. But those who turn to this in other ways, either as money making, or as athletics, or as philosophy, are neither said to desire nor are called lovers, but those who turn to this and are concerned with one particular <u>form,</u> they have the name of the whole: desire, desiring, and lovers. (*Symposium,* 205d).

The Phaedrus passage seems to point to a unique condition in which the cause of desire is obscure to the beloved and so it isn't even clear that it is desire. Most cases of not knowing our desire seem to differ from this form of aporetic desire. The typical case, as we noted above, is that I know that I desire but am uncertain what I (really) desire--my ignorance is de re, though not de dicto. Diotima, however, advances a stronger claim about desire. Desire deceives. All of our particular desires and all of the constellations of desires that form lives are in fact desire (ἔρως) deceiving us. Our interests and our urges, our wishes and our wants, are really all manifestations of desire, though we might not know this at the time. But this concealment, as described by Diotima, is not an opacity or an obscurity, neither is it withdrawal. Eros does not, as Heraclitus believed of φύσις, love to hide (φύσις κρύπτεσθαι φιλεῖ, Fr. 123). Rather, cunningly deceptive, δολερὸς ἔρως deceives us, only to surprise. It is by substitution and redirection--feints and gambits--that we are led by our desire. Thinking that we want one thing, we discover that our desire is, in fact, something of an entirely different order or origin. Alcibiades, without using Diotima's language would seem to confirm this in his paian to Socrates which is playfully substituted for a more serious paian to ἔρως. "Δολερὸς Σωκράτης"--Alcibiades might have said--"the clever manipulator who adopted in turn the role of lover, and then, the role of beloved, in a gambit aimed ultimately at seducing to philosophia."[51]

But, on Diotima's account, all desire is ultimately desire for the beautiful itself, for the truth of beauty, and so desire and knowledge at last

---

[51] Once again a detailed reading of this passage must be foregone at the risk of a certain oversimplification.

coincide in a knowledge that remains philosophical--that is, that remains a desire. Diotima then contends that all other desire is ultimately a sort of distracted and incipient philosophy, condemned to dissatisfaction because it misleads and substitutes an inadequate "knowledge" of beauty for a true philosophical knowledge. Our desires are mistaken philosophia.[52]

Is this Desire?

"What Desire desires is not immediately clear to me. If it coincides with "me" (in the sense of my deep, originary self), it is also true that I do not initially--and perhaps never will--know what "I" (*au fond*, originally) desire. What I ultimately desire, my Desideratum, is a secret. It fascinates and obsesses the human "soul" without being known. It is vaguely felt, obscurely suspected and surmised, yearningly presumed."[53]

If we, following Diotima, distinguish between the proper nature of desire and the misdirected and distracted desires, we find normativity and a criterion that allows us to restore the parallel between the question concerning desire and the question concerning knowledge. Where the elenkhos asks, "Is this really knowledge?" and measures the answer against a criterion whose origin is perhaps mysteriously grasped only in its negativity, identifying the philosopher requires determining whether they really desire and measures the answer against the standard of philosophical desire.

Adriaan argues in a similar yet importantly different way in Elements of Ethics that this "radical Desire of being and becoming good" "cannot be identified with any of the many limited wishes, wants, or tendencies that arise over the course of a life" (F.F., 79). Unlike Diotima, Adriaan does not identify some single object of Desire, some single content that would

---

[52] We would need to the *Phaedo* and the *Republic* for further elaboration of the question of knowledge and desire. In the former, *philosophia* is interpreted as a κάθαρσις of desire, a purification of desire that has been contaminated by *somatic* pleasures. Thus, all of our desires are in their purest form *philosophical*. In addition, however, the *Phaedo* seems to point to a bi-partite conception of desire depending upon whether the desire is pursued through the body or through the soul. The *Republic* continues this with the tripartite soul in which desires are differentiated by the part that houses them and their objects. In these latter texts, the highest desire becomes the *proper* desire for the whole.

[53] Peperzak, Adriaan, *Elements of Ethics*, Stanford University Press, 2003. p. 74. (*EE*, hereafter).

make Desire "merely" one more desire.[54] The Desire of being good is never, seemingly, present as a content of consciousness, as one desire among others. Its Desideratum "surpasses the World and history" yet haunts our our finite desiderata as "an "aspect," "moment" or a "hidden secret of its finite manifestations" (EE, 89).

This difference between Diotima's account and Adriaan's is significant. The object of Desire, the Good, is transcendent as ἐπέκεινα τῆς οὐσίας, as the beyond being. Therefore, it cannot provide a positive criterion for the purity of our desires, as Beauty itself appears to do for Diotima, but instead reveals the inherent transcendence of all desire. The normativity derives instead from the principle of correspondence--the demand "to respond appropriately to all that is given" (EE, 101). No longer measured by the Desideratum, since all desires will fall short of that "object," "pure desire desires what is truly desirable" (EE, 102). What is truly desirable cannot be established in the abstract but rather only within a life that has been "purified," and which strives for correspondence, for experiencing phenomena as they 'want' to be received" (EE, 108).

But Desire itself aims beyond every desirable, expressing an underlying restlessness of desire itself. The Good, which is never clearly grasped in a positive cognition, reveals itself through the inadequacy of each finite desideratum. Like Socrates' mysterious grasp of knowledge that makes possible his maieutic art and the elenkhos, revealing to himself and others that what they took to be knowledge is merely belief, Desire seems to be a condition of our grasp of the inadequacy of our finite desires, revealing to us that what we take to be Desire is merely desire.

---

54 For Diotima, ἔρως ultimately has for its object Beauty itself and strives after knowledge of Beauty though this knowledge of Beauty is not merely "theoretical" but practico-poetic, that is, procreative as well. Nevertheless, unlike, the Good of the *Republic*, the Beautiful itself does not seem to be beyond "being" and "knowledge" according to Diotima.

JESUS, REPUBLICANS, PEPERZAK AND ME: REFLECTIONS ON HOPE, GRATITUDE AND TRUST

§

Catriona Hanley

Preface: Something to Initiate

There has to be some beginning of conversation. Even if the words we speak together now elicit all the talking and tattling in all the world, all the chitchat and angry shouting, all the poetry and meandering solipsistic prose, all the authentic and pretentious philosophizing, all the pouting and pleading, all the speech that inflicts death, all the speech that promises redemption, all that long history of soul-killing talk and crushed response, every bit of the language of love: in short, even if every word that has ever been uttered in conversation still resounds (and even if all this is there only in the far reaches of our peripheral vision, a dim echo).... even so, when I encounter you face to face, I must still greet you. And you, well-- you must return the greeting.

Unless, of course, I kill you, or you kill me. James Bond and a plethora of fictional heroes and villains never start to fire before a polite exchange of witty pleasantries. But we know that murder is not an equal exchange between two conversing people, whether or not that conversation is authentic. To murder is always to silence the voice of the other, to smash the gaze of the other; it is a hubristic annulment of the other's claim to existence.

There are, certainly, ways of killing that do not deserve the nomination 'murder': everything that lives depends on the death of something else for its survival. The rabbit dies to feed the fox, though not willingly. This humble carrot, this sheaf of wheat has to die in order for me to live, even though I may forget to be grateful, failing to acknowledge my participation in this huge cycle of existence. The logic of *thanatos* belongs to self-sacrifice as well: a mother has deep physical understanding that she will choose her own death over that of her child. It would be absurd to even ask the question, since the answer has always already been given in late night negotiations at the bedside of a feverish child: please take me, not my child. *Please*. Alcestis agrees to take the place of Admetus in death, not for him, but for the sake of her children[55]. Socrates chooses death over life for the sake of philosophy, so that the human desire for truth be upheld and celebrated. Jesus accepts the cup of death for a vision of immortality for all humankind, a vision that sustains the simple truth that the Other matters more than me. In all these cases, there is an invocation, a call outside myself. The call is not always answered, or not in a way that satisfies my egoicity.

Still, finally, in any productive human exchange we do look at each other, look into the eyes of the other, sink into the voice of the other... and then we begin to listen and later to speak, and to be heard. We *recognize* each other. This simple exchange, which most of us run through hundreds of times a week, is what we most hope for in our lives and the lives of the generations that follow us. We must struggle to preserve this most elemental feature of human society, this constant casual exchange between humans, from the haggling at the farmer's market to the perfunctory hello to the bus driver, to the stale look from the wearied and grumpy colleague.

This simple recognition of the humanity of the other is at the core of our struggle against all propagandas, all hate mongering, all of those who

---

[55] Though the poignancy of her acceptance, highlighted by the horrible but almost understandable refusal of Admetus' parents to step up (which seems akin to a heroin addict's parents having, finally, to say no), is highlighted in versions other than Euripides: Rilke's poem "Alcestis" is one example.

seek to inflame hatred and fear of the other human being. Those who urge us on to war begin with dehumanizing the Other, making this little girl, this father, this strong young woman, this naïve little boy, this old lady dying in the hospital, making all these humans into The Enemy. But also the natural environment can be turned into the inimical other: terrestrial plants, from poison ivy to old growth forests that stand in the way; animals from mosquito to Grizzly bear; dynamic features of the natural world, from rivers and lakes, winds and snows, beating sun—all these are so easily seen as impediments.

We must remember to always resist the voracious spirit that urges us to eat up all in our path, or in the language of Levinas, to subsume all otherness to the same. This spirit is all too easily whipped to life by whispered voices that become angry multitudes. We must counter it with a return to simplicity in our everyday exchanges with human beings and with nature. Most powerfully, we must keep the path to the divine open, even in the most flat periods of dull materialism and despair. Peperzak's lovely and fruitful suggestion is that we keep hope alive through sincere and enjoyable conversations and philosophical reflections with our friends, in an open circle constantly enriched and renewed with new interlocutors. There is nothing naïve in what he has to say. Nothing at all.

Introduction: Something to Contextualize

The text below is written in the second person, which is the traditional form of the open letter. This was not simply a stylistic decision on my part. My remarks are lovingly addressed to Adriaan Peperzak, but in a public forum. They are thus doubly in the spirit of our conversational theme. I speak to Adriaan very personally about something, and through this speaking about and speaking to, I address also all of those who came to our gathering at Loyola University Maryland in honour of his 80th birthday in May of 2009, as well as those who will come "here", to this written text, later on. As I invited all of you here to this celebration of our beloved teacher, so also do I invite you to listen in to my conversation with him… or as much of it as I can reasonably share.

Gratitude was the hidden subject of my dissertation work with Dr. Peperzak.[56] That dissertation work became my first book[57], for which I am grateful to Adriaan: it seems that Aristotle is right that there is circularity to all things! Although my Aristotle/Heidegger book deals with questions of metaphysics and ontology in an explanatory and heuristic manner, it depends upon the notion of gratitude in two ways. Textually, gratitude is the bridge that I construct between the metaphysics of Aristotle and the phenomenological ontology of Heidegger. I see in Heidegger the space for construction of such a bridge, even if he was not willing to build it himself. As I construe it, the phenomenon of existential gratitude is-- in an admittedly rather Levinasian move—a way in which the infinite can be said to enter into Heideggerian ontology. There is, I argue there, space for such an entry, and Heidegger himself left that space open.

Secondly, my work depends on gratitude insofar as it is a response to my own life experience. Gratitude has long been present to my thinking. Hope and trust—the other elements that I draw upon in my subtitle to this present text-- have been rather more absent from my intellectual universe. Over the last twenty-five years, in all the time I have lived since formally leaving Adriaan's tutelage in Chicago, it has seemed to me more and more difficult to be both politically aware and to maintain hope and trust in the world. In this world, the mighty forever proclaim their right, the strong forever oppress kill, rape and mutilate the weak, and the truth is forever squashed under the weapons of war and law by the makers of violent myths. To return to the possibility of hope and trust and the belief that we (each individual understood as a collective member of a society of equals) can make a better world, I must always call myself back to gratitude.

Wide, existential gratitude—gratitude not only for all the gifts that the universe has delivered to *me*, but gratitude for this whole terrible, awesome mess, this complicated rat-trap of existence. I hate the suffering this world

---

[56] To note: I still want to *vouvoyer* Adriaan all these years later, and though I now adopt the more intimate *tu*, there is, strangely, in that expression an even greater sense of respect offered. And if we ever return to the *vous*, I hope it will be with ever more intimacy—an intimacy of the heart, mind, and finally one day, far way, soul.

[57] *Being and God in Aristotle and Heidegger: The Role of Method in Thinking the Infinite*: Roman and Littlefield, 2000: Lanham

contains, and, like many others, I feel quite literally ready to die when I hear about the torment of individuals from that bombed village, the agony of these particular people who must flee their country and are abused on the way, the degradation of an entire people, who though they have endured over 300 years of the trauma of slavery (*a history that cannot be captured here in a clause between commas even if italicized*), are still blamed for the social problems that beset them. I'm already in pain at the sight of a beaten dog, an abused horse, and an abandoned cat, let alone factory farmed animals; it hurts terribly to see the polluting of our city streams, the destruction of a forest, the desecration of our oceans. That this is the future being prepared for my child, and my future grandchildren, but also for this whale I am thrilled to see, and her children, for this mighty oak and his children...

Can it be that the sight of a suffering human being is too much for my eyes to see? Yes, but I must still have the courage to gaze upon it, and recognize that it is there, inexorably before me, telling me of my complicity, speaking of the historical involvement of my ancestors, showing the line of privilege that grows from my culture. Those peasants blindly or poetically tending the soil far away are my ancestors; those who would long to arise and go to a land of peace—those are my fellow humans.

Wallowing in stultifying guilt and inaction so easily calls attention to the one who is "meta-suffering", that is, one who is suffering because of the suffering of others. It is certainly possible to imagine that one is raised up or ennobled by "feeling sorry" for others, to somehow feel self-righteous by acceding to the pain of the Other. I am superior to you, since I recognize more fully the pain of the other. But how dare I think to be transfigured by empathy alone? But then, what to do? Here is a much more interesting question. In short, how shall I live? Maybe that is the question.

Something to Provoke

One of my students recently told me that he had taken my class in part because of what he'd read about me on "Rate my Professor.com". The entry that "sold" him was apparently "Hanley rocks: she hates Jesus and

Republicans". I found this tale initially amusing of course, but upon further reflection, it seemed disturbing—especially the Jesus part. A day or two later, I used this phrase in class, presenting it to students in a purely formal way as an example of a proposition. I confess that I was aiming for a laugh while getting students to understand the rules of argument, fallacy, *ad hominem*, etc. Without naming the student, I no doubt let it be known that the phrase was disturbing to me.

After class the student who had initially told me about the posting on "Rate my Professor" came up to the front of the room where I was (in that quintessentially professorial way) gathering up my papers. The student assured me that it was not worth worrying about the posting, and that there was no need to fret; it was clear to any reader of "Rate my Professor" that I hated Jesus "in a good way".[58]

It may seem rather odd that I call attention to the fact that at least two students consider that I hate Jesus, just when I am hosting a Colloquium in honour of my beloved dissertation director, who I know very well is an ardent Christian in the Catholic tradition. Indeed, Adriaan is a self-described philosopher of Christianity, or "a Christian who happens to be also a philosopher" as he puts it. He is also my friend-- one who has always invited me to consider myself a colleague (though up to now I have been unable to do so), and my spiritual advisor (perhaps—though not necessarily--unwittingly). Adriaan Peperzak has in fact thought and written a great deal about how the seeming opposition between philosophy and Christianity can quite convincingly be dispelled, so how will he, as my friend, react to my students describing me as "hating Jesus"?

Perhaps I am in the Freudian moment, trying finally to kill the father—in this case the Doktor-Vater-- and in public, at the rostrum. The "hating Republicans" part worries me less, Adriaan, as I know your political sensibilities, but the accusation that I "hate Jesus" is disturbing, especially as the very attribution of hatred is anathema to your thinking. Why then do I have to lay bare here my supposed hatred, and hatred of Jesus? Perhaps there is some inner voice, an inner compulsion that is now emerging from

---

58 I see that this entry has since been removed from "Rate my Professor"!

within me, as I *prepare* for this event in your honour, a voice that will lead me to publicly strip you of the respect I have hitherto felt for you?

But no.... I think not. That is not it at all. (Please relax.) I think that there is no need in my case to kill this particular father, and I plan here to say why that is, why, in other words, the bonds of the paternal or maternal force of love, the erotic relationship between teacher and student, the companionship and fraternity or sorority experienced in the shared quest— why these ties do not have to become oppressive, and why in our case, they did not. And why it is that I can be said to hate Jesus and Republicans, and still love you.

Before launching into that, I'd like to say this: preparation for writing this short piece has been very difficult, but also immensely pleasurable. I took some time to read back through some of your writings, especially *System and History in Philosophy*[59]; *Before Ethics*; *The Quest for Meaning*; *Thinking*, and it was tremendously uplifting to feel again your thoughts resonating in my mind, and I began to consider the impossible question of how and in what part precisely my thinking is indebted to yours, how I have been formed and guided by you, what part of me is me, and what part inherited from you. What does a student owe a teacher? It took a while for me to see just how foolish this question is.

Walking my beloved dog Gideon in the park or about the neighbourhood gives me time to think, and I do some of my best free thinking on these meandering walks—this is thinking that is not concerned with children, teaching, grading or errands. The other day while walking it came to me again, in a *newly* new kind of way, in the way that intellectual insights, like emotional ones, repeat themselves over and over again in the course of one's life, the same insight, the same suddenly perceived truth, but now understood in an entirely new way, a way that seems richer, more appropriate, deeper, fuller. This is the hermeneutic of thinking, of living, of thinking about living. The old-new thought was this: there is no separation of my Self as a philosopher from the experiences and influences that have formed

---

59 *System and History in Philosophy*, SUNY, 1986: Albany; *Before Ethics*: Humanities Press, 1997: New Jersey; *The Quest for Meaning*, Fordham 2003: New York; *Thinking*, Fordham, 2006: New York.

me. There is no possible positive attribution of thinking or development, such that this piece comes from here, and that there, as though the mind were a jigsaw puzzle, as if there were an ideal completeness possible and awaiting me in some foggy future. No genetic code can be cracked that will reveal all of who I am, and nor will any history of myself and or one that traces my education answer the question. This is an insight that, paradoxically, I can attribute in some of its manifestations to Adriaan Peperzak and his teachings on what it is to be a human being in a world of suffering.

In trying to describe what it is to be an animated human, Aristotle, in that most famous and most difficult passage from *De Anima* III chapter five says that the soul—or the mind-- *nous,* in one aspect *becomes* all things that it perceives. But *nous* in its other aspect *makes* all things. "Actual knowledge", he says," is identical with its object; potential [knowledge] is prior in time to actual knowledge in the individual, but in general it is not prior in time. *Nous* does not think intermittently".[60] His point here is that there is no given or set order of knowledge, no necessary progression from what we might know to what we do in fact know. For any given individual, of course, there is an order and progression: I had to know how to hold a fork before I could eat spaghetti on my own, though others might have learned with a knife and a spoon; I had to understand Aristotle in some way, before I began to understand Heidegger, though others might have found a route through Kant. But what is true, is true, and remains true independently of our tentative approach to it, and despite our looking through the glass darkly. Aristotle does think there is a way that things are, and he thinks, in my opinion, that the wisest among us can come close to perceiving what that is. But none of us has or can hope to have complete knowledge: no one can gain a God's eye perspective. At the same time, in order to come to know anything, we must be open to what we perceive—we must let the data in--and we must be able and willing to play with it, to question its origin, to interpret it, understand it, make it ours.

It is disconcerting to think that there might be a Truth of which we

---

60 Aristotle: *DA* 430 15-20 Tredennick trans., p. 171 (Loeb Classical Library, Harvard Univ. Press: Cambridge: 1936)

can never be aware: this is surely Kant's worry in the first of his Critiques. In the *Critique of Pure Reason*-- the one devoted to the unfolding and the limitations of knowledge-- Kant attempts to determine the conditions necessary for rational beings to attain knowledge. The strange existence of the noumenal "realm", inhabited by many of the same kinds of entities that Plato had posited 2000 years earlier (only this time even more inaccessible to human thought) provides a conceptual "out" within Kantian metaphysics. Here is the world as it really is, this noumenal *way-things-are*, the unperceivable standard that not only *is* the way things are, but which also deeply shapes what it is that we as humans perceive to be the reality of things. The entities of the noumenal cannot, by definition, enter into human perception or intellect, even though the existence of such a realm can be conceived. And the very thought of this potentially existing realm condemns us to posit its existence, and thus to see our own world as a mere shadow reality. We cannot ever, on this model, know how things really are. Nor do we need to develop any consistent relationship with what is—or rather, with what we think *is*.

Aristotle never feared the objective world, and never worried that the Truth was liminal. On the Aristotelian view, there is a way that things are, and we humans can have access to that, as long as we carefully measure our perceptions against what is there for us to see, or there for us to conceptualize. Aristotle's preoccupation was not so much that he might be structurally unaware of the real way things are, or that he might make a mistake in judgment about what the truth of things is. His great concern is, arguably, not that he might not come to know the truth, but rather that the Truth might not be not aware of him.

Surely Aristotle worried about that unmoved mover outside the edge of the universe, indifferent, unmoved in all possible senses of the word. He names this eternal thing "god", and then traced the mover also *in* the natural world, very formally present within it as a principle of order and regularity and thus understandability. The theological model here is that of a very distant, chilly pater; no warm friendly male or female spirits of the earth or creation or procreation need apply. Aristotle's god is not a *thing* at all, but is also not a *not-thing*. The unmoved mover is an abstraction, like the phrase "the terms of the argument", but in being this abstraction it keeps all the rest making sense. Aristotle subsumes all the nature gods under the one most powerful god: the god of reason.

Here then are two worries about the god of the philosophers: 1) Kant: that something like God might be unknowable, unreachable, but must be assumed to make sense of the human place in the world; or 2) Aristotle: that god be unknowable, unreachable, entirely unconcerned with human beings or any other inhabitants of the universe (precisely not "creatures"), and may just be the name for the interesting and undeniable fact that the world makes sense, and that the physical universe behaves in utterly predictable ways.

Peperzak, in his writings, quiets both kinds of fear, while raising another. He urges us to finally put aside childish things, like our fairy tale Christian conception of God as the old white man, long-bearded, sitting on a cloud, making a list of our rights and wrongs. God- and truth-- is not unknowable in Kant's sense, nor knowable, or a stand-in for the principle of knowability. For Peperzak, as for Levinas, God is outside of this epistemology, beyond this ontology. For Peperzak, God is the focus of meaning in a human life. What could this mean? Can it mean something to the non-believer as well?

****

But allow me to take a step backwards from this question for a moment. In the preface to *Before Ethics*, Adriaan talks of the discomfort one feels as a thinker and a writer in having to revisit one's old texts, old thoughts.[61] As Peperzak describes it there, the text I write encapsulates my thought as an engaged thinker at the time I write it, but a short time later, it is something almost alien. To write is already to fix the past, "and if no past is an absolute authority for thinking, no text can be accepted as a once-and-forever established basis for further construction, not even

---

61 I thus apologize to you Adriaan (though the apology is purely formal and purposely half-hearted) for making you face these old thoughts! Still I hope that in my formulation these lovely worries are made new again to you, even if you no longer agree with any of the neat solutions offered-- or with me.

by its author" (p.ix). There is then this strange dichotomy between the written text, which we think of as authoritative but from which each writer distances herself *ex post facto*, and the spoken word, to which each genuine, or authentic speaker can fully commit at the time of speech, yet may be hazy about later.

How is this to be explained? How to address the fear that there is no legitimate, firm ground in either text or speech? Is it that the truth is there but inaccessible, or is it accessible but incomprehensible? Or is it just *not* there... or, simply Other to all this? One of the most important lessons I have learned from you, Adriaan, is that philosophy is dialogical; that thinking, if it is to be meaningful, needs to be addressed to someone, that talking, discussing, sharing ideas is the very essence of philosophy, and that all the rest is a kind of decoration. Reading is fruitful only if it is experienced as a conversation with the text, as your worthy hero Plato tells us over and over again; writing has meaning only if it is directed to a reader; teaching is only meaningful if it is also listening and learning; and thinking? In writing this short paper in your honour, I address you, but also those of us who are here to discuss our similarities and differences in thought, and reaching out beyond this, to the larger community of students and scholars who might be present, or who might later come across this piece. But to whom is my thinking directed *in general*? Or more specifically, how can I determine the correct orientation for my thinking and for my life? First Nietzsche and then Heidegger quite effectively stripped us of grounds for our thinking. Is there any hope of return?

Aristotle is surely correct in saying in the *Nichomachean Ethics* that we need a good guide to get along in life; naturally, good circumstances of birth, good influences, a certain amount of money and property, respect of one's peers: these all make the path towards the well ordered life of wisdom, and thus happiness, easier. Plato is also right in the describing, in virtually every one of his dialogues, how resistant most people are to the guide, how unwilling we are to listen, to hear, to change, even if we are free to follow to best possible teachers, to hear the most sage of teachings. In *Before Ethics*, Peperzak writes:

> ...the experience of human freedom reveals its lack of self-sufficiency. Human beings cannot choose their own existence; they find themselves as given to their own awakening consciousness: their existence precedes their ability to choose. Instead of being causa sui, human individuals discover that their own given reality cannot be refused but must be accepted willingly. Acceptance and gratitude include hope, but they do not constitute an alibi for the heavy burden of humanization and self-realization that proceed from a fundamental sense of reality... [62]

Here we are, each of us, in the world, struggling with what has been given to us materially, intellectually, and spiritually. We are always already here in the midst of it all, in the middle of living which is for each of us a full time job. I, for one, spend my whole day every single day living my life, and being caught up in all the drama and all the ennui that living any life entails. Well, I can't live my life part-time-- even if I try to withdraw from the thrust of it all through drugs of any kind, be they narcotics, food, drink, sex or entertainment: in the end, it is still my experience that I awaken to or from. I am here in this reality, which, even if it is lived in what Peperzak calls "the desert of our cultural nihilism".[63] I cannot turn away; I cannot refuse. Peperzak suggests that I should therefore embrace it, be *grateful* for it, *trust* that it is right, *hope* that I can make it better: in short, that I should live in faith.

Faith, in Peperzak's interpretation, is much larger than dogmatism. In fact, as I have tried to make evident here in my discussion of the hermeneutics of truth seeking and truth telling, faith in Peperzak's interpretation is opposed to any simple declaration of apodictic propositional truth. In his 2006 work *Thinking*, Adriaan writes:

> ...The biggest mistake one can make in thinking about God is to absolutize any tool, concept, proposition, theory, language, genre, framework, or vision—thus erecting them as idols....In faith, God's "speaking"

---

62 See above: *BE*, p. 100-01
63 *Before Ethics*, p. 85

addresses me, who answer God in trust, gratitude and hope...⁶⁴

Without: a) the absolute epistemological truths of the Aristotelian universe; b) the Kantian creation of the unknowable grounds of the phenomenal; c) the Cartesian certainties, and without even d) the wild and persuasive arguments of bishop Berkeley: what do we have to go on? For Adriaan, it is a matter of faith, of profound and discursive faith, faith precisely as the decision, warranted or not, to live this reality, this life, this one-time-round, which is a gateway to another existence, this life here and now which is interpreted as a Good. I paraphrase his text here: *Trust* as the experience of having received everything, including faith, from God; *Gratitude* for the splendour of creation and history, even while recognizing its horrors and evils; *Hope* as the confidence that a caring God will continue to create and to liberate; these are the elements of faith (*Thinking* p.146). The direction of thinking, in Peperzak's mind, is to God; the orientation is to truth.

There is a lovely line in one of Adriaan's books: "not the right to eat, but only food stills our hunger, and a right to work is no consolation for the hopelessly unemployed".⁶⁵ I have never heard Adriaan's work as pious rumination on the platitudes of the general fully digested pap of Christianity. Rather, I have heard a protest against the injustices in the world, and a strong protest against the placid self-satisfaction of the "Christian believer".

When I hear that my students think I hate Jesus "in a good way", I hope it is this that they are thinking—that to reduce Christ's message to a screed *against*: against contraception, against women's voices, against homosexuals, against women's rights, against pleasure, is a travesty. There are many many evils that have been committed in the name of Christ, and some of these, arguably, are being committed now in Rome. But the Jew Jesus, philosopher, man of peace, friend of the poor, resident of an occupied territory, would in my interpretation condone none of it.

When I hear on the other hand that my students think I hate Republicans—"in a good way"—or that I hate America (since, according to

---

64 *Thinking*, ibid, pp. 146-7
65 *Before Ethics*, p.85

students and strangers, my accent shows, that I am not "from here"), then I try to turn back towards love. I suppose "Republicans", as conservatives, are meant to stand for the status quo; my goal in bringing to light the social ills besetting this country both in and outside the classroom are aimed expressly at upsetting the status quo. From an outsider perspective-- the perspective of a philosopher—it seems odd that putting into question the current actions and workings of a state is an assault on freedom. Rather, as Socrates so clearly demonstrated, questioning the status quo, calling all assumptions, all prejudices, all received opinion into question is at the very heart of democracy.

I try to remember that these 17-22 year old students have been encouraged to keep sleeping an adolescent dream. History lessons in high school are all too often exercises in blind nationalism. Language learning in the public school system is perfunctory, and despite teachers' best efforts, has little financial support. Nor would a parent expect anymore that recess, art, gym, music, as well as lessons in a second or third language, be offered in a public school in the US.

Sometimes this all leads me to the brink of despair. I fear that the entire misconception of society that this country in which I live is facing may be too Herculean a task. How can little people like us fight such stupid yet well-funded ideas? How can we persuade the easily persuaded that only with a continued effort towards truth, a dedication to the idea that truth is precisely *not* a series of propositions on stone tablets, but a living, breathing experiment in which we are all engaged, but which must, for the success of each and all, be oriented to the Good?

<u>Addendum: Something to Inspire</u>

Adriaan Peperzak has often told the story of how, while still a boy in grade school, his reading of Plato's *Symposium* set the course of his intellectual and spiritual life. As late as a week or two ago[66], he claimed again that to this day he has never recovered from that reading. It was the speech of Diotima, through Socrates, through Plato that uplifted and challenged him,

---

66 Only gentle teasing, not mockery here!

and I have always thought that the double or triple remove of her speech makes it all the more potent for Adriaan, this Christian who happens to b a philosopher. Diotima's vision exposes the possibility of an intellectually and spiritually erotic relationship to the Good. Love, even this focused love of another here and now, opens a path to the *epikeina tēs ousias*, to that which is the source of all this, but which is beyond this. It is beyond being, but still fully visible in the spectrum of being—if one knows how to look.

What do we talk about when we talk about love? So asks Raymond Carver in his devastating and illuminating short story, the central piece in a collection of stories Carver published under that very title: *What We Talk About When We Talk About Love* (1981)[67]. I have always read this story as a dystopian retelling of Plato's *Symposium*. I'm not sure if Carver had this in mind, and I haven't found much literature on the subject. But here is how I read his story: "What We Talk About…"[68] is a story about a reverse telling of Plato's *Symposium*. *Nota bene*: it is precisely not a reverse retelling, but a *story* about a retelling. In this framing, there is a double negative return to something more like a true Greek symposium. If in Plato, the participants decide not to *drink* until they have all made speeches on the topic of love, in Carver, the sextet of symposiasts tacitly agree not to *eat* until their conversation is over.

The six people in Carver's story meet for drinks before dinner, but as they get more and more gin-drunk, the prospect of dinner recedes. Dionysius takes precedence over Apollo. The conversation becomes increasingly unfocussed and incoherent. The experience of love, in examples the symposiasts reveal through their increasingly uninhibited behavior and the stories they tell, is far short of anything Diotima describes. The love they propose is degraded, violent, even pornographic, or else it is fleeting sentimentality, distraction. Yet through these dark, unhappy manifestations of some version of love, there still appears—in the shade—a truer form.

[67] My recent re-reading of that story is based on Carver's own original version, published in the *New Yorker* Magazine (December 24 2007 issue). The previously published version was heavily redacted by Carver's editor, Gordon Lish, and is now eschewed by most scholars. Sadly, this did not prevent the screenwriters of the 2014 film "Birdman" from using Lish's more crude and heavy-handed version of the story as the backdrop to Iñárritu's film.
[68] The unedited version of the story (as published in the New Yorker), goes under the title "Beginners".

Love as spiritual kinship mediated through the divine is alluded to as the long sought vision of the host of the party, an ex-seminarian. Are we stuck, as Carver might suggest, in longing for the spiritual meaning of love, while being utterly crushed by the cultural weight of the interpretation of love as physical?

Perhaps it is time for brief return to the beginning of this essay, and the problem posed there. What do we talk about when we talk about anything? First, we talk to each other, and so we are always directing our words and thoughts to another. We seek to be understood, and we try to understand, but we are also, always, grasping for communality. When that breaks down as it so often does, whether in political dispute, legal disagreement, maybe even a difference of ideas, what can we do to keep the spirit of conversation alive? Peperzak suggests, Diotima signals, Socrates notes, Plato writes that we can only keep our attention, our intellectual energy, our soul-searching, directed to the Good.

Something to Conclude:

In his inspired and inspiring book of 2006, *Thinking*, Adriaan writes,
> "*A pupil becomes a teacher when he has learned enough to educate others. When a listener answers a speaker, he is or begins to be a colleague by taking responsibility for presenting positive or negative or interrogative observations to the one who first instructed him.*" [69]

Far from killing you as my father then, in offering you this paper, Adriaan, I hope-- in the sense you lay out-- to present you to my students, friends, family as my colleague. And I present myself to you as yours.

---

[69] *Thinking*, p.45

ORIENTING ONESELF IN KANT: REFLECTIONS ON ADRIAAN PEPERZAK AS A PHILOSOPHER AND TEACHER
§

Kristi Sweet

<u>Preface</u>

While the piece that follows is in the minority in this collection insofar as it treats a thinker from the Modern era, I was struck in our conversations to discover the extent to which its question is shared by my friends, colleagues, and mentors. This may be, perhaps, because as students who share a common lineage, we share similar philosophical concerns and questions. We are, as it were, already in a dialogue with each other, and share a primary interlocutor in Professor Peperzak, from whom many of us received our orientation in philosophy. And, too, we belong to the same philosophical heritage, and the thinkers we study are also students within this heritage. One theme that stands out to me in our essays is that of the complex relation of activity and passivity that characterizes human existence, and comes to the fore in the task of living a good life. This shows up in the themes of friendship, the transformative character of education, and the way in which we are responsible for—and responsive to—one another and to nature. I would suggest that the explorations carried out in the rest of this collection give a much broader perspective and more sophisticated contours to my own work than I ever could have on my own. In this way, the collection is itself a testament to its theme of the importance of dialogue for thought, and I hope that readers will approach this particular essay with the insights of my friends in hand.

****

This past April, Prof. Peperzak gave the keynote address at the graduate conference on education at Boston College. I know this not because I am continually apprised of Prof. Peperzak's travel, rather, it came to my attention because a graduate student of mine was presenting a paper at this conference. This graduate student had written a fine paper for a graduate course I had taught on Kant's practical philosophy, which had been the topic of my own dissertation with Prof. Peperzak. The idea that one of my students would be presenting a paper written for my graduate course in front of my dissertation director occasioned all kinds of anxieties. While this student does really fine work, it nevertheless led me to worry whether I had been able to pass down what I have inherited from Prof. Peperzak to my own students. So, what is it that I have learned from Prof. Peperzak and hope to pass down in my scholarship on Kant as well as in my teaching?

No doubt each of us here can recognize the influence of Peperzak on our person, and I suspect this has left us with common sense of philosophical values and comportment to our vocation. The commonalities I think we share are put into even further relief as we look around and note the many different areas of teaching and research represented here: Plato, Aristotle, Hegel, Heidegger, Kant, and Levinas, and still others. For my part, one thing I have learned is

> that philosophy really has to address the question of how we are to live our lives. Another thing I have learned is to be generous and open to the text itself, and try to acknowledge how I am already a part of a philosophical tradition, claimed by and subject to it. And, I have learned to try to continue the dialogue I find myself in.

But what, specifically, has been the influence of Prof. Peperzak on my own work on Kant? This question has been especially present to me recently as I work on my first book on Kant's practical philosophy. I have moved from being a graduate student (though of course, I will always remain a student), and I now have to become a scholar, teacher, and, perhaps, even a philosopher. And, as Peperzak writes, "To become a philosopher is to respond to the live voice of someone who is already at home in the republic of philosophy—or rather, in one of its particular provinces, tendencies, waves, fashions or schools."[1] And again, "the impact of the teacher's style on the student's thought cannot be denied."[2] What is the impact of Prof. Peperzak's style on my approach to Kant? What, precisely, gives my work a distinctive profile? The recent proliferation of books on Kant may leave one wondering if, indeed, anything more could be said. This proliferation should no doubt be seen to be first and foremost arising from the utterly inexhaustible wellspring that is provided by Kant's own thought. Like all great thinkers, Kant's work continually occasions new meanings and interpretations and there can be no doubt that what sustains Kant studies so richly is the depth and expansiveness of Kant's philosophy. Nonetheless, as I seek to articulate my own vision of Kant—what our frame of interpretation ought to be and what we can learn from him—I am led to ask what can be gained from my reading. This, then, occasions a turn to investigate how my philosophical education with Adriaan Peperzak, being provoked by his voice and led by discussion with him, has given rise to how I orient myself in Kant's thought.

There are innumerable and certainly many hidden legacies of Peperzak's influence in my work, but there are a few that I would like to highlight as perhaps the most evident, or at least present to my consciousness about Kant and his thought. Perhaps the most overarching influence that Peperzak has had turns on Kant's sensitivity to human finitude. While Kant is often celebrated as the thinker who most fully articulates and endorses autonomy and independence, Peperzak has taught me to recognize that Kant's ethics is guided by an emphasis on human finitude. In Kant, human beings find themselves always already subject to what not only lies beyond their doing, but also calls for a response. The delineation of the ways that the human being is called to respond takes shape under the rubric of the relationship between reason and nature in the human will. Human beings, for Kant, are finite rational beings, constituted both by reason and participation in the natural order. It is this "wise constitution," as Kant names it, that yields Kant's vision of human life, indeed, of practical life. Some of what I plan to focus on in my book, and what I wish to share with you today, are three dimensions of this responsiveness. For Kant, we find ourselves responding to nature, to reason, and to community.

Perhaps the most prominent aspect of Kant's notion of human finitude is human beings' participation in nature. We can see this most clearly when we broach Kant's practical philosophy from the perspective of its guiding demand, namely, reason's demand for the unconditioned. It is this demand that is manifest in the presentation of the moral law, and expresses itself as an imperative to "be good." This demand, however, only ever arises, on Kant's account, in relation or response to a given nature, an inclination suggested to us by our condition. Thus reason's command to be good is always a response to a specific situation, person, context, or relation. In accord with this fundamentally responsive character of reason, moreover, our task of moral goodness—virtue—is one that Kant insists is never fully attainable. Kant contends that the best we can ever hope to attain is an "endless progress" toward securing virtue; we can never fully extirpate our inclinations, but only ever be strong in the face of our temptation to transgress the moral law. As Kant puts it, "Virtue is always in progress, and yet always starts from the beginning...virtue can never settle down in peace and quiet with its maxims adopted once and for all."[3] This is because to be alive is always to be called to respond to whatever situation, relation, in which we find ourselves. Were we no longer subject to the influence of nature, there would no longer be anything to which we are called to respond, no given nature against which the imperative of reason would take shape.

Kant not only believes that reason is called to respond to the givenness of nature. He also holds that reason itself places demands that call for a response. For Kant, we find ourselves always already obliged by respect for the law. We "experience" the command of reason as something unbidden—it subjects and subjugates us, in our natural aspect, to its presence. It is to this I think that Peperzak may be pointing when he writes that what Kant calls a "fact of reason"—the givenness of the moral law to us—"corresponds to the epiphany of the other's face and speech" in the thought of Levinas.[4] We find ourselves always already claimed by our rationality, and with this, our moral obligations. Peperzak goes on to write, "Kant's autonomy was, however, only a metaphor, because he knew very well that, before I become aware of it, I am not able to establish the law by which I discover myself to be ruled."[5] We do not chose to be moral beings, we do not ask: why be moral? The call to be good does not, in some sense, originate in our doing; our moral condition is one in which we find ourselves. Even our freedom, then, is finite. We are not free to choose whether we are subject to the call of moral goodness, but only how we respond. Our realization of freedom, then, is already predicated for Kant on a kind of responsiveness, both to the situations and relations in which we find ourselves, and to the imperative of reason.

I believe that both dimensions of finitude I see in Kant—our need to respond both to nature and to reason—can be seen as a kind of reflection of Peperzak's concern for the passivity, or affectedness, of a human life; we are always being affected and thus involved in what affects us.[6] We are simultaneously involved then, in our situations and relations (nature), and in the obligations we have to them (reason). What this interpretation of Kant brings into focus are the deepest underpinnings of his practical philosophy. Kant's philosophical approach to the demand that reason places on us, and the contexts in which it arises, suggests perhaps above all a phenomenology of ethical life. As we know, this is a perspective that is virtually absent in Anglophone literature on Kant's ethics, and maybe even contemporary ethics more generally. Even more, Kant's phenomenological sensibility undermines the idea that moral goodness is a mere testing of one's maxim against its potential for universalization, whose descriptions imply that we choose whether or not subject ourselves to reason's command at all. Kant's consideration of our finitude and situatedness in a web of contexts and relations reminds us that we already belong to a world animated by the demand to be morally good. Further, Kant's focus on the intractable influence of natural inclinations on the will calls attention to the difficulties and struggles that Kant believes to characterize practical life.

Kant's concern for the problem of moral responsiveness culminates in his conviction that we are obliged to embrace and engage in a world larger than ourselves. This concern becomes most evident, I contend, when we attend for the unity of his practical philosophy—encompassing his moral theory, and writings on politics, history, and religion. The unity of his practical philosophy can be discerned in the demand for the unconditioned that yields an ever-outwardly striving reason. It is this demand for the unconditioned that guides his practical philosophy. It animates, authors, governs, and organizes the various aspects of Kant's ethics, politics, and religion. This demand is always a demand for the absolute totality, for the thoroughgoing transformation of the natural order into a rational whole. Practically speaking, the demand to be good embodied in the categorical imperative is at the same time a command to bring about a moral whole, as represented in the highest good in the world. What emerges in my treatment is that the realization of individual freedom requires us to set for ourselves and pursue a whole constellation of social, political, and communal ends. Kant's point is not simply that we factually find ourselves in communities. More than this, Kant believes that one can only be good insofar as one works to participate in and promote political, ethical, and religious communities that accord with the principles of reason. The demand that reason places on the individual for the unconditioned can only be satisfied through the creation and pursuit of a world community of human beings. Our response to the command of reason must bring us out beyond our own individuality, and join with others in the universal exercise of human reason.

One will not be mistaken to sense something of an Hegelian impulse guiding much of this approach to Kant. In my judgment, Hegel's very attempts to supercede Kant put into relief many of the concerns that guide Kant's conception of the unconditioned. And, I believe there is another lesson learned from Prof. Peperzak that informs my sensibility here. I learned that philosophers need to be understood as part of the living history of thought which they help to shape and which in turn, sheds light on them. This has led me to the conclusion that my own reading cannot be divorced from the insights of the idealist tradition Kant initiated. For me, the passkey to Kant's philosophy has been Hegel's discernment that Kant recognizes the necessity of the unity of reason and nature, of freedom and necessity, even though Hegel is of course himself highly critical of Kant's own backing away from the constitutive role of this union, i.e., its status as absolute. I contend that without thematizing this demand as what unifies Kant's practical philosophy, our interpretation of Kant's practical philosophy, as well our own self-understanding in the realm of ethical life, is diminished.

These substantive aspects of my reading of Kant as influenced by Prof. Peperzak are no doubt present in my teaching as well. But the legacy of the values he has instilled in me about how to teach and do philosophy is of course much broader. First and foremost, I have learned to ask my students to do close readings. I encourage them to meditate on the text, and seek to follow its own directions and gestures. I offer that they should not take our own biases and concerns to be the sole frame through which we read. I can recall vividly a course in which we read Kant's Enlightenment essay (the piece that led me to decide to study Kant). This piece is, among other things, a rich defense of the right of free speech. In an effort to insure that we not let our own presumptions about such a right determine our understanding of Kant, Prof. Peperzak sought to highlight the restrictions Kant himself put on this right. Challenging the common view that the right to free speech means simply that all are entitled to say whatever they wish, he prompted us to have concern for the limits of this right, asking, "Who should speak? Even the French?" The call was to be true to Kant, to what he himself wrote, and seek to discern in that what was significant and meaningful about his actual claims. To read the text this way, to be led by it, is a challenge I certainly lay before my own students. I strive, in this spirit, to encourage my students not to succumb to simply asking Kant to answer to our debates, as this may only make him, indeed most great thinkers, smaller.

I also ask my students to pursue their reading with philosophical generosity and to consider what the philosopher is trying to do, rather than only whether they succeed or fail. In this, I try to convey that we should try to allow the spirit of philosophers' work to guide our interpretation of them. While there many ways into every author, and to Kant specifically, there is one that captures the thrust of his project for me. I would like to end with a quotation from Kant, that is, I think, his most strident affirmation of the spirit of his work, and is certainly appropriate to the occasion, and, I hope, to Prof. Peperzak's own work. It also reflects Kant's relation to someone whose voice he found himself responding to: Rousseau. The quotation appears in his notes, and it is how I introduce my students to Kant, "I am an inquirer by inclination. I feel a consuming thirst for knowledge, the unrest which goes with the desire to progress in it, the satisfaction at every advance in it. There was a time when I believed this constituted the honor of humanity, and I despised the people, who know nothing. Rousseau set me right about this. This blinding prejudice disappeared. I learned to honor humanity, and I would find myself more useless than the common laborer if I did not believe that this attitude of mine can give worth to all others in establishing the rights of humanity."[7]

Response to Peperzak

In his response to my piece "Orienting Oneself in Kant," Professor Peperzak summarizes with discerning insight the main lines of my concerns with Kant's philosophy. Prof. Peperzak remarks that the aspects of Kant that I emphasize remind us that Kant is to be admired for "not divinizing humanity." He has here picked up on a question I have long had about Kant, one that I have tried to think through in reference to the relation of finitude and transcendence. While Plato, with whom Kant is often compared, suggests to us that we ought to try and become like gods through a kind of death in life, and intimates to us that we leave behind that which imposes finitude on us, Kant offers no such prospect to us. Indeed, even his vision of immortality is one characterized by an "endless struggle" with our human nature. Yet, characterizing what Kant thinks our relation to our own finitude ought to be has proven, for me at least, more elusive to discern.

It may be that part of the reason it is difficult to tease out of Kant what he thinks our relation with our own finitude should be is that it is not only the case that we must struggle against a perpetually given nature. It may be, as Prof. Peperzak suggests, that we must look deeper, into a mysterious feature of human freedom itself. Namely, that human freedom has at its root a propensity for evil. This is what Prof. Peperzak names "an irreducible element of human irrationality."

Perhaps just as mysterious as the origin of evil in human beings is what Kant calls for as a response to this fact. That is, radical evil, while universal, is nonetheless something that we are each responsible for; it is something that each of us chooses for ourselves. Moreover, this choice is in Kant's mind not an anthropologically, empirically, or socially conditioned one. Nonetheless, Kant offers community—specifically religion—as the corrective for our fallen condition. The mystery of this suggestion can be seen by way of comparison with Kant's other forms of community, which each arise in response to a specific limit that nature imposes on us. Culture, for Kant, arises from our unsociable tendencies, and through discipline, seeks to transform our inner nature. In this, our naturally given inclinations are refined and restrained, making us more receptive to the moral law. The state takes its place as that which transforms our natural external relations; the unsociability that naturally characterizes our relations with others is harmonized and made subject to reason through lawfulness. Radical evil, though, has no natural cause that can be redressed and mitigated. Rather, it is originary in freedom itself. And yet, Kant still insists that we must pursue its overcoming in the context of a religious community.

I have wondered often about this aspect of Kant's thought, and about the extent to which Kant's pessimism about the possibility of human virtue permeates his thought. While much of his practical philosophy focuses on the difficult task—the struggle—that reason has to overcome the limits that nature imposes on us, in his writings on radical evil and religion, it strikes me that the hopeful character of his other work seems absent. This is most obvious, I think, in his turn to the notion of grace, which Kant seems to turn to as that which redeems us in the face our inability to attain virtue. No longer is it a matter of indefinite time that allows us to be good. Instead, we must give up this hope, and rely on something outside of ourselves. In this, I suspect perhaps that Kant acknowledges the impossibility of human freedom to realize itself in the world. The ontological guilt he describes in the *Religion* book may also be seen, perhaps, to throw new light on the task of reason to transform the world, and humanity, into its own image. And I wonder, too, if this gives new context on how we understand our relation to the duties we must pursue in realizing the ends of reason. From this standpoint, it is not only that reason compels us to strive ever outward, beyond ourselves into our communities. Rather, perhaps we must interpret this ever expanding domain of duties required by promoting the highest good as Kant's way of articulating the idea that I am responsible for more than I can do. I am responsible not only for myself, but for the state, for the creation of a world, of a highest good on earth.

Endnotes

1. Adriaan Peperzak, "Ethical Life," *Research in Phenomenology*, 33 (2003), 146.
2. Peperzak, "Ethical Life," 145.
3. Immanuel Kant, *Metaphysics of Morals*, in *Practical Philosophy* (New York: Cambridge University Press, 1999), 6:380.
4. Adriaan Peperzak, "Some Remarks on Hegel, Kant, and Levinas," *Face to Face With Levinas*, ed. Richard A. Cohen (Albany: State University of New York Press, 2007), 211.
5. Peperzak, "Some Remarks," 212.
6. Adriaan Peperzak, *Elements of Ethics* (Stanford: Stanford University Press, 2004), Chapter 3.
7. Immanuel Kant, cited in the Introduction to *Practical Philosophy*, 20:44.

THE TRUTH OF SOIL: PHILOSOPHIZING IN THE GARDEN
§

Norman Wirzba

In *Elements of Ethics* Adriaan Peperzak writes of the diverse realities that intersect and speak to human life: persons, plants, animals, schools, states, stars, the moon (to name but a few). These realities are not simply a stage or backdrop – mere fodder – for the actions of an autonomous and solitary ego. "Each reality affects and challenges me: I must respond – but is my response appropriate? Responsivity is part of responsibility. I will never be autarchic or autonomous: reality suggests, invites, commands, and often forces me, but I am free and forced to respond in my way to those challenges." [70] The world, in the various forms of beloved teachers and philosophical friends, but also chickens and tomatoes, sets our hearts (and stomachs!) aflame with the desire and the need to philosophize.

Responsivity, the invitation to witness to the grace and mystery of our life together, is at the core of a genuinely human life. More fundamental to our living than our acting or planning, our choosing and deciding, is the fact that even before we are born, and (later on) often without intention or thought, we are receiving and appropriating the gifts of those around us. As Jean-Louis Chrétien reminds us, "Whatever we do, or do not do for

---
70 Adriaan T. Peperzak. *Elements of Ethics* (Stanford: Stanford University Press, 2004), 54.

that matter, wherever we are, we are always already called and requested, and our first utterance, like our first glance, is already an answer to the request wherein it emerges." [71] Though we may choose to be silent about what is everywhere and always calling us, our silence is in fact a response, a testimony to personal and social boredom, disaffection, or blindness. But to those who heed the call, and so bear witness to the attention, patience, and love (*phileo, eros,* and *agape* each have a distinct role to play) that seeks to be faithful to the world, the possibility of a wisdom (*Sophia*) that appreciates and understands the coincidence of "being" and "being good" emerges. [72]

***

In this essay I argue that the *place* of philosophical reflection is vital because *where* one is, one's physical and not only cultural *Sitz im Leben*, inspires, shapes, and gives direction to thought's production. [73] Though philosophers often speak of the inter-human setting of philosophical work, giving thoughtful and necessary attention to the complexities and potential joys of dialogical life, they do not often enough appreciate that "we cannot discover the true reality of one single phenomenon without a full reconnaissance of the totality from which it emerges." [74] When we attend to the total contexts of things, aware that we will never be able to give an adequate or comprehensive accounting of those contexts, we are necessarily drawn into the diverse places in terms of which things can be what they are. Aristotle recognized this, which is why he noted that "place" is prior to all things. [75] To be is to be in a place because nothing can "be" without

---

71 Jean-Louis Chrétien, *The Call and the Response* (trans. Anne A. Davenport, New York: Fordham University Press, 2004), 14-15. In the face of our continually being called, Chrétien suggests that "Our task is not to give an answer that would in some sense erase the initial provocation by corresponding to it, but to offer ourselves up as such in response, without assigning in advance any limit to the gift" (13).

72 In *Elements of Ethics* Peperzak argues the thesis that because everything in the world makes an appeal to us, awakens, provokes, challenges, invites, and makes demands of us, "no being is without value; *being* and *being* (in some sense) *good* coincide" (46).

73 It should be noted that in its early Middle English usage the word "culture" referred to a piece of land. Gradually its meaning expanded to include the skills necessary to take care of the land. A cultured person was thus one who *knew* the land practically and intimately.

74 *Elements of Ethics*, 110.

75 For an excellent account on the importance of "place" in philosophical life see the two excellent books by Edward Casey *Getting Back Into Place: Toward a Renewed Understanding of the Place-World*

being "somewhere." Whatever exists draws its life and/or meaning from the material and spiritual contexts that give it a home and a bearing.

The point, however, is not simply that everything needs a container of some sort that holds it or feeds it. From a philosophical point of view it is not enough to describe the places that give a context to any particular thing. We must also attend to how places inspire, shape, and direct the work of philosophical description and reflection itself. The place in which one lives and converses – a prison, a field, a library or classroom, a war zone, a forest, an urban penthouse, a factory cubicle, a desert – opens and closes lines of vision, sympathy, and understanding. Habits of attention and affection, indeed the wide range of what we might call thought's sensitivity, develop their defining forms in response to what particular places recommend. What one thinks and how one thinks it – the very capabilities of thought, as well as the capacities for amazement, wonder, and responsibility – are formed decisively (though not exclusively) in the various modes of being in a place. [76] Meaning and sense, though clearly also taking abstract forms, find their most vital inspiration, bearing, and existential significance in the webs of concrete relationships that constitute life in a place.

To make this point clear I will focus on the place of gardens and the gardening work that occurs there. This may appear an odd place to locate distinctly philosophical reflection, particularly when we observe that: a) gardening has been relegated to a hobby or recreational affair for a shrinking percentage of the world's populations, and b) most philosophers spend their time with books inside rather than with soil and plants outside. In my view, this is a serious problem because gardening has long been the kind of work that trains humanity in several essential ways. When people garden they do not simply grow food and make the world more beautiful (as essential as these are!). They also develop dispositions and skills of attention,

---

(Bloomington: Indiana University Press, 1993) and *The Fate of Place: A Philosophical History* (Berkeley: University of California Press, 1997).

76 Martin Heidegger's analyses of *Dasein's* "being-in-the-world" are a rich point of departure for those seeking to understand the many philosophical dimensions of being in a place. For a lucid extension of Heidegger's insights with respect to "place" see Jeff Malpas's *Heidegger's Topology: Being, Place, World* (Cambridge: The MIT Press, 2007).

patience, learning, and humility that are indispensible for an honest and responsible life together. When people garden they have the potential to learn crucial insights about their place in the world and the responsibilities they have for each other. Amidst plants and animals, and in terms of the varying conditions of soil, water, and weather, humanity discovers what it means to be marked by finitude, ignorance, need, mortality, interdependence, and miracle.

Gardens are microcosms of the world in which human life and the forces productive of life meet. One does not need to be an expert gardener to appreciate the fact that insofar as we eat, drink, and breathe we are necessarily and beneficially bound to the geophysical and biochemical processes at work in a garden. Gardens, and by extension also farms, have been and will continue to be the places in terms of which our bodies and souls are fed. Without the life and death in gardens, none of us could survive, let alone thrive. This is why even non-gardeners must be sympathetic and committed to the preservation and nurture of healthy gardens and good gardening work. The health of all life depends on the vitality, resilience, and growth gardens embody. When people lose gardening sensitivities and sensibilities they run the risk of failing to appreciate the fact that they are first and foremost creatures in need of the help and nurture of others, creatures deeply embedded in the many memberships and food webs of creation. Failing to have this appreciation makes it more likely that we will then become accomplices in the destruction of fields, streams, forests, and oceans.

Gardening is hard, humbling work. It requires attention and patience and a tremendous amount of detailed knowledge about soil and plant and animal life, not to mention weather and the peculiarities of different growing zones and topographies. It presupposes that the schedules of the day and season are not entirely our own as we respond to the changing needs, limits, and possibilities of each garden. It would be a bad idea, for instance, to take a vacation when the raspberries are coming ripe, or to put off making salsa to the cooler days of October when the tomatoes and peppers have already rotted into the ground. The times and terms of planting and harvest, watering and weeding, are set by the plants, not by us. Gardening work, in short, reveals that we are benefited by and bound to the memberships of creation. For a garden sustainably to service our needs, we must also serve it.

To garden effectively is thus to bring human life into fairly close, appreciative, and sympathetic alignment with the life going on in the garden. This is what it means to be a creature. Being a human creature, however, does not mean that we are to become the slavish imitators of all creation's ways. People, for instance, are not to follow some animal creatures in their predatory ways, particularly when those ways entail what we would characterize as needless suffering or violence. [77] This is because human beings bear the responsibility of choosing how they will relate to each other, and in their relating contribute to the growth of good in the world. Though violence is a possible response, the accrued wisdom of great philosophical and spiritual traditions is that violence is ultimately self and world defeating and a destruction of what is good.

Gardening requires people to know a particular plot of land and understand its potential, and then work harmoniously with it. To garden is to unseat oneself as the center of primary importance, and to instead turn one's life into various forms of service that will strengthen and maintain the many memberships that make up the garden. It is to give up the much-trumpeted goal of modern and postmodern life – individual autonomy – and instead live the life of care and responsible interdependence. When people garden well, devoting themselves to the strengthening of the memberships of creation, personal ego gradually recedes from lines of sight so that the blessings and grace of life can shine through what is seen, smelled, and tasted.

All this is another way of saying that the land as well as people can be our teachers. In this teaching-learning relationship people have the opportunity to become more attentive, more knowledgeable, and more faithful to the places and communities in which they live. Wendell Berry,

---

[77] It is a very complex matter to know exactly how to describe, narrate, and then explain the actions of non-human animals. The danger of anthropomorphism with respect to animals is well known. What is not as well appreciated is how certain vocabularies – the conceptual frameworks of Darwinian competition and scientific materialism or the reductionist measures of econometric calculation – determine and shape how we think about these matters.

one of today's most perceptive and eloquent writers on place, often uses the language of marriage and husbandry to capture the kind of patience and fidelity we need if we are to know our places well and then live in them appropriately. Unlike the relationship and the economy of the one-night-stand, in which people get what they can without attention to costs and effects, people who are committed to a place know that it takes study and discipline to see clearly *where* one is and then make the steps necessary to correct the mistakes we make while being there.

This is difficult to do because people, often consumed by insecurity, anxiety, or ambition, are so readily tempted to transform reality by fantasy. Genuine perception, as Peperzak has also observed, compels us to face and correct the many ways we have for "distorting the givenness of the give." [78] Speaking of a farmer's first perception of a new farm, a perception shaped by dreams of success rather than steady work, Berry notes that with the correct discipline and time

"Truth begins to intrude with its matter-of-fact. One's work may be defined in part by one's visions, but it is defined in part too by problems, which the work leads to and reveals. And daily life, work, and problems gradually alter the visions. It invariably turns out, I think, that one's first vision of one's place was to some extent an imposition on it. But if one's sight is clear and if one stays on and works well, one's love gradually responds to the place as it really is, and one's visions gradually image possibilities that are really in it. Vision, possibility, work, and life – *all* have changed by mutual correction. Correct discipline, given enough time, gradually removes one's self from one's line of sight. One works to better purpose then and makes fewer mistakes, because at last one sees where one is. Two human possibilities of the highest order thus come within reach: what one wants can become the same as what one has, and one's knowledge can cause respect for what one knows." [79]

What Berry is describing is an apprenticeship to reality, a form of

---

[78] *Elements of Ethics*, 100. Peperzak continues: "I must open, adjust, attune, and adapt myself to the reality of what I want to be united with ... I must be open to the object without forcing it to fit into any preconceived pattern..." (100).

[79] Wendell Berry. "People, Land, and Community," in *The Art of the Commonplace: The Agrarian Essays of Wendell Berry* (ed. Norman Wirzba, Washington, D.C.: Counterpoint, 2002), 187.

teaching/learning that is realized in the disciplines of work, attention, patience, correction, and ultimately love.

When people serve a garden well by learning to calibrate their schedules and desires to complement gardening realities, life has the chance to thrive and smell and taste really good. A chance, however, is not a guarantee. One of the hardest lessons of gardening is that success is always under threat of disease and death. Though gardeners might do everything they know to be correct – proper soil preparation, sufficient moisture, appropriate plant maintenance and protection – there is always the possibility that calamity will intervene. Good gardeners are precisely those who do not run from the calamity. Michael Pollan put it this way:

"All the accomplished gardeners I know are surprisingly comfortable with failure. They may not be happy about it, but instead of reacting with anger or frustration, they seem fairly intrigued by the peony that, after years of being taken for granted, suddenly fails to bloom. They understand that, in the garden at least, failure speaks louder than success. By that I don't mean the gardener encounters *more* failure than success (though in some years he will), only that his failures have more to say to him – about his soil, the weather, the predilections of local pests, the character of his land. The gardener learns nothing when his carrots thrive, unless that success is won against a background of prior disappointment. Outright success is dumb, disaster frequently eloquent. At least to the gardener who learns how to listen." [80]

Could it be that our declining interest in, even disparagement of, gardening is rooted in our fear of failure and our impatience with loss? Very little in our culture prepares or encourages us to learn the eloquence that comes from disaster. We don't know how to face our own fragility, vulnerability, and ignorance. And so we shun the humus, the rich organic layer of soil, much like we shun the humility that comes from a life devoted to the land and its creatures. More than we care to admit, we resist the truth that we live more by gifts and mystery than by the cunning and might of our presumed power.

---

[80] Michael Pollan. *Second Nature: A Gardener's Education* (New York: Delta, 1991), 143-44.

Humility is not about self-debasement or self-loathing. [81] It is, rather, the realization that human life depends on many others, even the sacrifices of others. As people begin to take stock of the great number and variety of gifts that feed into their being – ranging from water and sunlight, earthworms and bees, green peppers and eggs, but also social nurture and help – they see how inappropriate and dishonest it is to think they could live alone or on their own terms, or live without constant reference to a place. Need and interdependence define the human condition. That people live at all is always already the sign that they have received, whether appreciatively or not, gift upon gift. Being an authentic creature presupposes knowing how to receive these gifts with humility and gratitude.

In his excellent, wide-ranging exploration of the meaning of gardening throughout the ages, Robert Pogue Harrison observes that "care is constantly being thrown back upon the limitations of its powers of action, is constantly reminded of its own inefficacy and essential passivity when it comes to phenomena like weather, blight, parasites, and rodents." Gardening does not proceed in mechanical, predictable fashion, where people can be sure that a particular input will net the desired output. Gardens are places of struggle, surprise, and deep mystery, places where gardeners are often reduced to silence and awe. Though they may desire this or that outcome – a succulent, blemish-free peach, for instance – in the end they must learn to receive humbly as a gift what the garden provides. Harrison concludes "The fall from Eden was as much a fall into the humility of impotence as it was into shame." [82]

But there is more. Gardeners have not only to contend with human arrogance and gardening failure and unpredictability. They also have to face the massive amount of death that every garden *by necessity* includes and presupposes. Though our culture encourages the hiding and denial of death, gardens are constant reminders of the fact that whatever lives, lives only for a short while, and that for anything to live at all, others must

---

81 I have developed the meaning of humility in "The Touch of Humility: An Invitation to Creatureliness," *Modern Theology* 24:2 (April, 2008), 225-244.
82 Robert Pogue Harrison. *Gardens: An Essay on the Human Condition* (Chicago: The University of Chicago Press, 2008), 28.

die, most often by being eaten. [83] The sight and aroma of death are simply unavoidable. Seed germinates into new life, then grows (hopefully) to maturity and fruitfulness, only to die back into the ground. Soil, we could say, is the ever-open receptacle for death. Deep in the bowels of earth countless bacteria, microorganisms, fungi, and insects are engaged in a feeding frenzy that absorbs life into death and death back into the conditions for life. Facing this ground, immersing one's hands in it, as every gardener does, is often too much of a reminder that we too will one day be welcomed by the ground in death: "you are dust, and to dust you shall return" (Genesis 3:19). It is a reminder that can turn into fear, but also revenge: "because the earth is the place where our death is at home, we have an urge to take revenge on it ... A great deal of the destructiveness in our dealings with nature arises, it seems, from a stubborn refusal to come to terms with our finitude, to accept our fundamental limitations." [84]

Gardeners and non-gardeners live in two considerably different worlds. Or, more exactly, they occupy a shared world in different ways. This is because gardeners *see* differently. Though they share eyes with everyone else, the disciplines of gardening life promote distinct forms of vision, giving gardeners special sensitivities and a complex, more detailed and comprehensive, focus. How they see is a feature of the kind of life they live, the patterns of their days, and the nature of the engagements they have with fellow creatures in a garden. It is a way of seeing that would, I believe, greatly enrich our philosophical lives.

Gardening is an indispensible activity for philosophers not only because it provides them with food. The work that gardening requires makes possible a joining of theory and practice that is too often absent from philosophical work. In her well-known essay "Against Dryness," Iris Murdoch observed that trends in modern philosophical and literary life encouraged a

---

[83] William Ralph Inge has observed that "The whole of nature ... is a conjugation of the verb to eat, in the active and passive" (quoted by Leon Kass in *The Hungry Soul: Eating and the Perfecting of Our Nature* [Chicago: University of Chicago Press, 1994], 17).

[84] Robert P. Harrison. "Toward a Philosophy of Nature," in *Uncommon Ground: Rethinking the Human Place in Nature* (Ed. William Cronon, New York: W.W. Norton & Company, 1995), 436. Harrison has developed this theme in *The Dominion of the Dead* (Chicago: The University of Chicago Press, 2003).

view of persons as solitary wills that then take the world by determination and by force. The instruction of particular places and communities, and the work their maintenance requires, did not seem to factor much in the manners and methods of philosophical reflection. People came to think of themselves as "isolated free choosers, monarchs of all [they] survey." Or to give a more contemporary metaphor, the temptation of people today, many of whom have been reduced to the status of the helpless and hapless consumer, is to treat the whole world as a store that we can enter in as we feel the need. How do we understand reality and the places of life when our primary means of encounter is through a shopping relationship? In a consumer world there is little appreciation for the fact that people live in terms of deep cultural traditions and complex backgrounds of lived experience, backgrounds that include bodily attachments to other bodies. This is why Murdoch urged that we need the skills and vocabulary of attention. [85] We need to find the ways that will enable us to enter deeply in the life-giving places of the world. My point is that gardening can be one powerful and practical (and enjoyable!) means for precisely this kind of engagement.

The skill of attention is crucial because it enables a reconfiguration of self-identity as connected to and deeply immersed in a specific place and time. Failing careful attention it is virtually inevitable that people will experience themselves as lost in this world and without a deep sense of belonging and responsibility. They become lost not simply because they are without direction, but more fundamentally because they don't know *where* they are. Not knowing their *place*, they are unable to see the many ways in which they are mutually implicated *in* and benefited *by* and responsible *for* the lives of each other. Living in the age of simulation and the spectacle – we are all mostly spectators and consumers now – people are addicted to virtual reality, the merely surface images and highly stylized representations of life rather than the complex world itself. What people are losing is not simply reality, but the ability to sense life deeply, to feel and taste its vitality and fragility. People look at the world around and see little that is

---

85 Iris Murdoch. "Against Dryness," in *Existentialists and Mystics: Writings in Philosophy and Literature* (ed. Peter Conradi, New York: Penguin Books, 1998), 290-93.

compelling, little that feeds and ennobles life. And so they become bored and restless, the easy prey of marketers who promise to fill voids with a glitzy, convenient product. Rowan Williams describes this situation succinctly: "The skills have been lost of being present for and in an other, and what remains is mistrust and violence." [86]

When people become more attentive a most important result becomes possible: they begin to see the world as it more nearly is, rather than as they (fearfully, anxiously, or arrogantly) wish it to be. They begin to name the world more truly. To be attentive is to know that we are always already in a world that touches us and responds to us in bewildering varieties of ways. It is to see how frequently and how easily egos get in the way of others because people are so intent on imposing their way. At root, the skill of attention manifests a willingness to love the world. The discipline of attention works to remove ego so that what lies before us can speak for itself. Attention testifies to the desire to work with rather than against others so that they can be all they can be. In its deepest and most concentrated forms, attention becomes a form of prayer, a practice in which the truth and integrity of the world and the grace of the world shines, inspiring hearts and minds with the desire to greater fidelity and love. [87]

Much more needs to be said about how gardening enables the development of key philosophical virtues like attention, propriety, humility, honest speech, and responsibility. In this brief treatment I have highlighted only some of the features of how the practice of gardening introduces us to a more detailed and honest understanding of our place in the world (dishonesty would result in gardening failure and the diminishment of livelihood). In a time when many people believe philosophers to be out of touch with the world and their words to be (often torturous!) flights of fancy, there is hope for philosophy if lovers of wisdom can make their way to gardens and become lovers of the soil and considerate eaters and sharers of its life. But not only hope. The great joy of submitting to the

---

86 Rowan Williams. *Lost Icons: Reflections on Cultural Bereavement* (Edinburgh: T & T Clark, 2000), 175.

87 In *Gravity and Grace* Simone Weil says "Absolutely unmixed attention is prayer." I have developed this insight in "Attention and Responsibility: The Work of Prayer," in *The Phenomenology of Prayer* (eds. Bruce Ellis Benson & Norman Wirzba, New York: Fordham University Press, 2005), 88-100.

teaching-learning relationship – a joy many of us in the Peperzak circle of influence have known – is that we may also come to experience our world and our neighbors as a source of delight.

Continuing the Conversation

The more attentive and reflectively aware I become – "progress" in this direction is hardly steady or linear! – the more I discover how difficult it is to be faithful and true to the places and communities that give me life. My temptation is to assume that I know *where* I am and *who* I am with, and so rest content with superficial or readily available accounts. Adriaan's admission that after years of study he is still learning to understand even a few of the great philosophers is made richly complex for me because of my interests in ecology and agricultural life. I am trying to become "friends" with books and with plants and dirt. I am constantly testing what I learn in books with what I see, touch, hear, taste, and smell in my garden, in my community, and in our world.

So many valuable themes were broached in our conversation in Baltimore: invitation, desire, community, voice, vocation, humility, teaching, learning, the tension between theory and practice. These go to the heart of who we are as philosophers. Having the leisurely time and the welcoming place to have this conversation – many thanks again to Catriona – made me realize how rare it is that genuine philosophical conversation occurs. We are all so busy, caught up with institutional, professional, family, and personal demands that I left our time together longing for more. Being in Baltimore helped me see how precious and how fruitful genuine conversation can be. Being amongst friends and colleagues who are sympathetic but also willing to engage and challenge is a great gift.

Conversation is indispensible. I need it precisely so that the assumptions and categories through which I attempt to make sense of the world can be refined, corrected, and inspired to move in new directions. The skill of *attention* that I highlight in my essay is not an individually acquired skill. Nor is it a private possession. It is a faculty that develops and deepens through conversation and a shared life together. How I wish you all were close by so that we could continue the work begun and the insight received in Baltimore! I have resolved to create welcoming places and times here in Durham where conversations of a similar sort can occur.

Adriaan asks how we should respond to the power of nature, a power that is often shocking, terrifying, and violent in its expressions. The more I reflect on this question the more I see that we need to attend to two prior concerns: a) how do we come to have the descriptive terms like "nature" or "violence"? and b) how do we get into the practical position that will enable us to judge the suitability of our descriptive and evaluative schemes?

When I was younger I was a farmer. Working on the land, attending to animals, participating in the life and death of multiple organisms showed me that the way I saw and thought about the world differed significantly from my city friends. My position in the world, a position made possible by the distinct forms of work I performed, opened lines of questioning that have remained with me. Should we describe our world as "natural"? I realize that the word "nature" carries an enormously complex cluster of meanings, but I think it is safe to say that in our post-Darwinian era many people understand by nature a random, accidental, competitive, and amoral sphere that surrounds human life and culture. This was not my experience. Though there were clear signs of competition, cooperation abounded. Though there were many signs of accident, there were also many indications of movement in the service of achieving a goal or end. The "natural" world did not seem to me to be an "amoral" space, but rather a place of beauty, mystery, joy, suffering, terror, delight, and immense hospitality. I don't know that the word "violence" was a big part of my imagination, even though I witnessed up close plenty of death.

I make these observations because I am not sure that we know where we are, or that we know how to describe where we are. If it is accurate to say that we live in a consumer culture, in a society of the spectacle where simulation reigns, then I am not sure how people will get into the practical position where "nature" – would a better term be "creation" or "wildness" or "maya" or "earth"? – can teach us about itself. The teaching/learning relationship that we have come to love and continue in our philosophical conversations needs to be extended into a conversation with the "places" in which we live. No doubt, this will be an unusual sort of conversation since places "speak" in ways quite unlike humans do. But it is an indispensable conversation nonetheless. Just as inter-human conversations train us to live well – more honestly, attentively, responsibly, and joyfully – with each other, so too will our conversations with particular places enable us to live well in our life-giving homes. The exhaustion and destruction of the many places of life in our world shows us that the conversation is now more necessary than ever before.

    I am not suggesting that we all become farmers, or even that farmers be given some exalted status. It would be grand, however, if agricultural work and insight were to make a more regular appearance in our philosophical conversations. The same goes for hunters and gatherers (the few that are left), or any other group of people having intimate and practical understanding of humanity's place in the world. As the scope of our conversation grows, and the love of our teachers increases, my hope is that the range of our love will also increase. My sense is that the wisdom made possible by an enlarged love will serve the good we already have come to enjoy.

TEACHING AND THE ACTIVE LIFE ACCORDING TO ST. THOMAS

§

Ryan D. Madison

Preface

"*Il maestro di color che sanno*"—such, in Dante's memorable phrase, is Aristotle. But can a master engage in dialogue? Teaching presupposes, does it not, knowledge, and knowledge, in its turn, mastery? The Greek word for knowledge, *epistēme*, means standing on top of something, a symbol of the commanding mastery traditionally associated with knowledge. Aristotle and, even more so, the scholastics when compared with Plato seem less interested in engaging in conversation than in finding students to instruct and before whom they can display their sophisticated and technical mastery. Such a picture however would be misleading.

There are conditions to every dialogue as anyone who has ever tried to engage in one knows. Every fruitful conversation relies upon common, shared presuppositions, things that can be taken for granted by the participants. Without this common ground, dialogue must come to an end or be condemned to endless repetition and stagnation. But what is the common ground upon which all genuine philosophical conversation depends? Aristotle and St. Thomas would answer that it is first principles, the source of all rational discourse. But are not these principles immune from dialogue? Are not the very conditions that make meaningful discourse possible themselves exempt from discussion? The dogmatist would answer in the affirmative—but neither Aristotle nor St. Thomas would. Discussing first principles however appears impossible, for is not their certainty and stability necessarily destroyed when subject to the scrutiny of doubt and questioning? The skeptic would answer yes—but neither Aristotle nor St. Thomas would. And their position is the only one capable of preserving the necessary conditions for real, philosophical conversation, for dialogue is equally threatened by dogmatism *and* skepticism, as each fails to recognize that there is something prior to reflexive discourse from which all of our conversations emanate. This is the common ground of all dialogue, the world of shared experience, a world in which we live and move and have our being. This is not a philosophical construct or a theoretical doctrine but rather something prior. In spite of all their complexity and technical mastery, neither Aristotle nor St. Thomas ever forgot this fundamental fact and this is what makes them our eternal partners in conversation, the true masters of dialogue.

Presentation

There are two important places in the *Corpus Thomisicum* that explicitly and thematically discuss the nature of teaching in its relation to the active and contemplative lives.[88] The first treatment occurs in the eleventh question of the *Quaestiones disputatae de veritate*, an early work completed in Paris between the years 1256-1259, just after Thomas had finished his commentary on the *Sentences* of Peter Lombard. The second is found near the end of *Summa theologiae* II-II, the treatise on the virtues, and was almost certainly composed towards the end of his second stay in Paris, probably around the years 1271-1272, just two or three years before

---

[88] There are just two other works that discuss the topic: *III Sent.* d. 35, q. 1, art. 3, qc. 1, ad. 3 and *Contra retrahentes*, C. 7, ad. 7. The first discussion is extremely brief and does nothing more than anticipate the later discussions in both the *De veritate* and the *Summa theologiae* while the latter, which appears in a work dedicated to a defense of the mendicant orders, was composed at the end of the 1269-1270 school year, approximately ten years after the discussion contained in the *De veritate*, does not contribute anything new to St. Thomas's earlier position.

his death.⁸⁹ In both places the question posed is whether or not teaching is a work of the active or contemplative life and, relying upon the authority of St. Gregory the Great,⁹⁰ Thomas argues that the act of teaching (*actus docendi*) belongs primarily to the active life, though in a certain respect it must also be said to belong to the contemplative life. This position however raises an important question, for it apparently contradicts St. Thomas's often repeated thesis that acts are specified by their objects. Acts derive their species or nature from their object and just as the nature of a thing can be of only one kind—otherwise it would not be one thing but two— so too it would seem that the species of an act can be of only one kind. Yet in the case of teaching there appear to be two distinct objects. On the one hand, teaching presupposes knowledge, or the possession of the true, apprehension of that which is. As Aristotle says, the ability to teach is a sign of wisdom, for the wise are those who instruct us in the causes of things.⁹¹ And yet mere knowing is not teaching. To teach is to communicate a truth already possessed *to* another, it is the communication of knowledge to someone. The object of the teacher seems therefore to include two distinct things, the one to whom the teaching directed and the content or knowledge conveyed. Does the act of teaching have a single object, is it a specifically unified act, or is it rather an accidental composite constituted by two essentially different acts aimed at specifically different objects? In order to answer this question it is necessary to investigate the relation between the theoretical and practical dimensions of human life and the unique role of charity (*caritas*) in relation to the virtues. In a phrase of St. Thomas's that was eventually to become the motto of the Dominican Order, *contemplare et contemplata aliis tradere*, it is charity that binds the act of contemplation and the communication of truth.⁹²

---

89 P. Mandonnet, "Chronologie des Questions disputées de S. Thomas," *Revue thomiste* 23 (1918): 266-287; 341-371. See also, M.-D. Chenu, O.P., *Toward Understanding Saint Thomas*, tran. By A.-M. Landry, O.P. and D. Hughes, O.P., (Chicago: Regnery, 1963), 281-283; J. A. Weisheipl, *Friar Thomas d'Aquino. His Life, Thought, and Works* 2ⁿᵈ Ed. (Washington D.C.: The Catholic University of America Press, 1983), 55-60, J.-P. Torrell, *Saint Thomas Aquinas: The Person and His Work*, trans. R. Royal, (Washington, D. C.: Catholic University of America Press, 1996), 197-223.
90 Gregory the Great, *In Ezechiel*, II, 2 (*PL* 76: 954). See also, *Homélies sur Ézéchiel*, Livre II, trad. Charles Morel, S.J., (Paris: Les Éditions du Cerf, 1990), 106.
91 Aristotle, *Metaphysics*, I, 2, 982a28-30.
92 *ST*, II-II, Q. 188, art. 7, "Manifestum est autem quod maiorem sollicitudinem spiritualium requirit

In spite of the great temporal distance that separates Thomas's two discussions of teaching there is no serious doctrinal divergence between them, though the practical aspect receives slightly more emphasis in the earlier than in the later treatment. The first account is the fourth and final question in the brief but important treatise known as the *De magistro*, "On the Teacher," and which constitutes the eleventh of the *Disputed Questions on Truth*. The *De veritate* as a whole is devoted almost exclusively to discussions regarding the nature of knowledge and truth and the ideas of St. Augustine loom large in nearly every question. St. Thomas is often at pains to demonstrate how the more Platonically inspired spiritualism of St. Augustine can be reconciled with the more mundane Aristotelian doctrines regarding the nature and origins of human knowledge.[93] The first question of the *De magistro* contains an extremely condensed summary of the fundamental metaphysical principles that underlie the Aristotelian approach of St. Thomas as well as a masterful attempt to demonstrate how a substance ontology rooted in the real distinction between essence and existence provides the key to reconciling the Platonic-Augustinian tradition with Aristotelianism.

There is no doubt that this same concern extends to his discussion of teaching, for what is at stake ultimately in this question is a broader issue regarding the relations between the contemplative and active lives, between theory and practice. Historically, the Platonic and Aristotelian traditions have diverged fundamentally on this issue. Plato and the Platonic tradition do not admit the sharp distinction between theoretical and practical reason that is so fundamental to Aristotle's account of moral reason, action, and virtue in the *Nicomachean Ethics*.[94] St. Thomas's primary philosophical allegiance is to Aristotle of course but his commitment to the Fathers in general and to St. Augustine in particular places upon him the burden of reconciling their Platonic emphasis on the continuity of theory and prac-

---

religio quae est instituta ad contemplandum et contemplata aliis tradendum per doctrinam et praedicationem, quam illa quae est instituta ad contemplandum tantum."

93 See William Wade, S.J., *A Comparison of the 'De Magistro' of Saint Augustine With the 'De Magistro' of Saint Thomas* (Ph. D. diss., St. Louis University, 1935).

94 Aristotle, *Nicomachean Ethics*, VI, 5, 1140a33-1040b6. See also, *In VI Eth.*, lect. 4, nn. 1-4; *ST*, I, Q. 1, art. 3-4; *ST*, I, Q. 14, art. 16; *ST*, I-II, Q. 56, art. 3; *ST*, II-II, Q. 57, art. 1; *ST*, II-II, Q. 58, arts. 2-4.

tice with a sharp Aristotelian distinction between the two.

Both in the *Summa* and in the *De veritate* the thesis that governs his discussion is that teaching bears upon a twofold matter, that is, has a twofold object, for the matter of an act is that which it is "about," or that upon which it bears. The matter of an act is otherwise known as its object.[95] It is in virtue of one of these objects that teaching is said to belong to the contemplative life while the other object places it in the active life. The existence of an act with a twofold object is peculiar. Fortitude, for example, has as its object fear of death in battle,[96] and this object is the cause of the act's species or unity. Likewise, the object of sobriety is the drinking of intoxicants and the object of abstinence is the "pleasures of the table" (*delectationes ciborum*).[97] In each case the nature of the virtue is defined in terms of its formal object. Teaching, however, since it has two objects, seemingly possesses a two-fold nature since the species or form of an act, which constitutes the principle by which the act is determined, is derived from its object. Hence, an act that is determined by two specifically distinct objects gives the appearance of being not *one* kind of act but rather two. But if such is really the case then one might reasonably ask whether or not the act of teaching is rightly said to be *one* act rather than two. Is teaching in other words a single kind of act or rather a hybrid, a fusion of two essentially different kinds of acts? And if the latter turns out to be true, is there *any* sense in which we may speak of its unity? In order to address these questions it is necessary to lay out some of the fundamental principles that underlie St. Thomas's analysis.

According to Aristotle and St. Thomas, the various human sciences, habits, and ways of life are distinguished by their subject-matter or, more properly, by their formal object. This doctrine is based upon a fundamental axiom that governs St. Thomas's entire discussion of anthropology and the virtues: potencies are distinguished by their acts and their objects (*potentiae distinguuntur per actus et obiecta*). This axiom in fact

---

[95] *ST*, I-II, Q. 18, art. 2, ad. 2, "obiectum non est materia ex qua, sed materia circa quam, et habet quodammodo rationem formae, inquantum dat speciem."
[96] *ST*, II-II, Q. 123, art. 5, "... concedendum est quod fortitudo proprie est circa pericula mortis quae est in bello."
[97] *ST*, II-II, Q. 149, art. 2; *ST*, Q. 146, art. 2.

contains two distinct principles, the first being that potency is specified by its act, the second that acts are specified by their objects. In other words, every potency is of its nature ordered towards and specified by its correlative or proper act, and since every act is in turn determined by its object, potencies must be diversified according to the diversity of objects.[98] The first part of the axiom, that potencies are specified by their acts, rests upon a central tenet of Aristotelian metaphysics, namely the priority of act over potency. This priority is expressed by the axiom *potentia dicitur ad actum*, potency is relative to act, and is explained in detail in Aristotle's *Metaphysics*, IX. The most important sense in which act is prior to potency is ontological, a priority not of time but of nature. Potency, because it is essentially incomplete, always exists for the sake of and in relation to the actual, a thesis expressed by Aristotle when he says that "man is prior to the boy" or more generally that becoming is for the sake of being.[99] Since movement and becoming are imperfect actualities their explanation lies in the perfection or completion towards which they are ordered and directed—the imperfect or potential, in other words, cannot be ontologically prior to or causative of the perfect or actual.[100] More emphatically, the potential could not exist and would not be what it is, were it not for the actuality towards which it is ontologically ordered.

Turning to the second part of the axiom, Aristotle distinguishes between active and passive powers, that is, between potency in the sense of agency or efficient causality, the capacity to do or change something, and potency in the sense of a positive capacity to suffer or undergo a change.[101] Now acts, whether of a passive or of an active potency, are specified by their objects. This thesis constitutes another of the fundamental principles of St. Thomas's account of moral agency and what it means is that acts

---

[98] *ST*, I, Q. 77, art. 3, "Dicendum quod potentia, secundum illud quod est potentia, ordinatur ad actum. Unde oportet rationem potentiae accipi ex actu ad quem ordinatur; et per consequens oportet quod ratio potentiae diversificetur, ut diversificatur ratio actus. Ratio autem actus diversificatur secundum diversam rationem obiecti." See also Aristotle, *De Anima*, II, 4, 415a14-24 and St. Thomas, *ST*, I-II, Q. 18, art. 5; *In I Sent.*, dist. 17, q. 1, art. 4; *In II Sent.*, dist. 44, q. 2, art. 1; *In II De Anima*, lect. 6; *Quaestiones de anima*, Q. 13.
[99] Aristotle, *Metaphysics*, IX, 8, 1049b4-12.
[100] Ibid., 1050a4-12.
[101] Aristotle, *Metaphysics*, IX, 1, 1046a19-29.

receive their nature or species from their formal cause.[102] The object is the cause that specifies the act and in the case of a passive power this is the efficient cause, whereas in the case of an active power this is the end (*finis*). A similar analysis is applied to the virtues, for virtue is a quality that resides in a power of the soul and constitutes in itself a special capacity for certain kinds of acts. The virtues too, in other words, are specified by their acts and their objects.[103]

Now, since the intellect is an active power, it follows that the habits that perfect it must be distinguished in virtue of their different ends. Accordingly, we find that both Aristotle and St. Thomas distinguish theoretical and practical knowledge by a diversity of ends. Theoretical knowledge aims at truth for the sake of itself whereas practical knowledge aims at truth for the sake of action or making; its act is consequently ordered to something beyond the mere consideration of reality (*consideratio veritatis*).[104] As St. Thomas argues, speculative and practical sciences are both concerned with knowing the objective order of things, but he distinguishes between different types of order which can be known. The speculative sciences, which include philosophy of nature, mathematics, and metaphysics, are concerned with the sort of order that human reason considers or discerns in the world but which it does not in any way make; logic, through the very consideration of the proper ordering of thought *introduces* this

---

[102] *ST*, I-II, Q. 18, art. 2, "Sicut autem res naturalis habet speciem ex sua forma, ita actio habet speciem ex obiecto; sicut et motus ex termino." See also, *ST*, I-II, Q. 18, art. 2, ad. 2; *ST*, I-II, Q. 18. art. 5.

[103] *ST*, I-II, Q. 49, art. 1; I-II, Q. 49, art. 3, "Si igitur natura rei in qua est habitus, consistat in ipso ordine ad actum, sequitur quod habitus principaliter importet ordinem ad actum. Manifestum est autem quod natura et ratio potentiae est ut sit principium actus. Unde omnis habitus qui est alicuius potentiae ut subiecti, principaliter importat ordinem ad actum." *ST*, I-II, Q. 54, art. 1, ad. 1; *ST*, Q. 54, art. 2.

[104] Aristotle, *Metaphysics*, II, 1, 993b19-23; *De Anima*, III, 10, 433a14-15. St. Thomas, *In Boeth. De. Trin.*, Q. 5, art. 1, "Dicendum quod theoreticus sive speculativus intellectus, in hoc proprie ab operativo sive practico distinguitur, quod speculativus habet pro fine veritatem quam considerat, practicus vero veritatem consideratam ordinat in operationem tamquam in finem;" *Ibid.*, Q. 5, art. 1, ad. 4, "Cum enim philosophia vel etiam artes per theoricum et practicum distinguuntur, oportet accipere distinctionem eorum ex fine, ut theoricum dicatur illud, quod ordinatur ad solam cognitionem veritatis, practicum vero, quod ordinatur ad operationem." *ST*, I, Q. 14, art. 16, "Intellectus enim practicus ordinatur ad finem operationis; finis autem intellectus speculative est consideratio veritatis." See also St. Thomas, *De Veritate*, Q. 2, art. 8; Q. 3, art. 3. John of St. Thomas, *Cursus Philosophicus Thomisticus*, pars IV, Q. 10, art. 6, "Speculativum autem et practicum distinguuntur per hoc, quod speculativum apprehendit res, ut sciat illas, practicum autem dirigit, ut exequatur seu faciat extra intellectum."

order into its own thinking and so is not a purely speculative science; moral philosophy considers the sort of order that introduces rectitude into the appetites; and finally, the mechanical and productive arts consider the kind of order that can be realized in the world of external, material objects.[105] The kind of order that constitutes the object of the theoretical sciences is therefore an order that does not depend for its existence or its constitution upon an act of the intellect, will, or bodily action of man. Upon this ground the Aristotelian tradition has always tended to identify, *pars pro toto*, speculative philosophy with philosophy itself, for the etymology of the word 'philosophy' is *amor sapientiae*, or *amor scientiae*, the love of wisdom or knowledge simply for the sake of itself.[106] It is this feature that grounds the distinction between theoretical science and practical or productive knowledge: the latter aim not at knowledge for the sake of itself but rather at an intelligible order for the sake of being actualized, that is, an order sought under the aspect of what can be made or done (*factibile, agibile*).[107]

It is important however not to misunderstand this distinction. As Aristotle says, while the practical intellect differs from the speculative in virtue of its end, this does not imply that there are two distinct rational powers of the human soul.[108] Only where there is an essential difference in the nature of the formal objects are there diverse powers of the soul.[109] As St. Thomas says, speculative intellect becomes practical by extension; and this means that whether or not a truth apprehended by the intellect is directed to action or operation is something incidental to that very apprehension. Consequently, while the speculative and practical intellects have

---

[105] *In I Eth.*, lect. 1, nn. 1-2.
[106] John of St. Thomas, *Cursus philosophicus thomisticus*, pars I, Proœmium, "Philosophia si in tota latitudine suae significationis sumatur, omnem complectitur scientiam; dicitur enim Philosophia quasi 'amor' seu 'amicitia scientiae,' qua ratione sapientia a D.Thoma in proœmio Ethic. Et sic Philosophia est scientia generica complectens sub se omnem scientiam naturaliter acquisibilem, praesertim speculativem, cuius amor proprie est amor scientiae, quia tantum scire amatur."
[107] *ST*, I-II, Q. 57, art. 3-4.
[108] Aristotle, *De Anima*, III, 10, 433a15.
[109] *ST*, I, Q. 77, art. 3, "Sed tamen considerandum est quod ea quae sunt per accidens, non diversificant speciem … Sic igitur non quaecumque diversitas obiectorum diversificat potentias animae; sed differentia eius ad quod per se potentia respicit." See also, *In VI Eth.*, lect. 1, nn. 1119-1123. John of St. Thomas, *Cursus philosophicus thomisticus*, pars IV, Q. 10, art. 6.

diverse ends they do not have specifically, that is, formally, distinct objects and so are not really different powers of the soul.[110]

St. Thomas bases the division of life into active and contemplative upon the diversity of the ends and aims of practical and theoretical knowledge.[111] This division is peculiar to the life of man (*vita hominis*) since only rational beings can order their lives according to practical or speculative reason.[112] As Thomas explains, the empirical basis for the distinction lies in the fact that some are more inclined to the contemplation of truth while others are more inclined towards external actions. Yet it would be a mistake to think that this division means that anyone who lives the active or contemplative life engages exclusively either in contemplative or practical acts. What it means is simply that either kind of life is characterized by a primary tendency or intention towards speculative or practical activity and that each life is organized with a view to this goal.[113]

In the *De veritate* St. Thomas explains the diversity of lives in terms of a difference both of matter and end. The matter of the speculative life, the object so to speak upon which it bears, is the intelligible natures of things (*rerum scibiles rationes*), whereas the matter of the active life is temporal affairs (*temporalia*). But, relying upon an axiom of Aristotelian metaphysics, it is the end that must ultimately explain this diversity of matter since matter exists for the sake of form. Now the end of the

---

110 *ST*, I, 79, art. 11, "Accidit autem alicui apprehenso per intellectum, quod ordinetur ad opus, vel non ordinetur. Secundum hoc autem differunt intellectus speculativus et practicus. Nam intellectus speculativus est, qui quod apprehendit, non ordinat ad opus, sed ad solam veritatis considerationem, practicus vero intellectus dicitur, qui hoc quod apprehendit, ordinat ad opus. Et hoc est quod philosophus dicit in III de anima, quod *speculativus differt a practico, fine*. Unde et a fine denominatur uterque, hic quidem speculativus, ille vero practicus, idest operativus."
111 *ST*, II-II, Q. 179, art 2, "divisio ista datur de vita humana, quae quidem attenditur secundum intellectum. Intellectus autem dividitur per activum et contemplativum, quia finis intellectivae cognitionis vel est ipsa cognitio veritatis, quod pertinet ad intellectum contemplativum; vel est aliqua exterior actio, quod pertinet ad intellectum practicum sive activum. Et ideo vita etiam sufficienter dividitur per activam et contemplativam."
112 *ST*, II-II, Q. 179, art 1, ad. 2, "vita universaliter sumpta non dividitur per activam et contemplativam, sed vita hominis, qui speciem sortitur ex hoc quod habet intellectum. Et ideo eadem est divisio intellectus et vitae humanae."
113 *ST*, II-II, Q. 179, art. 1,"Unde etiam et in hominibus vita uniuscuiusque hominis videtur esse id in quo maxime delectatur, et cui maxime intendit, et in hoc praecipue vult quilibet convivere amico, ut dicitur in IX Ethic. Quia ergo quidam homines praecipue intendunt contemplationi veritatis, quidam principaliter intendunt exterioribus actionibus, inde est quod vita hominis convenienter dividitur per activam et contemplativam."

contemplative life is distinguished from the active life in that the former is directed towards the consideration of truth (*inspectio veritatis*), whereas the latter is directed principally towards exterior action and in particular to the help of our neighbor.[114] So the question that naturally arises is whether teaching is an activity of the active or contemplative life. To the extent that it is concerned with speculative truth it seems to belong to the contemplative life, for one can only teach what has been grasped through an exercise of theoretical reason. Yet teaching is not simply concerned with speculative truth, for teaching consists precisely in the *communication* of truth *to another*. It is precisely the fact that teaching aims at this communication (*locutio, communicatio*) to another, the fact that it is directed to others, that it pertains to the active life.[115] And yet it cannot be defined *simply* as a communication to another, for teaching, particularly the teaching of theoretical truth, always involves a complex act, the communication *of something* to another. In the *De veritate* St. Thomas argues that since teaching reaches its end precisely in this communication to another it more properly belongs to the active life, but in the *Summa* no such claim can be found.[116] In any case, in both treatments Thomas affirms that the object of teaching is twofold, speculative and practical, and therefore that it belongs in some sense both to the active and to the contemplative lives.

To return then to the original question with which the essay began, if the object of teaching is both practical and speculative, if it bears both

---

114 *De vertitate*, Q. 11, art. 4, "Dicendum, quod contemplativa et activa vita ad invicem fine et materia distinguuntur. Materia namque activae vitae sunt temporalia, circa quae humanus actus versatur; materia autem contemplativae sunt rerum scibiles rationes, quibus contemplator insistit. Et haec materiae diversitas provenit ex diversitate finis: sicut et in omnibus aliis materia secundum finis exigentiam determinatur. Finis enim contemplativae vitae est inspectio veritatis ... Sed activae finis est operatio, qua proximorum utilitati intenditur. "

115 *De veritate*, Q. 11, art. 4, "In actu autem docendi invenimus duplicem materiam, in cuius signum etiam actus docendi duplici accusativo coniungitur. Est, siquidem, una eius materia res ipsa quae docetur, alia vero cui scientia traditur. Ratione igitur primae materiae, actus doctrinae ad vitam contemplativam pertinet, sed ratione secundae pertinet ad vitam activam." *ST*, II-II, Q. 181, art. 3, "actus doctrinae habet duplex obiectum ... Est igitur unum obiectum doctrinae id quod est materia sive obiectum interioris conceptionis ... Aliud vero obiectum doctrinae est ex parte sermonis audibilis. Et sic obiectum doctrinae est ipse audiens. Et quantum ad hoc obiectum, omnis doctrina pertinet ad vitam activam, ad quam pertinent exteriores actiones."

116 *De veritate*, Q. 11, art. 4, "Sed ex parte finis doctrina solummodo ad vitam activam pertinere invenitur, quia ultima materia eius, in qua finem intentum consequitur, est activae vitae materia. Unde magis ad activam vitam pertinet quam ad contemplativam, quamvis etiam aliquo modo ad contemplativam pertineat, ut ex dictis patet."

upon speculative truth sought for the sake of itself *and* upon the communication of this truth to another, if the act of teaching has two specifically different "matters" upon which it bears, then how can it be understood as a single, unified act?

In the first place, it must be emphasized that the distinction between *temporalia* or contingent matters and principles is not a formal but only a material distinction. Even though Aristotle appears to think otherwise in the *Nicomachean Ethics*,[117] St. Thomas is emphatic that there is not a formal difference between contingent and necessary things with regard to our faculty of knowledge but merely a difference with regard to the mode according to which our intellect acts (*modus agendi*).[118] As being is the formal object of the intellect, the contingent and the necessary can be apprehended by the intellect only to the extent that they share in being. To deny this would be to deny the fundamental unity of being, the only formality under which our intellect can apprehend anything at all. Even with regard to practical and productive knowledge, what is known is known in the light of being and in terms of that which is necessary. The human intellect therefore knows the contingent as it knows the singular, by an indirect or reflex activity upon its knowledge of being and the universal.[119]

Yet this does not entirely resolve the question. It explains why St. Thomas holds that teaching belongs primarily to the active order, for teaching bears primarily upon contingent matters, upon *temporalia*. It also explains why he does not see a great problem in the fact that it also bears upon eternal natures and first principles. The unity of the human intellect as a faculty of being ensures that whatever the mind grasps it will grasp under one and the same formality, the formality of being (*ratio*

---

117 *Nichomachean Ethics*, VI, 1, 1139a5-15. For St. Thomas's interpretation of this passage see *In VI Eth.*, lect. 1, nn. 1123.

118 *ST*, I-II, Q. 79, art. 9, ad 3, "Nec tamen est simpliciter dicendum quod sit alia potentia qua intellectus cognoscit necessaria, et alia qua cognoscit contingentia, quia utraque cognoscit secundum eandem rationem obiecti, scilicet secundum rationem entis et veri. Unde et necessaria, quae habent perfectum esse in veritate, perfecte cognoscit; utpote ad eorum quidditatem pertingens, per quam propria accidentia de his demonstrat. Contingentia vero imperfecte cognoscit; sicut et habent imperfectum esse et veritatem. Perfectum autem et imperfectum in actu non diversificant potentiam; sed diversificant actus quantum ad modum agendi, et per consequens principia actuum et ipsos habitus."

119 *ST*, I-II, Q. 87, arts. 1 and 3.

entis). But when teaching enters into the realm of the contingent it also enters into the moral realm, the realm of virtue. If teaching were merely an art then while it would belong to the realm of the contingent, it would bear much greater resemblance to theoretical virtue than to moral virtue. Art is an intellectual habit that perfects merely the intellect, not the appetite, and is therefore, as art, entirely free of the aim of moral virtue, i.e., the perfection of the moral agent with respect to the end of human life.[120] As St. Thomas explains, art aims at the good of the work to be made, not at the perfection of the moral agent, and therefore it does not require right appetite or desire.[121] But since teaching aims at the good of another, not at the production of an external work existing in matter, it presupposes on the part of the teacher some good will towards the student. Teaching, in other words, is a work of love and of good will. It cannot therefore be classified as an art. But if this is the case, then teaching belongs to the ethical realm and requires the exercise of moral virtue. Yet in this case teaching would seem to fall entirely outside the realm of intellectual virtue and the activity of contemplation in exactly the same way as the life of virtue does. To put the question simply, what *philosophic* motive would a philosopher have to communicate theoretical truth to another?

If we turn to St. Thomas's discussion of charity some light can be shed upon this question. Since charity is a kind of intellectual love (*amor intellectivus*), that is, a movement or act of the rational appetite, and since the proper object of love is the good, then the object of charity must be some special good.[122] This good according to St. Thomas is the divine good. Hence, the love of charity (*amor caritatis*), which is directed to God as its object, is a kind of friendship based upon a communication (*communicatio*) of the divine happiness to us.[123] Yet charity is also directed to our neighbor and not simply to God, which raises the question of whether or

---

120 Aristotle, *Nicomachean Ethics*, VI, 5, 1140b20-30.
121 *ST*, I-II, Q. 57, art. 3.
122 *ST*, I-II, Q. 26, art. 1; *ST*, I-II, Q. 27, art. 1, "Oportet igitur ut illud sit proprie causa amoris quod est amoris obiectum. Amoris autem proprium obiectum est bonum, quia, ut dictum est, amor importat quandam connaturalitatem vel complacentiam amantis ad amatum; unicuique autem est bonum id quod est sibi connaturale et proportionatum. Unde relinquitur quod bonum sit propria causa amoris."
123 *ST*, II-II, Q. 23, art. 1.

not the virtue of charity is specifically one or two. St. Thomas explains that since the species of an act is derived from its object considered under its formal aspect (*ratio objecti*), and since our neighbor is to be loved under the aspect (*ratio*) of God—for we love our neighbor *in* God—then it is specifically one and the same act whereby we love God and whereby we love our neighbor.[124]

Now one of the most important teachings of St. Thomas on the nature of charity is that it is the form of the virtues (*forma virtutum*), and what this means is that charity directs all the acts of the virtues to the ultimate end or good, which is God.[125] Charity is the "bond of perfection" that orders all of the virtues to a single end, namely, to the divine good, and because of this order the acts of the virtues receive a new form, the form of charity.[126]

In order to understand this it is helpful to compare it with Aristotle's conception of the unity of the virtues. In the *Nicomachean Ethics* he argues that it is not possible to be good without practical wisdom and that, conversely, it is not possible to be practically wise without moral virtue since we are rightly disposed towards the end by virtue.[127] In other words, as St. Thomas explains, prudence is right reason about what is to be done (*recta ratio agibilium*) and this requires rightly apprehending the end for the sake of which we act; but right apprehension in turn presupposes that our appetites be properly disposed towards this end. Hence, all the moral virtues will exist together with, and *only* together with, practical wisdom. The one who has prudence has *all* the virtues.[128] It does not follow from

124 *ST*, II-II, Q. 25, art. 1, "Ratio autem diligendi proximum Deus est, hoc enim debemus in proximo diligere, ut in Deo sit. Unde manifestum est quod idem specie actus est quo diligitur Deus, et quo diligitur proximus. Et propter hoc habitus caritatis non solum se extendit ad dilectionem Dei, sed etiam ad dilectionem proximi."
125 *ST*, II-II, Q. 24, arts. 7-8.
126 Col. 3:14.
127 *Nicomachean Ethics*, VI, 13, 1144b30-1145a12. *ST*, I-II, Q. 64, art. 1, "ad rectam autem electionem non solum sufficit inclinatio in debitum finem, quod est directe per habitum virtutis moralis; sed etiam quod aliquis directe eligat ea quae sunt ad finem, quod fit per prudentiam, quae est consiliativa et indicativa et praeceptiva eorum quae sunt ad finem. Similiter etiam prudentia non potest haberi nisi habeantur virtutes morales, cum prudentia sit recta ratio agibilium, quae, sicut ex principiis, procedit ex finibus agibilium, ad quos aliquis recte se habet per virtutes morales. Unde sicut scientia speculativa non potest haberi sine intellectu principiorum, ita nec prudentia sine virtutibus moralibus. Ex quo manifeste sequitur virtutes morales esse connexas."
128 *ST*, I-II, Q. 64, art. 1, "ad rectam autem electionem non solum sufficit inclinatio in debitum finem,

this however that all virtues are specifically one and same or that they are reducible to prudence. The virtues retain their distinct natures and species, which they receive from their relation to reason, even though they are essentially dependent upon prudence and upon each other.[129]

Charity plays a similar role with regard to the infused moral virtues that prudence plays with regard to the acquired moral virtues. The infused moral virtues, as opposed to the acquired moral virtues, are directed to a different end or good, one that surpasses the power of human nature and can therefore be acquired only through divine operation.[130] The acquired moral virtues, while they cannot exist without prudence, can exist without divine charity because they are directed to an end that does not exceed the natural human power.[131] Yet when separated from divine charity these virtues remain imperfect and possess the constitutive character of virtue only in a relative sense (*secundum quid*).[132] While they are really and genuinely virtues they are only imperfectly so. Such is not the case however with the infused virtues which, since they order us to our ultimate divine end, possess the fullness of virtue and are accordingly said to be virtues in an

---

quod est directe per habitum virtutis moralis; sed etiam quod aliquis directe eligat ea quae sunt ad finem, quod fit per prudentiam, quae est consiliativa et iudicativa et praeceptiva eorum quae sunt ad finem. Similiter etiam prudentia non potest haberi nisi habeantur virtutes morales, cum prudentia sit recta ratio agibilium, quae, sicut ex principiis, procedit ex finibus agibilium, ad quos aliquis recte se habet per virtutes morales. Unde sicut scientia speculativa non potest haberi sine intellectu principiorum, ita nec prudentia sine virtutibus moralibus. Ex quo manifeste sequitur virtutes morales esse connexas." John of St. Thomas, *Cursus theologicus*, disp. XVII, art. 2, 14, "Et quidem ex parte prudentiae petitur ista connexio, quia prudentia est una virtus directiva omnium actionum humanarum, praesupponensque rectam intentionem de fine. At non potest recta intentio de fine haberi, sine rectificatione, quae fit per omnes virtutes morales; ergo non potest dari una prudentia nisi habeant connexionem omnes virtutes cum ipsa. Et sic qui habet prudentiam habet omnes virtutes, et qui caret prudentia nullam habet virtutem perfectam; ergo perfectae virtutes connexae esse debent."

129 *ST*, I-II, Q. 60, art. 1.
130 *ST*, I-II, Q. 63, art. 2, "Virtus igitur hominis ordinata ad bonum quod modificatur secundum regulam rationis humanae, potest ex actibus humanis causari, inquantum huiusmodi actus procedunt a ratione, sub cuius potestate et regula tale bonum consistit. Virtus vero ordinans hominem ad bonum secundum quod modificatur per legem divinam, et non per rationem humanam, non potest causari per actus humanos, quorum principium est ratio, sed causatur solum in nobis per operationem divinam."
131 *ST*, I-II, Q. 65, art. 2, " ... virtutes morales prout sunt operativae boni in ordine ad finem qui non excedit facultatem naturalem hominis, possunt per opera humana acquiri. "
132 Ibid. "Patet igitur ex dictis quod solae virtutes infusae sunt perfectae, et simpliciter dicendae virtutes, quia bene ordinant hominem ad finem ultimum simpliciter. Aliae vero virtutes, scilicet acquisitae, sunt secundum quid virtutes, non autem simpliciter, ordinant enim hominem bene respectu finis ultimi in aliquo genere, non autem respectu finis ultimi simpliciter."

unqualified sense (*simplicter*). The infused virtues have the divine good as their end and consequently cannot exist without the proper disposition towards this end. It is divine charity, and this alone, that disposes us rightly towards this end.[133] The infused moral virtues therefore are unified or "interconnected" with and by *caritas* in a manner similar to the way acquired moral virtues are by prudence. If it is true to say that the acquired moral virtues exist together with, and *only* together with, prudence then it is equally true to say that the infused moral virtues exist together with, and *only* together with, charity.

Thomas's thesis that charity is the form of the virtues must therefore be understood first of all in relation to the role it plays with regard to the infused moral virtues. It functions in a manner analogous to prudence in relation to the acquired moral virtues. It is the "bond of unity" because, like prudence, without it there can be no infused virtue. In the second place, with regard to the supernatural virtues of faith and hope, Thomas teaches that it is their form as well. Charity is the form of faith because it perfects it by referring it to the divine good.[134] When it is said that faith is "informed" by charity what is meant is not that the act of faith is transformed into a different species of act but rather that it is perfected by an accidental form.[135] Charity is the form of faith because it informs it by bringing it to perfection and causing it to be living and effective, not by transmuting it into a completely different sort of act.[136] Faith without charity is dead, since the end for the sake of which faith is given is love and union with God.

With regard to the acquired moral virtues, which compared to the infused virtues are imperfect, charity directs them to a higher end and

---

[133] Ibid. *ST*, II-II, Q. 23, art. 7. John of St. Thomas, *Cursus theologicus*, disp. XVII, art. 2, 46, "Sed prudentia supponit rectam intentionem circa finem, et adhaesionem ad ipsum; tum circa fines particularis in ipsis materiis agibilibus; tum a fortiori circa ipsum finem ultimum, a quo particularis fines dependent, et cui per se subordinatur; ergo si supponunt prudentiam, eique connectuntur virtutes morales, a fortiori supponunt charitatem sine qua non est recta intentio in fine ultimo supernaturali."

[134] *ST*, II-II, Q. 4, art. 3.

[135] *ST*, II-II, Q. 4, art. 4, ad 2, "Sed id quod facit fidem esse formatam vel vivam non est de essentia fidei."

[136] *ST*, II-II, Q. 4, art. 3, ad1, "caritas dicitur esse forma fidei inquantum informat actum ipsius;" See also, Ibid., ad 2.

therefore causes a unity and perfection among them that in and of themselves they lack because, taken by themselves, they are ordered merely to particular goods. When all of the virtues are motivated by an act of charity, however, they are referred to the ultimate and universal good whereby they are united through the reception of a new form. As in the case of faith, this new form does not destroy the particular virtues by replacing their object and species with a different form but simply sets them in order and brings them to perfection by referring them to a higher end.[137]

In an analogous sense the theoretical or intellectual virtues can be perfected by charity to the extent that they proceed from and are motivated by an act of the will directed to the divine good.[138] Any act, according to St. Thomas, can be meritorious to the extent that it is ordered by charity. In the case of theoretical contemplation, the consideration of truth for the sake of itself, such an act would have to be directed to a higher end and thus in some sense cease to be a purely philosophical act directed to a truth naturally proportioned to the human intellect and be directed to the contemplation of divine truth. Acquired intellectual virtue differs from infused intellectual virtue just as the acquired moral virtues differ from the infused. The former has a naturally attainable object and is acquired by unaided human effort whereas the latter is directed to a higher object and comes from above.[139] Human wisdom is able to attain to a knowledge of the first causes and principles of things within a certain order (*secudum quid*) whereas infused wisdom, *sapientia*, considers the highest cause of things absolutely (*simpliciter*).[140] The latter kind of wisdom, because it attains to God absolutely, extends to more things than does philosophical or theoretical wisdom, including, among other things, contingent and practical matters. Infused wisdom, while principally a theoretical virtue, is not *merely* theoretical but practical as well.[141] As St. Thomas explains,

---

137 *ST*, II-II, Q. 23, art. 8, ad 1.
138 *ST*, II, Q. 182, art. 2, ad 3.
139 *ST*, II-II, Q. 45, art. 2, ad 2.
140 *ST*, II-II, Q. 45, art. 1.
141 *ST*, II-II, Q. 45, art. 3, ad 1, "Unde ex hoc ipso quod sapientia quae est donum est excellentior quam sapientia quae est virtus intellectualis, utpote magis de propinquo Deum attingens, per quandam scilicet unionem animae ad ipsum, habet quod non solum dirigat in contemplatione, sed etiam in actione."

though infused wisdom is of its very nature an intellectual virtue, its cause lies in the will, that is, in an act of charity.[142] Consequently, it includes within its sphere of concern and competence the practical as well as the purely theoretical.

In a similar way, the act of *communicating* truth and not merely of contemplating it can be motivated by an act of charity, that is, if the ultimate intention behind the act be the love of our neighbor in God. The act of teaching, of communicating a truth already contemplated, is in perfect continuity with infused wisdom because the latter embraces within itself both the purely speculative and the practical. In the case of merely acquired wisdom however this would not be true. Philosophical wisdom, since it does not perfect the appetitive part of the soul but *only* the intellectual part does not embrace those contingent and practical matters that belong to the moral realm, the realm of prudence. But when the contemplation of truth is done out of charity, that is, when merely acquired wisdom is transformed into infused wisdom, then the communication of this truth to others is *also* motivated by an act of the will that is continuous with and of the same nature as the act that generates infused wisdom. In other words, when contemplation and teaching are done out of true charity, when they are genuine acts of love, then and only then do they become integrated and connected by being referred to one and the same end, the love of God. The discontinuity between contemplation and teaching that results from the distinction between theory and practice at the natural level is overcome to a certain degree when these acts are elevated to a higher level, that is, when they are ordered to the divine good.

This is not to say that the tension arising from the twofold object is completely overcome, even at the level of infused wisdom. As Thomas explains, there will always be a sense in which the contemplative and active lives are in competition since action, while it may dispose one to contemplation by introducing right order among the passions, is in itself a hindrance to contemplation since it is impossible to engage in external

---

142 *ST*, II-II, Q. 45, art. 2, "Sic igitur sapientia quae est donum causam quidem habet in voluntate, scilicet caritatem, sed essentiam habet in intellectu, cuius actus est recte iudicare …"

acts and to contemplate at one and the same time.¹⁴³ Yet, in the presence of charity the decision to teach makes sense because the communication of the fruits of contemplation is done for the very same reason as the act of contemplation. Charity embraces both God and our neighbor under the same formal aspect and so when contemplation is undertaken out of the love of God then teaching this truth to others is a natural extension of this love. Without the virtue of charity however the inner connection between the pursuit of theoretical truth and the sharing of this truth with others remains unclear. Thus, devoting one's life to teaching, *contemplare et contemplata aliis tradere*, to contemplating the truth and communicating it to others, makes the most sense from the vantage point of charity. This love does not totally eliminate the tension between contemplation and action but, like the very gift of wisdom, one of its fruits is to make that which is bitter, sweet.¹⁴⁴

<u>Response</u>

Gratia non tollit naturam, sed perficit. Grace does not destroy nature but perfects it. Perhaps my contribution has cast doubt upon this hallowed principle? If *caritas* is the form of the virtues then what room is there for any virtue besides love? As I reflected upon Adriaan's comments it seemed as though his questions anticipated my very own—so much in fact that I've incorporated into the revised version of the essay what I think is a more sensitive account of the unique role of charity in the life of natural moral virtue. But it seems to me that the fundamental, underlying issue is precisely the role of nature and grace in St. Thomas's thought. I do not wish to rehearse the disputes from sixty years ago regarding the natural desire for the supernatural but it seems appropriate to engage in a kind of *retractatio* of the problem of teaching with the intention of affirming what seems to be denied in the essay.

The statement in which St. Thomas articulates the famous principle that "grace builds upon nature" is worth quoting in full: "Since therefore <u>grace does not destroy</u> nature but perfects it, natural reason should minis-

---
143 *ST*, II-II, Q. 180, arts. 2-3.
144 *ST*, II-II, Q. 45, art. 3, ad. 3.

ter (subserviat) to faith as the natural bent of the will ministers to charity" (ST, I, Q. 1, art. 8, ad 2). The analogy is an interesting one: reason assists faith just as the natural bent of the will ministers to charity (naturalis inclinatio voluntatis obsequitur caritati). What is the nature of this "natural inclination of the will?" And in what sense is it proper to refer to it as an obsequium to charity?

To begin with the first question, the will according to St. Thomas pertains to the appetitive power of the soul, a power whose proper object is the good. Appetite or desire however is a universal phenomenon, a reality coextensive with being. Thomas is fond of quoting the opening lines of Aristotle's *Nicomachean Ethics*, "the good is that which *all* things desire," for this expresses the universality of appetite. *Quamlibet formam sequitur aliqua inclinatio*, upon any form whatever there follows some inclination. Desire or appetite is an inclination to act in a certain, determinate manner and it is something that all things have in virtue of their nature or form, in virtue, that is, of their very being. *Agere sequitur esse*, action follows being, and the inclination towards this activity follows upon a thing's nature. This thesis expresses an idea that goes back to the ancient Greek philosophers and reminds us of Plato's *Symposium*. The will however is a peculiar form of appetite, for its root lies in the intellect which, as Aristotle says in the *De Anima*, is in a way all things. Unlike the natural tendency (*appetitus naturalis*) of stone to move in a determined manner appropriate to its nature, the will is an appetite consequent upon the nature of the intellect, which is a form whose peculiar nature is to be the "place of forms." The nature of the intellect in other words is transcendence, which requires that it be undetermined or in potency to all things, for if, like the things of nature, it were determined to one particular mode of being it would be incapable of becoming all things. The will is the rational appetite (*appetitus rationalis*) or the inclination that follows upon the nature of the intellect and, like the sensitive appetite (*appetitus sensitivus*), it differs from natural appetite in being an inclination that follows upon a cognitive faculty. But it transcends the sensitive appetite as well precisely as the intellect transcends the power of sensation. The sensitive appetite aims only at a good grasped by the senses whereas the will is ordered to a purely intelligible good.

It is upon the distinction between sense and intellect that St. Thomas founds the distinction between the love of concupiscence (*amor concupiscentiae*) and the love of friendship (*amor amicitiae*). To love, as Aristotle says in the *Rhetorica* (II, 4, 1380b35), is to wish good to someone. There is accordingly a twofold tendency in love corresponding to two distinct objects or goods, the good *that* is wished to someone, the *bonum quod*, and the one *to whom* that good is wished, *illud cui*. The love of concupiscence aims at the former good while the love of friendship aims at the latter. Moreover, these goods are related as primary and secondary, for that which is loved with the love of friendship, the one *to whom* we wish good, is loved simply and for the sake of itself (*simpliciter et per se amatur*), whereas what is loved with the love of concupiscence is loved for the sake of something else (*alteri amatur*). The love of concupiscence therefore only attains to the *bonum alteri*, which is merely a relative good, whereas the love of friendship, a love that has its root in the intellective faculty, attains to the *bonum simpliciter*. To these two kinds of goods there correspond two kinds of love, one of which is love absolutely speaking (*amor simpliciter*) while the other is love only in a relative sense (*amor secundum quid*).

Love in the absolute sense, a love that we may call a kind of spiritual love insofar as it is based upon the intellectual nature of the soul, is the root of perfect friendship as Aristotle describes it in the *Nicomachean Ethics* (VIII, 3, 1156b6-19). The friend is loved in an absolute way, *simpliciter*, and not in a relative way with a love of concupiscence, that is, not with a love that sees in the other merely a relative good, a good *for me* or *for another*. It loves the other precisely as an absolute good, the one *to whom* we wish good in an absolute way. Friendship in the highest sense, as Aristotle points out, requires that this love be mutual and that each of the partners be aware of their love for one another. But the foundation and source that makes perfect friendship possible is our intellectual nature which, precisely to the degree that it transcends the limitations of the sense power, is capable of reaching the other precisely as an absolute good, a good of the spiritual order.

The love of the will, *amor amicitiae*, a kind of "good will" by which we love the other as an absolute good and *to whom* we wish good things, a love which is also the foundation of perfect friendship, is what St. Thomas refers to when he speaks of the "natural bent of the will" that ministers to charity. It seems to me that in the natural order it is precisely this love, the love of friendship, that lies at the basis of all good teaching. Do we not teach students precisely because we really believe that knowledge is something good for them? And to desire this good for them, is this not to love our students with a love of friendship, a love that wants what is truly good for them as persons?

Charity simply builds upon this love. But that is not all it does. Just as the acquired moral virtues remain in a state of imperfection without the influence of grace, so too this natural love of friendship remains merely a "bent" or inclination of the will because it lacks the stability and firmness of divine charity. This is not to say that true friendship at the natural level is impossible or that the activity of teaching, which is rooted in the very same love out of which perfect friendship arises, is not based upon a true love of the student, *amor simpliciter*. It is however to say that, just as the natural moral virtues apart from grace are virtues *secundum quid*, in a relative way, so also teaching remains imperfect without charity. Such would seem to be the conclusion if, as St. Thomas teaches, grace perfects nature even as it presupposes and builds upon it.

JACOBI'S REVENGE: DELEUZE'S CRITIQUE OF HEGEL

§

Brent Adkins

<u>Preface</u>

I would like place the paper that follows within two contexts. The first context is the occasion that brings us together, celebrating the profound and enduring influence that Adriaan Peperzak has had on our teaching and scholarship. I think I can safely say that while we greatly admire Dr. Peperzak's keen and thorough scholarship, the primary reason we are gathered here is the way he affected us as a teacher. Even though his classes were very demanding, they were always a pleasure. Every session would bring new food for thought. It is precisely in this way that I think we all hope to emulate Dr. Peperzak. That we might be able to create a sense of anticipation around whatever we were teaching. That we might draw our students into a discussion of more excellent things, and they might take the same pleasure in them as well. It is here that we find the nexus of teaching, love, communication, and desire that everyone has spoken about so eloquently.

Within this first context, my paper on Deleuze and Hegel represents somewhat of a departure from the other papers. First, it takes up Hegel's role in shaping contemporary philosophy. Second, it takes up Deleuze's account of philosophy as the production of concepts as a way of doing philosophy in a mode other than Hegelian. Finally, given Deleuze's definition of philosophy, the paper takes up the relation between philosophy and religion in order to reconceive both.

The second context within which I would like to place this paper is the context of a larger project that traces the development of both philosophy and religion after Kant. While I can only pursue a small portion of this project here, it's my contention that post-Kantian philosophy and theology is beholden to Kant in a methodological way such that talk of God is reduced to a kind of apophaticism. In response to this, I think Deleuze's understanding of both philosophy and religion makes a kataphaticism possible again. As a way to begin thinking about this project, I would like to begin with the pantheism controversy instigated by Jacobi and note some strange and unremarked parallels between Deleuze and Jacobi.

Introduction

In the continuing attempt to locate Deleuze within the history of philosophy the names most likely to come up are Spinoza, Nietzsche, and Bergson. Kant, Klossowski, and Stoicism also appear in the gallery, and sometimes Hegel appears, but only as the villain; as Deleuze says of Hegel, "somebody has to play the traitor."[1] I would like to add a new name to this list of Deleuze's friends and enemies, F.H. Jacobi. My claim is not that Deleuze read Jacobi, but that at the crucial moment where Deleuze seeks to distinguish religion and philosophy, the distinction that Deleuze proposes is structurally identical to Jacobi's distinction. Furthermore, even though, Deleuze maintains a structurally Jacobian position, he does not fall victim to Hegel's criticisms of Jacobi on this score. In fact, Deleuze is able to turn his homology with Jacobi into a criticism of Hegel.

Hegel

In 1785 F.H. Jacobi upended the German intellectual community with the revelation of G.E. Lessing's Spinozism. Mendelssohn took up Lessing's defense, while Jacobi widened his offensive to include all of philosophy. Jacobi argued that all philosophy, insofar as it is thought consistently, tends toward Spinozism, atheism, and nihilism (a term coined by Jacobi).[2] Jacobi's scathing condemnation of philosophy had wide-ranging consequences for years to come. Fichte lost his position at Jena when he was charged with atheism. Schelling and Hegel, who remained at Jena after Fichte's departure, were scrupulous in their writings about God to avoid the same censure, even as they were trying to further their philosophical projects.[3] Hegel goes out of his way in *Glauben und Wissen* to praise Jacobi even as he criticizes him as a manifestation of the subjective tendency in current philosophy. The subjective tendency in philosophy, Hegel argues, results in an untenable split between faith and knowledge. The solution to this difficulty for Hegel is to reconcile the opposition in terms of content and form. Faith, explicitly trinitarian faith, provides the content that is given philosophical form in speculative philosophy. This is the call for a "speculative Good Friday" with which Hegel ends *Glauben und Wissen*.[4] And, this is the promise that Hegel fulfills in the *Phenomenology of Spirit*.[5]

That Hegel sees the trinity as the essential content of philosophy does not mean that Hegel is trying to Christianize philosophy or turn philosophy into theology. Rather, Hegel is trying to account for the basic historical fact that the rise and spread of Christianity has profoundly changed the nature of thought in Europe and has become determinative for European identity. In short, Europe would not be what it is in any sense (material, cultural, moral, etc.) without Christianity. The task of philosophy for Hegel is to account for this change in order to show the contradictions that arise in a culture because of this change, as well as what is new in thought because of this change. Hegel articulates this change in terms of freedom in *Die Vernunft in der Geschichte*. Under oriental despotism only the despot is free. All others are in bondage to the ruler. In Greece and Rome some, the citizens, are free. With the coming of Christianity, Hegel says that all are in principle free, but that this freedom is not actualized until the Reformation. In order for philosophy to fulfill its purpose it must account for this expansion of freedom and it cannot do so without taking Christianity into account.[6]

In Hegel's *Lectures on the History of Philosophy*, he repeatedly notes that what separates philosophy proper from its origins in Eleatic philosophy is Christianity. Thus, in discussing the difference between Heraclitus and Parmenides, Hegel notes that Heraclitus is superior because he makes negativity immanent within the very concept of philosophy itself. Parmenides, since he fails to do this, is left with a "dead infinite." The crucial moment comes when Hegel compares the immanent negativity of Heraclitus with the trinity. "All that is concrete, as that God created the world, divided Himself, begot a Son, is contained in this determination."[7] Here we see that Hegel identifies the essence of the trinity with negation, and it is precisely this that must be thought in order for philosophy to be philosophy. At the same time, there must also be a process of historical actualization by which the thought of the negative becomes real in a particular community. So, while Heraclitus is to be revered for first thinking immanent negativity, philosophy itself must wait until this thought takes shape and makes its appearance in Europe.

Similarly, when Hegel notes the fundamental parallel between Spinoza and Parminedes, the issue of both negativity and Christianity arise again. "The difference between our standpoint and that of the Eleatic philosophy is only this, that through the agency of Christianity concrete individuality is in the modern world present throughout in spirit."[8] What makes modernity different from past ages is the change wrought by Christianity that makes concrete individuality possible. The reason that Eleatic philosophy (whether Parmindean or Spinozist) fails to do this is that it eschews the particular in order to think the One. In doing this Eleatic philosophy necessarily fails to think the negative and make it immanent to the concept.

In the *Phenomenology*, Hegel makes explicit exactly what he means when he says that faith is the content of philosophy. At the conclusion of the section on revealed religion, the community of Protestant Christianity comes on the scene. Historically, this community is centuries beyond the sensuous appearance of God's incarnation. Furthermore, God and incarnated is seen as both dead and resurrected. The resurrection is crucial for two reasons for this community. First, it indicates the overcoming of death, though, not as an empirical fact, but as an organizing principle for the community. Second, it makes room for the coming of the Holy Spirit, the third person of the trinity through which each person can be fully reconciled to God. This reconciliation is commemorated in the Eucharist through which the members of the community participate in this reconciliation as a daily death and resurrection.[9] The limitation of this community lies in the representational way it takes up the negativity of the incarnation and resurrection. All the pieces are in place. The community pictures a self-sundering absolute that takes on concrete form, dies, and in the negativity of death reconciles the absolute and the particular. The incorporation of negativity within revealed religion's concept of itself requires this incorporation to take the shape of a universal, transcendent God that creates the world and becomes incarnated as the concrete unity of the divine and the human. This incarnation is pictured as happening in the past and creating the reconciliation in principle, though the reconciliation will not be actualized until some point in the future. The task of philosophy is to take up this universal process of immanent negativity pictured in trinitarian religion and give it philosophical form.

Philosophy thus thinks what is already actualized in a community. The owl of Minerva takes flight at dusk. Philosophy arises within a specific community in order to reconcile the contradictions that arise in the thought of that community. What arises with the advent of Christianity is the thought of the concrete individual, which can be thought from either the standpoint of the subject or the standpoint of object (which could be nature or the community). Thus, for Hegel the fundamental contradiction (as the *Differenzschrift* makes clear) is between the subjective and objective viewpoints.[10] The problem with contemporary philosophy's attempt at a solution is that for the most part it has attempted to resolve this problem from the side of the subject (hence Fichte's radicalization of the Kantian project in which the *Ich* produces the non-*Ich*). *Glauben und Wissen* shows that despite all of their differences Kant, Jacobi, and Fichte remain trapped within the subjective viewpoint, which is why they are unable to come to terms with the relation between faith and knowledge. A one-sided approach, however, can never produce a reconciliation, it only reaffirms the contradiction between the viewpoints. What is needed is a standpoint that is neither subjective nor objective but out of which this opposition is produced. This is the absolute, the philosophy that is able to take up faith as its content and not something opposed to philosophy.

Deleuze

In the retrospective *What is Philosophy?* Deleuze and Guattari reflect about the nature of philosophy as they practice it and the ways in which it differs from other creative endeavors, such as science and art. Philosophy is the creation of concepts, and the ground on which philosophy creates its concepts is the prephilosophical plane of immanence. The great danger that continually haunts philosophy is taking the plane of immanence and making it immanent to something else, substance, being, or God, for example. Making immanence immanent to something other than itself transforms immanence into transcendence. At precisely this moment, philosophy ceases to be philosophy and becomes religion. "Whenever there is transcendence, vertical Being, imperial State in the sky or on earth, there is religion; and there is Philosophy whenever there is immanence...."[11] If Deleuze and Guattari's account is accurate, though, it would seem that philosophy has rarely been philosophy. The history of philosophy has rather been dominated by the continual attempt to subdue immanence, make it immanent to something. The primary exception here is Spinoza.

Spinoza was the philosopher who knew full well that immanence was only immanent to itself and therefore that it was a plane traversed by movements of the infinite, filled with intensive ordinates. He is therefore the prince of philosophers. Perhaps he is the only philosopher never to have compromised with transcendence and to have hunted it down everywhere....He discovered that freedom exists only within immanence. He fulfilled philosophy because he satisfied its prephilosophical presupposition.[12]

Spinoza thus becomes the hero (and savior) in Deleuze and Guattari's history of philosophy, the only one who understands the true nature of philosophy, which he pursues relentlessly.

In their description of the nature of philosophy and their evaluation of Spinoza's role in it, Deleuze and Guattari come remarkably close to Jacobi. For both, religion and philosophy are mutually exclusive. For both, Spinoza represents the culmination of philosophical endeavor; that is, to the degree that philosophy consistently follows its own presuppositions it tends toward Spinozism. All philosophers are Spinozists of some kind. The only issue is whether they are consistent in their Spinozism. The crucial difference, of course, is that Jacobi recoils in horror at this possibility, while Deleuze and Guattari embrace it as the path to freedom. What I would like to explore here is the way in which Deleuze and Guattari take up (in some respects) Jacobi's position, but at the same time do it such a way that they do not fall under Hegel's charge of subjectivism. The way in which Deleuze and Guattari avoid this criticism is first and foremost by reconceiving philosophy as a productive activity. The second way that they do this is by turning to the fundamental role of the affects in shaping thought. Thus, subjectivity is not the ground of philosophy it is the result of an affective process. It is precisely by these two means that Deleuze and Guattari criticize Hegel.

Philosophy as Productive

As we saw above, for Hegel, philosophy cannot be philosophy without thinking the negative. Deleuze's thought in general along with his work with Guattari can be seen as an attempt to remove the thought of the negative from philosophy. In *Difference and Repetition* Deleuze argues that negation is the last bastion of representation, the means by which Hegel stretches difference to the point of contradiction.[13] The dialectic, however, only ensures that difference remains external and subjugated to a greater unity, "the identity of identity and difference" as Hegel says in the *Logic*. It is precisely here that we see why Deleuze accuses Hegel of a "false Spinozism."[14] Hegel has taken the plane of immanence and made it immanent to something else, namely spirit in the *Phenomenology* and the *Encyclopedia* or the Idea in the *Logic*.[15]

In contrast to the Hegelian dialectic, Deleuze proposes a different model of thought and experience. Rather than introducing negation as the means by which movement is introduced into thought, Deleuze proposes that thought is self-moving, that it already differs from itself without this difference being a negation or rising to the level of contradiction, which would externalize the difference. Deleuze's first attempts to think internal difference come from an early essay entitled, "Bergson's Conception of Difference." Deleuze writes, "In Bergson, thanks to the notion of the virtual, the thing differs from itself first, immediately. According to Hegel the thing differs from itself because it differs first from everything it is not, and thus difference goes as far as contradiction."[16] There are numerous ways that Deleuze takes up the notion of internal self-differentiation throughout his work. In many texts he retains the notion of the virtual as the abstract, machinic account of actual processes. He also pursues this same notion in terms of possible connections among partial-objects and the way in which these connections are channeled by their limit. At bottom, though, lies a conception of philosophy, even life itself, as productive. Life, experience, philosophy simply is that process of making new connections. In philosophy these connection are conceptual and are articulated on a plane of immanence. There is desire but it is not predicated on a lack.

Affectivity and Subjectivity

Hegel would agree with Deleuze and Guattari that the subject is the result of a process. This idea encapsulates Hegel's criticism of Spinoza and Eleatic philosophy in general. Substance must become subject, as Hegel says in the *Phenomenology*.[17] The crucial difference, though, lies in the way that Hegel thinks the result. While result certainly indicates the culmination of a process, this process is at the same time what Hegel calls in the *Logic*, "a retreat into the ground." Hegel writes,

[P]rogress in philosophy is rather a retrogression and a grounding or establishing by means of which we first obtain the result that what we began with is not something merely arbitrarily assumed but is in fact the truth, and also the primary truth.... [T]he advance is a retreat into the ground, to what is primary and true.[18]

Hegel's point here is the Aristotelian point that epistemological grounds are inversely related to ontological grounds, that what is primary in the order of knowing is secondary in the order of being and vice versa. Thus, all of Hegel's works begin with what is immediate and through the process of determinate negation the immediate is shown to be grounded on the mediated. The truth of immediacy lies in mediation, but this can only be achieved as the result of a process. In the same way, the truth of substance lies in subject (as the concrete, self-conscious whole of spirit), but this moment can only be reached through the dialectic. Thus, the subject is an achieved moment for Hegel but it is also the ground and truth of all that preceded it.

The process that Deleuze and Guattari have in mind for the production of the subject is much different. Deleuze and Guattari take up Klossowski's *Nietzsche and the Vicious Circle* as emblematic of their account of the subject as the result of affective states. What is common to Deleuze's articulation of Spinoza and Nietzsche and Klossowski's articulation of Nietzsche is a fundamental affectivity that underlies and results in subjectivity. At the same time, however, subjectivity is not seen as more fundamental than affectivity. Rather, for Deleuze and Guattari, "the subject is a residuum."[19] Each individual, rather than being a self-posting whole is in fact constructed as the intersection of various affective forces. Thus Klossowski writes concerning Nietzsche, "The body is a product of chance; it is nothing but the locus where a group of individuated impulses confront each other so as to produce this interval that constitutes a human life, impulses whose sole ambition is to de-individuate themselves."[20] Thus, in sharp contrast to Hegel's account in which the more one pursues consciousness the more one uncovers its ground in the self-positing subject of reason, Deleuze and Guattari, following Klossowski argue that the subject is not the ground but the aleatory nexus of affects that are only chosen in retrospect as constitutive. This is why Deleuze and Guattari discuss the subject as the reflective moment by which one selects some affects, some intensities as representative and declares, "so, that's who I am."[21] This declaration is the final moment in the complexification of desiring-production in which the connective and disjunctive syntheses of desire interact with their limit in the body without organs. This third synthesis of desire Deleuze and Guattari call "celibate" because it neither produces nor grounds anything. It is merely the aorist moment that freezes the continuous circuit of desire.

Conclusion

Thus, even though Deleuze and Jacobi distinguish philosophy and religion in the same way. Deleuze does not fall prey to the same criticisms that Hegel makes against Jacobi. Deleuze's philosophy cannot be characterized as subjectivist. In fact, it's precisely because Deleuze sees the subject as the non-grounding, non-teleological residuum of an affective process that he is able to criticize Hegel's conception of the subject. Furthermore, insofar as Deleuze sees philosophy as a productive process of creating concepts and not as the labor of the negative that he avoids the dialectical recuperation of difference.

Response to Dr. Peperzak

Dr. Peperzak rightly points out in his gracious and perceptive comments that it is not entirely clear how Deleuze intends to separate himself from Hegel. This has been one of the most frustrating things about working with Deleuze. While he rarely discusses Hegel at any length or is plainly dismissive of him, there are no extended analyses of Hegel or attempts to think through him in the way that he did in the early works on Nietzsche, Kant, Spinoza, or Proust. In fact, the overriding sense one gets of Deleuze's relation to Hegel is simply one of refusal. It's almost as if rather than being anti-Hegelian, Deleuze is attempting to be non-Hegelian, if you'll allow the Kantian distinction here between negative and infinite judgment. As a result, any encounter between Deleuze and Hegel needs to be staged. My hope is that I'm being fair to both Hegel and Deleuze in this staging, so that each may have his say, even if, ultimately my sympathies lie with Deleuze.

Dr. Peperzak's first set of questions aims directly at these sympathies by asking how exactly Deleuze and Hegel are different. Both privilege the immanent production of concepts. Hegel would even go so far as to say that this production of concepts must be presuppositionless in order to be properly philosophical. Deleuze, however, is adamant that Hegel's production of concepts is not immanent but transcendent. It is transcendent precisely because the production of concepts is subordinated to the concept, or as you say "one all-embracing syllogism of syllogisms." This is what Deleuze refers to as "the illusion of transcendence" in which the immanent is made immanent to something else, in Hegel's case "spirit."[22]

There is, of course, more to the story in both Hegel and Deleuze. In particular it would be important to go beyond the creation of concepts and discuss what Deleuze calls "the plane of immanence" and "conceptual personae" both in relation to concepts, and more importantly all of these in relation to other domains of thought such as science and art, which are creative but they do not create concepts. Unfortunately, there is no space to explicate these issues here, and we will have to save them for another conversation.

What I would like to take up, though, is the point where Dr. Peperzak seems to find the most agreement, namely the affective dimension of Deleuze's thought. I, too, find this the most exciting part of Deleuze's thought. I also think Deleuze's notion of affectivity "could rehabilitate the conditional and receptive character of human activity." On this score I think that Deleuze follows Spinoza and Nietzsche very closely. Spinoza thinks through the notion very clearly that if individuals are not defined according to substance, then they can only be defined by their ways of affecting and being affected. On this reading, Part III of the *Ethics* becomes a taxonomy of possible ways of affecting and being affected. Accordingly, Spinoza notes that all of these affects are the result of living in a world incomparably larger and more powerful than any one individual. In this recognition we see not only the impetus behind the social and the political, but also the reason why, as Ovid says, "*Video meliora proboque deteriora sequor.*" Seeing the better path but following the worse, Spinoza calls "bondage."

Nietzsche takes up this same basic standpoint with regard to the affects as we can see in this aphorism from *The Gay Science*, "*Thoughts.*—Thoughts are the shadows of our feelings—always darker, emptier, and simpler."[23] To this Nietzsche adds the genealogical insight that cultural and institutional forces also shape and channel the ways in which we affect and are affected. Within this context philosophy becomes one of the ways in which we affect and are affected. It is different from art, religion, or science. That is, each of these domains describes a different way of affecting and being affected, but these domains are not hermetically sealed off from one another. Each borrows materials from the other, but then in the borrowing the material becomes transformed. Thus, when philosophy borrows the functions of science to construct its concepts, it is not doing science but philosophy.

In your final comments on my paper, Dr. Peperzak, you hope that despite what some might claim, metaphysics is not dead. This is my hope is well and it is one of the things that draws me to Deleuze. In the face of Heidegger's proclamation of the end of metaphysics, Deleuze has unabashedly pursued metaphysics. He has pursued a metaphysics that he traces through Lucretius and Duns Scotus to Spinoza, Nietzsche and Bergson that takes the univocity of being to be its founding principle and difference to be the necessary correlate of this univocity. You often say that philosophers build cathedrals, and that you like to walk around in them to see if they're beautiful. I think Deleuze also built a cathedral (or perhaps several), but he used many materials that previously were not thought suitable for building. As a result, his cathedral doesn't look like other cathedrals. Much of it is underground. It doesn't have the expected aborescent plan, but rather the endless branching of a rhizome. I don't know if it's beautiful, yet, but I'd like to explore a little further.

I'd like to thank Catriona for her tireless and thoughtful efforts at putting this conversation together. I'd like to thank the other participants for their willingness to contribute to this fruitful and ongoing conversation. Most of all, I'd like to thank Dr. Peperzak for his boundless charity in teaching and scholarship and without whom this present conversation would be impossible.

Endnotes

1 Deleuze, "Gilles Deleuze Talks Philosophy," *Desert Islands and Other Texts 1953-1974*, Mike Taormina, translator, (New York: Semiotext(e), 2004), 144.
2 See, Frederick Beiser's *The Fate of Reason: German Philosophy from Kant to Fichte*, (Cambridge: Harvard University Press, 1987) for a fuller account of the *Pantheismusstreit*, 44-91.
3 See, Terry Pinkard's *Hegel: A Biography*, (Cambridge: Cambridge University Press, 2000), for an account of Hegel's arrival at Jena, 118-202.
4 Hegel, *Faith and Knowledge*, Walter Cerf and H.S. Harris, translator, (Albany: SUNY Press, 1977), 190-91.
5 Hegel, Phenomenology of Spirit, A.V. Miller, translator, (New York: Oxford University Press), §784ff.
6 Hegel, *Reason in History*, Robert S. Hartman, translator, (Upper Saddle River, NJ: Prentice-Hall, 1997), 23-24.
7 Hegel, *Lectures on the History of Philosophy*, 3 vols., E. S. Haldane, translator, (Lincoln: University of Nebraska Press, 1995), 1:284.
8 Ibid., 3:258.
9 *Phenomenology*, §784.
10 Hegel, *The Difference between the Fichtean and Schellingian Systems of Philosophy*, Jere P. Surber, translator, (Atascadero, CA: Ridgeview Publishing Co.).
11 Deleuze and Guattari, *What is Philosophy?*, Hugh Tomlinson and Graham Burchell, translators, (New York: Columbia University Press, 1994), 43.
12 Ibid., 48.
13 Deleuze, *Difference and Repetition*. Paul Patton, translator, (New York: Columbia University Press, 1994), 262-63.
14 Deleuze, *Spinoza: Practical Philosophy*. Robert Hurley, translator, (San Francisco: City Lights Books, 1988), 128-29.
15 In the *Phenomenology*, for example, Hegel notes that the task of consciousness is to "arrive at a point at which it gets rid of its semblance of being burdened with something alien...so that its exposition will coincide...with the authentic science of spirit" (§89).
16 Deleuze, "Bergson's Conception of Difference," in *Desert Islands*, 42.
17 *Phenomenology*, §25.
18 Hegel, *Hegel's Science of Logic*. A. V. Miller, translator, (Atlantic Highlands, NJ: Humanities Paperback Library, 1989), 70-71.
19 Deleuze and Guattari, *Anti-Oedipus: Capitalism and Schizophrenia*, Robert Hurley, et al., translators, (Minneapolis: University of Minnesota Press, 1983), 17.
20 Pierre Klossowski, *Nietzsche and the Vicious Circle*, Daniel W. Smith, translator, (Chicago: University of Chicago Press, 1997) 27.
21 *Anti-Oedipus*, 20.
22 *What is Philosophy?*, 49-50.
23 Friedrich Nietzsche, *The Gay Science*, Walter Kaufmann, translator (New York: Vintage, 1974), §179.

RESPONSES TO SYMPOSIASTS
§

Adriaan Peperzak

Dear Friends,

"*So, here we are again, souls aflame, gathered to philosophize.*"

Greg will allow me to add one word to his sentence, which, I feel, summarized accurately the wonderful event of our Baltimore symposium. Now, after half a year, we remember that event with gratitude and amazement – an amazement that gives us much to think about and to rethink. Of course, three days were not enough to fully assimilate the many thoughts and suggestions that we offered and contemplated together. So, allow me to follow up by sending you some delayed associations that still occupy my mind.

It was a joy to speak with the ten of you, who, in the last two decades, had changed from doctoral students into colleagues, while knowing that several others, who could not come, participated in spirit. To enjoy our speaking face to face and together in philosophical friendship was delightful, but equally amazing and delightful was the fact that, although some of us had never met, we experienced a kind of belonging together that came by itself.

In his "phenomenology of invitation," Greg showed how an inviting word or gesture calls for a response: participation in a common meal, a shared discovery, a dialogue with friends, for example. An invitation presupposes at least: *someone* who invites and a *purpose* that is recognized as

169

sufficiently *desirable* to be adopted as motivation for an effective response. If the invitation is accepted, the desires of the accepting invitees join the desire that motivated the inviter. Their gathering thus is effectuated by the force of their joined desires. And, if all of them are in love with philosophy, "suddenly a light, as it were, is kindled by a flame that […] sustains itself," as Greg quotes from Plato's *Seventh Letter*.

A teacher invites students to ask questions and think; Catriona invited us for a discussion about reading, writing, teaching and discussing. Once the call was heard, we could not continue to live as if nothing had happened. One cannot avoid responding: you accept or refuse or you do not react at all; but inaction or silence *are* responses, although they may be perceived, or even meant, as insulting. Acceptance implies elements of obedience to the invitation, which thus develops a force of its own. By involving the invitees in a collective pursuit, for which no singular person can claim a separate responsibility, it produces a communion of interests and activities. As union of several persons, a community has a destiny or a fate of its own. The conversation that brought us together produced a kind of nuclear community. Could it serve as a model for the understanding of more extended communities in philosophy?

As the beginning of a new event, an invitation is not wholly initial, because it is prepared by many conditions and contingencies. The gathering call resulted from and responded to an utterly unpredictable combination of preceding calls, responses, and events. The temporality of our event, for example, was conditioned by the surprising convergence of personal relations that grew over time between a teacher and formerly unknown students, who changed into colleagues.

When a student joins a teacher, the latter transmits in the form of an appropriate transformation what he learned from his teachers: the professors he knew and the people behind the texts he studied. His students do the same and consequently become quite similar, though also very different, teachers. While transmitting the same old, but again transformed, heritage to their students, they prompt them to do the same, and so on. In other words, we are agents of a tradition, who enjoy the timely identity-in-transformation (or the loyal transformation of the same) that remains inspiring if it is saved from death by able hands and voices. Teaching and learning feed on a tradition that owes its life to them.

=/=

Whereas *Greg's* approach focuses on the communal force of a successful invitation, the inter-individual or face-to-face aspect of our gathering was analyzed by several others. We enjoyed and began to exploit the refreshing variety of their perspectives and the affinity between them.

Corinne models her description of the Socratic ideal as a personal vocation that calls for responsibility and growing wisdom. You emphasize the student's spiritual needs and the union of theory and practice as a primary condition of all education, without forgetting the limits of the human condition. While emphasizing the difference between concentration on serious matters and empty curiosity, you insist on the particular contingencies of a teacher's singular place, time, language, belonging, mood, pathos, and culture. Thus you show the relevance of a philosopher's singularity for her exchange with her students, who are equally unique and uniquely different. In addition to your sketch of an ideal teacher's virtues, you sketch some of the philosophical vices that threaten the virtuous "procreation in beauty," as Plato calls the transmission of philosophy to new generations. Your phenomenology of excellence in teaching shows how, instead of simply repeating that "philosophy is a way of life," we must show how a philosophical life realizes itself in concrete manners and exercises.

I believe that all of us gratefully agree with Corinne's encompassing portrait of excellence in teaching philosophy. Since vocation, responsibility, and wisdom are not entirely exempt from religious connotations, however, further discussion could perhaps involve us in a comparison of the various traditions that have developed within the horizon of such excellence. We could, for instance, ask in what sense we, after medieval and modern philosophy, still can and have to be authentically Socratic or Platonic in word and manners.

=/=

Aron reminds all of us how we, as beginning students, had to find a voice. You analyze how one's own philosophical voice develops in the trace of preceding voices, among which an influential teacher's spoken and written work might play a role. Closely related to the meditations of Corinne and Kristi, your paper shows not only how a student experiences the teacher's influence on his exercises as a beginning philosopher, but also how a good teacher cooperates by awakening and assisting the student in wondering, shaking off irrelevant opinions, avoiding dogmatisms and trivial orthodoxies, in order to become open for that which really is relevant. Relevant for what? If philosophy is indeed integral to a philosopher's life, it cannot fulfill its purpose, unless it speaks in the name and in favor of that life's search for meaning. Aron gives his reading of Platonic dialogues between a sympathetic teacher and an eager student, where several voices compete in responding to the fundamental question of the life-fostering good that truly matters. What is this good? It cannot be found in dogmatic propositions, definitions, universal laws or systems (although universality can be understood as an element of it), but it must belong to the core of each one's singular and unique, irreplaceable and unrepeatable destiny, which Plato called a "divine lot" (*theia moira*) and which we again are allowed to call – even in philosophy – a call or – if you do not want to exclude religion from human life – a vocation.

Much could be discussed about the birth and the aqcquired gift of each philosopher's unique, and yet communicating, voice, and its being part of a philosophical tradition that belongs to all. But let's also reflect on Aron's acquaintance with a writer's Dutch voice that prompted his American voice to produce philosophical texts, which indeed, Aron *wrote* and concretely recognized as *his own*. Aron's explanation of his experience with translation is a beautiful example of being supported by anterior voices in becoming a philosopher. The transmission of a heritage and the explanation of original thoughts would not be possible if we did not accept to listen, and, in general, to make ourselves dependent on living or reanimated philosophers. While speaking to us from a sympathetic distance, they prompt us to accept responsibility for our own living, thinking, teaching, and writing, but, at the same time for caring and encouraging others to be responsible for their philosophical adventures and successors.

=/=

As for my own experience with translation, Aron's analysis does not only remind me of my gratitude to Ricoeur, Levinas, and Hegel, who lend their thought, language, and style to me, when I tried to let them speak in Dutch or English, but also and perhaps even more passionately, my deep gratitude to *Catriona*, who, when I arrived at Loyola Chicago, was the first to change my clumsy English into a readable text; to *Aron*, who – fortunately for me – knew Dutch and translated many chapters and articles; to *Laurel*, who somewhat later edited many papers; to *Ryan*, who translated my French into English; and to *Marjolein*, who not only translated a series of Dutch essays but also cooperated in editing the final version of a book in Italian.

=/=

Marjolein's paper refers also to Plato, but then turns to his best and most original alumnus for an illuminating unfolding of the interpersonal relation that unites teacher and student. What strikes me most in Aristotle's analysis is not only the thesis that that relationship presupposes a form of friendship (*philia*), but also that the intertwining of teaching and learning in one activity that is accomplished from two centers of actions, constitutes one single movement. "Teaching and learning are *identical* in that they both inhere in the same substratum."

Allow me to formulate somewhat freely what I learned here from Aristotle through Marjolein. If a teacher cannot teach without pupils, the double activity of teaching-and-learning performed by a teacher and her student is not only conditioned, but also *constituted* by the unity of what each of them is doing in response to one another. Without a listener, a speaker is mute; without a student, a teacher does not have anything to say. If teachers nevertheless vent their philosophical wisdom, they are marketing their knowledge in the hope that someone will approach them for their guidance. (The same is true for writers, of course: writing books that no one reads is vain, even if they are treasure troves of wisdom). The teachers are as dependent on students as the students are on the teachers.

Moreover, teacher and student cannot communicate with one another unless they share a specific kind of affinity; both have to belong and to be "at home" (*oikeioi*) in the dimension of philosophical sensibility and exploration. In other words, both teacher and students must be moved by a common – or, at least, convergent – desire, which, ultimately and initially, is a desire for *eudaimonia*, enlightened by the knowledge that *eudaimonia* without (*philo-*)*sophia* is impossible.

Apparently it would be too simplistic to contrast the difference between the teacher and the one who is taught as the difference between the active and the passive, the giving and the receiving, or the full and the empty poles in the teaching/learning process. Learning, and all its moments, such as paying attention, reception, concentration, integration, reproduction, application, and so on, compose a complex sort of activity, whereas a good teacher must learn to listen, make pauses, interrupt his own speaking when a student speaks, and – yes! – learn from the students who belong to a generation that feels and thinks differently from their teacher. Teacher and student are at the same time, in many respects, like and, in other aspects, unlike; they are identical (for example, in eloquence) *and* different (in specialization).

However, if teachers can learn from their students, even in philosophy, would it then not also be possible to amend Aristotle's image of the one ladder on which teacher and learner walk in contrary directions, by allowing for an intermittent movement up-and-down on both sides (doesn't my doctoral student know more about Bergson or Plotinus than I?). If so, then their interaction is not only caused by the same *eros*, which (as generated by *poros* and *penia*) is smart and poor at the same time, but also by the complementarity of their own explorations. Is the dialogue that emerges from that interaction then structured dialectically or rather dialogically? But do we know what we ask here? For besides the very different Zenonian, Aristotelian, Kantian, Hegelian, and Marxian dialectics, a truly polyvocal dialogic has perhaps not yet been discovered within philosophy – not even by Plato or Aristotle.

In any case we should continue to reflect about the unique substratum, which you, Marjolein, call the "underlying phenomenon" of the didactic cooperation. Your remark that it "throws a spell" over the persons involved reminds us of the force that Greg spotted in the invitation. What sort of spell drives potential – and then actual – friends together in an at once erotic and agonic struggle for becoming wiser by going back and forth on the ladder that joins heaven and earth?

And: Does *eros* – as agonic *pathos* – have any affinity with Ryan's appeal to charity in his explanation of Thomas's philosophy of teaching as a synthesis of theory and *praxis* in didactic communication?

=/=

Whereas Marjolein shows how Plato and Aristotle discover friendship (*philia*) in the union of teaching and learning that unites teacher and students, you, *Ryan* show how Thomas, in Aristotle's trace but within the horizon of an Augustinian universe, analyzes the tense unity that connects teaching with *contemplation*. Teaching is in this context defined as *contemplata tradere*: the transmission or tradition of a body of knowledge that has been acquired by spiritual, philosophical, and theological recollection and meditation. Thomas sharply distinguishes theoretical knowledge, as knowledge of the truth for the sake of itself, from practical knowledge, which is related to action or making. Theoretical knowledge concentrates on insight and remains *internal* to the meditating, speculating, or contemplating mind, whereas practical knowledge is meant to be *externalized* by action or production of external objects. Because contemplation is a form of theory, it is, as such, not interested in going out into the world and thus it is reluctant to teach, if practical considerations do not convince the contemplative person (e.g., the happy philosopher) to communicate his or her wisdom to others, who have not yet discovered what the former knows.

Teaching is an externalizing activity. True philosophers do not want to be distracted from their delightful concentration on the highest realities; but compassion, responsibility, obedience or other obligations might demand that at least some of them develop teaching skills and sacrifice time and energy to communication. If so, it is not the truth that urges their teaching, but some other noble or not so noble motivation (for example, money or fame).

This analysis shows how a teacher who has a taste for theory or contemplation must overcome an inner tension. Indeed, the two activities that must be accomplished are driven by contrasting interests: contemplation wants more time and attention for speculative interiority, whereas teaching takes time and attention away for didactic formulations and external exercises with the students, who must learn what the teacher already knows. How is it possible to not be divided by these contrary interests and activities? Only by dedicating oneself to the overarching "form (or rather "meta-form"?) of all virtues": *charity*.

Caritas (charity) is not one virtue among others, not even one of the greatest virtues, but instead the supervirtue of all virtues: the virtue that gives all virtues their final perfection. Only love of God and the neighbor (two aspects of one single love that cannot be separated) is capable of unifying the internal (contemplative) and the external (communicative) aspects of the teaching activity.

The understanding of *caritas* as (super- or meta-)form of all virtues has always impressed and convinced me as the summit and cornerstone of any ethics that is true to the Biblical inspiration, and it saddens me that this basic insight does not often receive the place it deserves in modern or contemporary ethics. However, to make a long story short, I have some questions with regard to the role Thomas seems to attribute to it in his analysis of the relation between research and teaching.

A first question is this: if charity unifies the double activity that constitutes teaching, doesn't he use this form of forms as a *passe-partout*? Don't *all* virtues form one unified virtue insofar as all of them are "formed" by one and the same universal charity? What exactly is then the specific working of this general supervirtue in unifying the contemplative interiority and the practical externality of communication? Does Thomas also show that neither education nor civilization is possible without the tradition of knowledge and that, even if we bracket the religious perspective on love as divine caritas, teaching of that knowledge constitutes a union of the teacher's (and the student's?) spirit and its practical incarnation in an external world? Behind the first question lurks, of course, the question of whether Thomas's distinctions between theory and practice or between interiority and exteriority are not much too clear cut and abstract. But there are a host of other questions waiting in line regarding the relations between thinking and speaking. For example: Does contemplation want us to be silent? Is teaching not at the same time learning? Do we never discover truth while we, like Socrates, are speaking and listening? Does dialogue, did our conversation, not include a contemplative enrichment? And does working for the poor really hamper growth in wisdom?.

Perhaps I miss here something very important. If so, I embrace the opportunity to get a hint from you, Ryan. I know that a real answer would demand many hours, but perhaps it is possible to correct some misunderstandings.

If we had much more time or space, we could arrange a confrontation between the papers of Marjolein and Ryan. Although they do not focus on the same questions, they seem to have some Aristotelian assumptions in common, while differing in their affinity and their views on the intertwining of theory and friendship (is *philia* in Thomas's work entirely replaced by *caritas*?)

=/=

In "Orienting Oneself in Kant," *Kristi* reflects on (1) her Kant research, and – like Marjolein, Corinne, Catriona, and Aron – on (2) her own experience with the links that connect teachers in philosophy with their teachers. Of the latter, Kant is of course a genius who never stops being an "utterly inexhaustible wellspring," and, as such, a companion whose influence lasts an entire life. Although Kant's philosophy is not the unconditional itself, one never finishes meditating on its articulation of the relations between the epistemic, practical, and affective limitations of the human condition and the unconditioned on which we depend. Teaching, as a result of learning *and* responsibility for respectable traditions, is a good illustration of human conditionality; but you, Kristi, set an even wider stage for further reflection by stating that, "For Kant, we find ourselves responding to *nature,* to *reason,* and to *community."* You succinctly summarize how Kant stratifies these three dimensions and develops his *Critiques* and subsequent treatises on *metaphysics.*

Much of my teaching on Kant bears traces of André Wylleman, a professor in Louvain, an excellent teacher who published little, and Paul Ricoeur, who was not only a prolific writer, but also an excellent teacher. Nevertheless, as several of you, and especially Catriona, have expressed, it is difficult to sort out what exactly stems from our teachers and from other influences. In any case, my teachers mediated between (e.g.) Kant, me, and all of you who accepted responsibility for further development. And Kant was generated by others, to begin with, by Plato and Aristotle, even if he read them rarely. Isn't it great and delightful to be part of such a history?

As Kristi shows, Kant, more than Hegel, deserves admiration and gratitude for not divinizing humanity by balancing his enthusiasm for autonomy, as rational freedom, in all its configurations, with a deep awareness of our passivity – not only regarding our corporeal and sensible constitution, but also with regard to reason and freedom themselves. Not choice but human "nature," as given and pre-arbitrary reasonability, is the origin that rules, directs, obligates, and constitutes human dignity. This – and not a contract – is the truly radical and primordial origin of rights, and justice is his highest qualification of the Origin itself (*Fiat iustitia, pereat mundus!*).

However, Kant's philosophy of dependence and humility reaches deeper – or lower – than the recognition of human conditionality. He is one of the very few modern thinkers who does not obscure the factual phenomena of evil and its source, which he thematizes as mysterious, but universal. What impedes or destroys being good is giving in to a fundamental declination in us that resists human theoretical deduction and practical loyalty to universal dignity. Could we say that it is Kant's honesty which motivates his final conclusions about an irreducible element of human irrationality? And that his faith in a definitive triumph of justice as ultimate meaning was his defense against the greatest scandal of human history?

In Praise of Speaking

=/=

In "Jacobi's Revenge," *Brent* shows how several links with familiar classics can facilitate entrance into the frame of Deleuze's thought: Parmenides, Heraclitus, Aristotle, the Stoics, Spinoza, Jacobi, Hegel, Nietzsche, Bergson, and even Klossowski, are present in the background. Plato might also hide there, but that is questionable.

As a student, I heard and admired Deleuze's lucid explanations of Kant's third *Critique,* and somewhat later he became known as a critic of Hegel during the years in which the Parisian Hegel wave began to ebb away. I must recognize, however, that I have not closely followed his later development, because the pursuit of my own philosophical interests demanded other readings. Since I am not well-equipped for a discussion about Deleuze's attempt at a fundamental renewal of philosophy I will restrict my response to a few questions. In part, these questions overlap with questions I also direct to Hegel, who dominated many – too many? – years of my academic research. But Brent is better prepared to pursue the contrast between Hegel and Deleuze which we began to explore in Baltimore.

What I admire is the risky, but necessary scope of a project that encompasses the entire horizon of philosophy and its history, from Parmenides and Heraclitus via the modern classics to the second half of the last century. Deleuze's exclusion of medieval philosophy is in line with the French secular tradition. Though symptomatic of a huge, loss of collective memory, it is coherent with Deleuze's characterization of philosophy as faithful to the immanence of conceptual production and its strict separation from Christianity.

I am not sure whether I understand Deleuze's motivation for making this separation. Hegel's system is also an immanent production of coherent concepts, and even as one all-embracing syllogism of syllogisms, within which all concepts emerge from one another in order to constitute a tightly-woven web. And this prompts in me the question of why philosophy should exclude all forms of transcendence or why conceptual production without any reference to pre-, post- or metaconceptual truth(s) should be the ultimate horizon of philosophy. What is here at stake? Is it the *definition* of philosophy, a proud *decision* about its horizon and competence, a *faith* in conceptual immanence, or perhaps a sort of *indifference* with regard to any appeal to ultimate meaning? I think that I know Hegel's answers to these questions; but I do not know whether Deleuze's standpoint can be understood as a transformation, a mutation, or a wholesale rejection of Hegel's logic.

Brent has taught us that *negation* plays a crucially different role in Deleuze's and Hegel's logic. Many objections have been raised against the use of *negativity* in Hegel's explanation of movement and limitation, and against his identification of being and becoming (or identity and difference). But it remains to be seen whether Deleuze has produced less ambiguous concepts in order to support his conviction concerning a basic and terminal immanence.

What I find attractive in Brent's portrait of Deleuze's explorations is "the fundamental role of the affects in shaping thought," and I would like to learn more about the relation of this role to the production of concepts. Deleuz's thesis reminds me of Plato, Augustine, Pascal, and several post-Hegelian philosophers. I presume that it implies an attack on Hegel, who, around 1800, chose to subject all forms of feeling to the control of reason, which from then on became the supreme manager of the Spirit. A philosophy of affectivity could rehabilitate the conditional and receptive character of human activity, perhaps even without necessarily disrupting the all-encompassing horizon of the universe and its philosophical reproduction. Does Deleuze give hints in this direction? Whereas Kant's reference to the transcendence of the unconditioned allows for humility, I suppose that Deleuze has little sympathy for any philosophy in which this attitude fulfills a basic or central role.

I am aware that these questions, and the many others implied in them, testify more to my ignorance than to anyone's deficiencies. I also understand that at this moment we do not have enough space and time for a serious discussion. Therefore, Brent, please accept my remarks as expressions of my interest in further wrestling with contemporary attempts at correcting, destroying, or revitalizing some of the most radical and metaphysical, tradition, which, I think and hope, has not died, whatever some famous (and less famous) philosophers proclaim.

=/=

Conditionality and humility are clearly at the center of *Norman's* contribution, "The Truth of Soil." It can be read as a new interpretation of the natural conditions that rule and limit our possibilities. We are situated in nature, a specific landscape, a characteristic soil and vegetation, subject to the seasons and their volatility. We count on the availability of water and sun, a harvest and regularity in growth. We are associated with or even befriended by certain animals, and we enjoy a host of amenities – until suddenly we are overwhelmed by horrific outbursts of natural but hostile violence.

Norman eloquently shows how much our being "placed" in nature conditions and determines the entirety of our corporeal, affective, spiritual, and religious vitality. You remind us of the massive network of interdependence in which we are caught, without much choice on our part. You focus on the garden as a *microcosmos* that mirrors, on a small scale, what the *macrocosmos* grants us and demands of us. We easily forget that our lives are interwoven with natural processes from the outside or from within our symbiosis with nature. Technology especially overpowers and obscures large domains and natural energies, but let's not underestimate the philosophical habits that make us insensitive: abstraction, forgetfulness, and all the processes that we take for granted as obvious, trivial, "natural" – until we are shocked and terrified by overpowering disasters.

Contingency, unpredictability, non-necessary and non-universal events decide about human destinies, although they are the most forgotten and repressed subjects of philosophy. We rather stick to universal laws, universally valid definitions, calculable and predictable regularities, and the exclusion of all unpleasant surprises. But Norman shows that nature has its own ways and manners and that we, consequently, must adapt and adjust ourselves, while developing flexible associations with nature through a kind of osmotic befriending. Such a relationship is not compatible with the conviction that humanity is the center, master, or lord of nature. But how then should we qualify our most appropriate attitude toward the power of nature, which allows us a place in it?

You show which virtues protect us against the *hybris* of proud illusions. By dispelling a typically modern misunderstanding of *humility* and helps us to understand that a well-measured form of acceptance, in wonder and gratitude, is a better response to the human condition than the will of becoming a powerful god of the material universe.

=/=

Until here, I have tried to suppress most of the affective reactions and responses that interfered with the thoughts that your papers triggered in my "brain." However, after rereading *Catriona's* delightfully personal combination of letter and text, I can no longer follow that procedure. Let me then begin by repeating once more how profoundly touched, grateful, and encouraged I feel by each one of your exceptional, personal as well as philosophically outstanding, papers together with the oral explanations you gave during our symposium. I do not find anything trivial, uninteresting, un-thought, or insincere in these expressions of friendship with philosophy and with me. The way in which each of your lives has matured and found its footing fills me with awe and confidence; and again with thanksgiving for the greatest gift that emerged from my teaching in Chicago. Of course, my gratitude to my own teachers, from Plato to Ricoeur and Levinas, is great, but to have cooperated in the growth and self-discovery of others "in beauty" (as Diotima calls it), is at least as deep, because you keep likewise alive what long ago began. Philosophy does not live in fleeting words or muted texts, but only in thinking lives. Enabled by thoughtful remembering, you now take care of philosophy's splendor in revival.

=/=

How can I respond to you, *Catriona*, with equal depth and simplicity? Should we not already be *wise* to try it? And *loving*!

Let me talk about our love of Truth and its hiding, which converts that love into a desire as long and stubborn as life itself – a life that nobody chose, but everybody discovered after it had already settled and mobilized each of us. Life – meaning – desire – love: how do they long for truths and, underneath, for Truth!

For me, Desire began in high school, while deciphering the Greek of Diotima's revelations to Socrates. It resonated because my faith had already installed a post-Platonic orientation. In hindsight, big words pop up to name the *mania*, (as Plato calls it) that caught me. Did I fall madly in love with a quest for *Sophia*? I had still to undergo many disillusions in order to learn – with ups and downs and not without pains – what such a seeking meant. One truth, however, was clear: becoming wise does not necessarily pass through erudition, scholarship, or research, but once you are caught by philosophy, you cannot treat it as an entertaining puzzle in the margins of your search for meaning – the meaning of your and others' destiny. Therefore, besides Plato, Saint Francis became a hero, and somewhat later, Saint Augustine, who somehow seemed to combine some of their best inspirations. The practice of faith and philosophy, and soon the theory of their conjunction in theology occupied my daily life and remained my hobby and profession.

Loyola Chicago was for me a new beginning, where you taught me how to write papers in English, like several others of our friends somewhat later did. If my English has become less clumsy, I owe it to you in the first place. However, I have learned much more in America, especially about the friendship (*philia* as well as *caritas*) that grows when converging minds discover converging tracks that lead to the origin of their affinity, even if their contacts are few. What strikes me more than ever is that such affinities are associated with communal traditions, thanks to those who revive them while communicating them. *Contemplata tradere, philosophy as communication,* is perhaps a fitting name for a type of wisdom, in which theory and practice, thanks to friendship on more than one level of life, are intertwined without monopolizing time or mental and corporeal energy for either theory or practice.

One of the great delights for teachers and writers lies in the experience of being referred to through critical, corrective, and transformative approval. Innovative handling of lessons once received show the fecundity of such lessons, fecunded again by new incentives. Your essay, Catriona, shows, in a delightful manner, how affinity with Plato, Aristotle, Heidegger, and so many others receives a quite different manifestation in different lives, while strongly maintaining a shared hope and solidarity in the seeking of "the Sought" (as one of my favorite texts from Gregory of Nyssa calls the absolutely Desirable). Thank you for reminding us of the truth that the hidden Beloved does not grant its proximity to its seekers *unless* they extend their friendship with truth and justice to all victims of narcissism, *pleonexia*, and other monopolies.

=/=

So, "here we are, each of us, in the world, struggling with what has been given to us materially, intellectually, and spiritually."

Catriona, may I borrow this sentence as an *envoi* that rhymes with Greg's invitation? Here are some of my most immediate responses to the wonderful papers which I joyfully read and reread. As you see, I have emphasized our agreements and asked some questions, which might trigger answers from you. Obviously, complete responses and clarification must wait for other occasions; but hints or aphorisms are very welcome.

What I sent you today still needs some revision and perhaps a few additions. Since my responses are already overdue, as measured by my promise, I do not want to prolong your waiting time, however.

Enjoy life, love, and thought as intensely as it is given to you.

PART TWO
In Praise of Speaking: Living with Philosophy

INTRODUCTION TO CHICAGO SYMPOSIUM

§

Adriaan Peperzak

<u>Notes on the Loyola Chicago symposium, April 1-3 2016</u>

Before we started our symposium with a dinner and a first session, many friends from among the leaders, colleagues, administrators, staff, and students participated in a reception to which they were invited. I used the opportunity to cordially thank the provost, Dr. John Pelissero, the dean of the College of Arts and Sciences, Tom Regan S.J., and the chair of the Philosophy Department, Mark Waymack, who had permitted me to continue the use of my office and other facilities even after the date of my official retirement, and all my colleagues and students with whom I had a joyful experience over many years at the university.

The text of our invitation was the following:

> *On Friday, April 1, about 20 alumni of Loyola will join Adriaan Peperzak for a discussion of three days about "Living with Philosophy" from the perspective of those who, since earning their Doctorates in Philosophy, have become teachers or otherwise engaged in teaching philosophy. Our discussions will last until the noon of Sunday, April 3. To emphasize the festive character of our colloquium, our conference will begin with a reception on Friday from 4:00-5:30 pm in Piper Hall, to which you are cordially invited.*

We were gratified to host a pleasantly crowded reception, followed by a fine dinner and our first discussion of the symposium.

SPEAKING (LISTENING, HEARING, CONVERSING) AS THE MEANING OF LIVING WITH PHILOSOPHY

§

Catriona Hanley

What fitting sequel could there be to a mini-conference celebrating the spoken word through carefully prepared papers written in advance and read by the authors, each one defending the primacy of the discursive arts, and lauding the professor who taught them how to speak/listen? That was the challenge facing Giancarlo Tarantino, Justin Nordin and Jean Clifford, PhD candidates in Philosophy at Loyola University Chicago, and students of Adriaan Peperzak, who, at 86 was about to retire from teaching. Randy Newman, Adriaan's tireless assistant, was also of course drawn into the challenge. How could they honour and celebrate Peperzak in a fitting, interesting and even ground-breaking way, one that would be a real tribute to the profound and inescapable influence that a beloved professor had on the lives of so many students?

That Chicago crew had quite a task ahead of them, particularly as the symposium I had organized six years earlier at Loyola University Maryland, in honour of Peperzak's eightieth birthday was (with no false modesty) a resounding success. That put extra pressure on the organizers (which included Adriaan Peperzak himself, of course): could they find a way to make this new symposium congruent with the last?

The answer to both questions is simply, **_yes._** The wonderful event that took place in Chicago on April 2016 was both extraordinarily appropriate to the thinking and the life of Adriaan Peperzak, and very much in harmony with the previous symposium. It seems now in retrospect that it was the only possible direction open to us in order to continue the conversation. Briefly, where the symposium in Baltimore was in traditional conference form, with each participant in turn reading a paper aloud, and then opening the table for discussion, in Chicago there were no papers presented. True, we had mostly all written a page or two in advance, mulling over the theme *Living with Philosophy*; and true we had all read each other's musings before we arrived in Chicago. But at the seven sessions that made up our weekend of philosophy, no one read a word, or (except obliquely) referred to her own writings. General topics had been proposed in advance for each session, with a few contextual hints, and discussion took off from there, completely on the wing. And the discussion flew! This model was so successful that many of us are planning to propose it to our various specialty philosophy meetings.

Still, we do need to ask: what was gained? What was the point? I hope that the short papers that follow here will go some way to answering these questions. It is justice we want; a world in which justice rules is the only one where peace can be found. And to get to justice, Diotima tells us: we need love, a love that is sometimes desperate, passionate, dedicated, devoted to the beauty of telling the truth.

Thanks so much to the organizers of the Chicago event for opening our minds to what initially seemed to be a new way of doing philosophy. And thanks most of all to you, Adriaan, for showing us that this way was anything other than new. You reminded us forcefully with this experiment that ancient wisdom is not just a collection of aimless speculation on a page, ready to be deciphered and consumed. Rather, we must listen hard to the voice speaking to us across centuries; these pale whispers can only reach us across thousands of years if we open ourselves to hearing.

THE SPIRIT OF GRATITUDE
§

Giancarlo Tarantino

In the spring of 2015, Justin Nordin, Jean Clifford, and I began thinking about possibilities for commemorating Dr. Peperzak's retirement (his 2nd retirement, no less!). For us, it was important to propose something that fit with Dr. Peperzak's unique and creative approach to a rigorous engagement with the philosophic tradition, past and present.

Having worked as Dr. Peperzak's assistant for the last five or so years, I've had the terrific chance to hear lots of stories - stories about other thinkers, old memories, his own life as a doctoral student in Paris, and about those previous students who worked on their dissertations with him in The Netherlands and again here in Chicago. The delight with which Dr. Peperzak speaks about the lives, character, personalities, and philosophical work of those students is always evident. Naturally, then, when the idea was proposed to invite several of his former doctoral students back to Loyola Chicago, it seemed the perfect way to celebrate Dr. Peperzak, and for his students to express the gratitude I know they have felt for him in his role as teacher and mentor.

Dr. Peperzak had other ideas and other concerns than being "honored" however. Gratitude toward one's teachers is appropriate, but I suppose that for a philosopher, gratitude should not come at the cost of neglecting the rigorous and unending quest for meaning. As Aristotle notes at the beginning of his *Nichomachean Ethics*, both our friends and the philosophic quest are "dear to us; yet tis our duty to prefer the truth". Embracing the spirit of that remark, Dr. Peperzak was equally interested in speaking to and learning from his students, and in hearing about their own attempts at "living with philosophy."

What follows is a series of letters, responses, and replies to responses about the meaning of "living with philosophy" . This initial correspondence set the stage for the live conversations that took place in Chicago at the beginning of April 2016. In many ways, the 2016 symposium was a chance to extend, renew, and follow up the Baltimore gathering of 2009. I have no doubt that by putting the two conferences side by side, as Catriona has generously done here for us, many new lines of thought will emerge for the reader.

The Philosopher may have a "duty to prefer the truth", but Dr. Peperzak, I think, has also shown us how a spirit of gratitude supports and guides that "duty" along the way, wherever it might go. In the philosophical discussions that follow, the reader will find that very gratitude at work.

EPISTOLARY

§

Our gathering on the Lakeshore Campus of Loyola University Chicago began with the following letter of August 3, 2015, addressed to all who had obtained their PhD in philosophy in cooperation with Peperzak, and some still working on their dissertations. Here is a lightly re-edited text of this letter:

<u>First Letter</u>

August 3, 2015

Dear Friends,

Before I retire from teaching, I would very much like to enjoy one more conversation with all of you, whose dedication to philosophy has made me your companion in "doing philosophy." This is one of the reasons why this letter invites you to be part of a colloquium during which we, from face to face and together, might look back and forth to our involvements as teachers who continue to learn, while guiding others how to do the same.

Inspired by the joyful event that Catriona Hanley brilliantly organized some years ago in Baltimore, and encouraged by conversations with some of you, I would like to propose that we again engage in a lively dialogue – which could begin and continue online until it culminates in a dialogical type of getting together during the Spring of 2016. Since, at that time, we will have already explained and discussed several questions and thoughts that occupy our minds, we will then no longer need to present extensive papers, but use the available time for a true exchange of various interests, perspectives, and ways of wondering and clarification.

What shall we discuss? Which experiences and problems do we want to focus on? This is what we must discover very soon. It would be wonderful if all of us are struck by tightly connected questions that relate to our most cherished passions. To discover such questions, may I ask you to send me before August 25 a response in which you let me know (1) whether you want and can accept this invitation, and (2) which philosophical questions or perplexities you would like to recommend for a concerted discussion?

Please, let me also know whether you would like to amend the procedure sketched above and whether the proposed date for our meeting, provisionally planned on April 1-3, 2016, is convenient for you.

If I may, by way of suggestions, propose some questions for your meditation and subsequent discussion, I will here indicate only two of them, but I count on you to add many other questions that compete for being put on our list of urgency.

My main question – a not very original but sometimes forgotten one – is always: What can, must, and should philosophy – the philosophy of the great philosophers as much as that of myself and my friends – offer to the most radical Desire that drives us: our Desire of living *well*? Or: How does philosophy relate to – and thus is interested in – becoming wiser with regard to the amazing occurrence of our singularly lived human lives?

Less enormous questions are, of course, safer, such as the ones that are born from wondering about *things*. But if our wondering and reflecting about things imply some truth, shouldn't we also ask whether all elements and parts or aspects of whatever being are not primarily *human* factors in the overall drama of real history?

My most inexhaustible question, however, cannot be formulated clearly, because obscurity belongs to all the terms in which it might be expressed. Is that one of the reasons why modern philosophy tended to be rather silent about it and ended by ignoring or even hating it? Let me just try to evoke that question by asking why Plato's shattering reference to "the Good" (or the "Good-and-Beautiful") – as too radical for being caught by way of *eidē*, essences, *ideai*, or *universalia* – refuses any imprisonment in whatever ontic, logical, or ontological network of conceptual arrogance?

I look forward to your responses. In the meantime, I wish you a lucid mind and vivid inspiration during the preparation of new tasks. I often think of you, while enjoying your successes. In the hope that sad events will disturb you rarely, I wish you a wonderful life.

> *Having received the responses, all of which were positive, a second letter was sent on September 28, 2015, from which some main passages are quoted here:*

SECOND LETTER

September 28, 2015

Dear Friends,

Thank you very much for your answers to the invitation letter of August 2015. I read your responses and questions with joy and gratitude. It is wonderful that all of you can join in April; you can imagine how eagerly I look forward to seeing, listening, and speaking to each one and all of you face to face.

You sent many important and exciting questions, each of which deserves thorough discussion. It is not easy to extract from them one central problem that immediately could be specified into all the directions you indicate. I trust, however, that each question can play a role of its own within the web woven by our converging affinities.

If we want now to begin an all-of-us-inclusive conversation, we must at least agree on some broad and common interest. The letter of August 3 mentions one very general question with which all of you seem to sympathize. It is the question of how our involvement in *philosophy* (in all its particular forms of reading, thinking, discussing, teaching, writing, etc.) relates to our *living* an every-time-singular-but-also-shared *human life*. If all of us want to live well and if philosophy has become an important ingredient of our individual and shared lives, how then does our desired and realized way of "doing" philosophy fit into (or with and within) our (unfolding) lives? And how do these lives, insofar as they have become what they already are, fit into our philosophy? Or, in short, how does *philosophy* (and "doing" it *well*, despite failures) relate to *living* well (despite its failures)?

While Giancarlo, Justin, Jean, and I were seeking for a comprehensive theme or domain that would be hospitable to all your proposals, *"Living with Philosophy"* struck us as an acceptable title for our exchanges during the coming six months and our gathering in April.

Wishing you a happy semester full of inspired and well-received work, I send you my delightful memories with hopeful expectations for your own and your friends' lives and for a prosperous growth in philosophy.

—Adriaan Peperzak

THIRD LETTER

Outline of our Meeting

While trying to single out for every session a focus that might suggest enough points of interaction between the many questions and thoughts proposed in the papers, we realize that the discussion itself will probably lead to other questions that are not named in this all too compressed overview. We will however count on the leader of each session to guide our exchange along the surprising directions that might open up.

Friday, April 1
- 2pm – 3:30pm: *Arrival* and Informal gathering
- 3:30pm – 4:00pm: *Official Welcome* to symposiasts and special guests
- 4:00pm – 5:30pm: *Reception* of participants and invited guests
- 5:30pm – 7:30pm: Dinner for participants
- 7:45pm – 9:00pm: Opening of symposium and First Session. Welcome and short overview of some recurring topics, as highlighted in the received papers that were sent online.

Saturday, April 2
- 8:30am – 9am: Continental breakfast
- 9am – 10:30am: *Second Session*, led by Kristi Sweet: *Retrieving Plato's Symposium (201D-212C)*
- 10:30am – 11am: Break

- 11am – 12:30pm: *Third Session*, led by Brent Adkins: *Autonomy versus Docility*. *"I think,"* as confronted with classics, tradition, and established (e.g., American) cultures with their ethos and *doxai*, pundits, and promissory notes.
- 12:30pm – 2pm: Lunch break
- 2pm – 3:30pm: *Fourth Session,* led by Norman Wirzba*: Perspectives.* From above as a voice of solitude; as a service from the bottom; from the center; in response or correspondence; as interlocutor in conversation; as challenger in combat; as part of a choir after tragedy; or as actors of a comedy, because "it does not matter"?
- 3:30pm – 4pm: Break
- 4pm – 5:30pm: *Fifth Session,* led by Jeff Courtright*: Experience.* Old and new; including all corporeal becoming and fading, and all affective impressions, intuitions, experiments, and responses, insofar as they determine our living and thinking.
- 6pm: Dinner at *Francesca's* with Toasts.

<u>Sunday, April 3</u>
- 8:30am – 9am: Continental breakfast
- 9am – 10:30am: *Sixth Session,* led by Marjolein Oele*: Reaching out to the Good?* (Cf. *Politeia,* 498B-521C): Are we – can we be – content with a transcendentally understood universe (*ousia/ideas*) or can't we refrain from transcendence? What is the role of *eros, philia, agape, caritas, love* in our attachment to *Sophia*?
- 10:30am – 11am: Break
- 11am – 12:30pm: *Seventh Session,* led by Catriona Hanley*: Wrapping Up, Farewell*
- 12:30pm: Lunch and au revoir

OVERVIEW: WHAT WAS SAID IN CHICAGO?

§

Catriona Hanley

Presented here is a quick review of seven loosely themed dialogue sessions that took place in Chicago in April 2016. These were to note and to honour Adriaan Theodore Peperzak's retirement from his formal University position, and from formal teaching (underline *formal*, as we all know that he cannot—and should not—stop, even if we do *formally* release him to the study of garden tulips, and will demand no more of him!).

My hasty scribbles during hours of intensely focused and passionate dialogue with colleagues are bound to be distorted by my own perspective and to miss a lot of important threads and themes. Such is the hermeneutic of the philosophical practice that Plato began; here I avoided fiction perhaps overmuch, rendering the reconstructed conversations rather dry. As a corrective, note please that we were all (mostly) in great spirits throughout the three exhausting days. When we were tired, we turned to absurd humour and caffeine; there were belly laughs and giggles along with somber reflection, sharp irony next to grim assessment, and joyous hope next to quiet despair. And above all, there was a strong bond of intellectual fellowship and friendship: love radiating from our mentor touched and bound us all, even as we openly and trustingly voiced our disagreements and variations.

I hope that what follows catches some of the gist and feeling of our dialogues from sessions I- VI. Presentation of a version of these notes was my contribution in session VII. My colleagues did not protest at my rendering, so I have just enough courage to submit these notes as a partial retelling of our fruitful conversations. Thanks all for entrusting me with this happy/risky task.

I. First session: *Welcome and short overview of some recurring topics as highlighted in the received papers. Giancarlo Tarantino, Jean Clifford, Joe Linn and Chicago organizers led this session.*

This initial discussion sought to identify major areas of inquiry-- overarching themes-- that symposiasts thought necessary to explore. All agreed to study these questions over the next days of the Symposium:

- 1) *pedagogy*: how can we make philosophy central in teaching/learning?;
- 2) *suffering*: how can the luxury of philosophy meaningfully address deep suffering and pain in the world?;
- 3) *experience*: what does it mean to have, or *be had by* experience, and what are the grounds for being open to experience?

II. Second session: *Reading and Actualization of Plato:* Symposium 201D-212: *Examination of the prime text in Adriaan Peperzak's early formation as a philosopher. Kristi Sweet led this session.*

- The good is everywhere; we need to train our eyes to see it;
- Living, striving for reproduction in beauty: problems of the meaning of "in";
- Is *eros* divine? It is not a god, but that which throws you; it is not human, and not even godlike: rather it is that which makes it possible to *see* the good/beautiful:

- The approach of 'admirability': what accounts for the strange disappearance of this notion from modern/contemporary philosophy;
- "Dissatisfaction": a useful notion: there is a strong positive sense to the word, positing a destiny that has an immortal character and that can lift me out of the world of ideas;
  - There is a strong sense that the ladder of beauty/good presents steps along the way to being able to see (feel?)(touch?) the Good/Beautiful
    - What would it be to prioritize touch over sight?
  - Then we repeat the steps again and again until... transfiguration?
  - Or maybe we need to kick away the ladder à la Wittgenstein: a more direct approach... more direct than platonic.
- Discussion about the power and necessity versus the obstructive endeavour of the will.
- Is there a scandal in Kant, so that freedom =submission? Or is this a naïve reading?
- Two possible readings of Kant:
  - 1) the world is unfolding independent of my participation in it, and I'm doing what I can with and "in" it;
  - 2) there is a much more complex order than this terrestrial one: there are spiritual demands that may or may not have been met in advance of my being here. What I experience does not match up with reality, so I have to "force" reality to meet my constructive spiritual demands.
    - Doing so renders me "free".

III. Third Session: *Autonomy versus Docility: "I think" as confronted with classics, tradition, and established (e.g. American) cultures with their* ethos *and* doxai, *with their pundits and promissory notes. Brent Adkins led this session.*
- Time will run out before we get to docility: symbolic? [Editor's note: ... and it did in fact run out].
- Autonomy conceived as borders/constraints/territory: freedom

versus autonomy needs exploration also…
- Peperzak: our first attitude should be gratitude, before any positioning of the self as *auto nomos*.
  - Philosophy as a logic story about affectivity: Plato, Augustine, Bonaventure, Cusanus
  - Levinas: myth of autonomy as necessary to ethics (as Kant's ideas, God, Freedom and immortality of the soul)
  - Cartesian toxic distortion of the notion of autonomy
- Contemporary world: constraint is "sold" as freedom (Foucault)
  - Note: in the prison-industrial complex: incarceration of others= freedom for me
  - Note: in the contemporary world, enslavement to technology is read as freedom
- What "violence" can we use on students to shift their opinions?
  - How to persuade them to be autonomous—the paradox here.
    - This first noted in the philosophy teacher's best friend: Plato's *Allegory of the Cave*
- What do we mean when we talk about "style"?
  - Expression of character (authentic/inauthentic)
  - Engaging texts/ideas "in" a style
  - Is style an expression of my *auto nomos* "self"? or is the self fictionalized through style?
    - The work of consumer capitalist society on self-understanding of style; or surely we mean something other than that? Either way, it persists
      - How do I come (in)to style, or how does it come (in)to me?

IV. Fourth Session: *Perspectives: From above as a voice of solitude; as a service from the bottom; from the centre; in response or correspondence; as interlocutor in conversation; as challenger in combat; as part of a choir after tragedy; or as actors in a comedy, because "it does not matter".*

Norman Wirzba led this session:
- Problematic split between nature and culture;
    - Modern cultural bifurcation between the two tremendously damaging
    - Thoughts on nature/the natural; as if we humans could ever not be natural
    - Multiculture and nature
- How to think about my embodied *position* in the world;
    - What does it mean to be embodied?
- How has urbanization negatively remade *place*;
    - What is "place" versus "space"?
- Homelessness [*unheimlichkeit*], versus homesickness [*nostalgia?*], versus longing for home [*saudade*];
- The quadrangle: nature/culture, and person/world
    - Is this Heidegger's fourfold?
- Hospitality as *mending rifts*;
    - Deep roots of hospitality culture in the Western tradition; *Iliad*
- Equal rights for all easily ends in war:
    - The beginning of the assertion of *my* rights (as equally defensible as yours) can lead to irresolvable conflict; why should my rights be any more important/valuable/defensible than yours?
    - Rights culture critique leaves a gap in understanding contemporary political culture; can hospitality bridge that gap?
    - In the comedy of life, it does matter!
- Mass movement today of displaced peoples:
    - What can our thinking do in response?
    - The difficulty of removing myself from *a particular* perspective: the impossibility of Nagel's "view from nowhere", as removal of all potential, necessarily subjective perspectives.
    - Being here, being now, being honest.

V. Fifth Session: *Experience. Old and new, including all corporeal becoming and fading, and all affective impressions, intuitions, experiments, responses, insofar as*

they determine our living and thinking. Jeffrey Courtright led this session.
- Trust: "experience" of trust is preverbal. Is it then an experience?
- What role does experience play in provoking philosophy?
  - Is experience a failure of trust?
  - What phenomenological experience can function as a start to philosophy?
- Problem: how do we characterize, describe, become aware of the perspective from which we start?
- Or to just start, to speak to someone, to enter into conversation
- Experience: my attempt to experience the other *as* other: does this demand a spiritual transformation, or at the least deep spiritual work?
  - *Askesis*, a kind of withdrawal to work deeply on the self: but on the spiritual self; hard, concentrated work…
    - Relationship to psychoanalysis?
    - Is this a true experience of self?
    - Or is this more the old trope of the "solitary philosopher"?
- Starting again with the question of experience: the meaning of philosophy is, after all, the clarification of what is important to us, and with how we engage with others [Peperzak].
- Philosophy is not a map, not a discovery of a path, whether that be learned or pointed out by an expert.
  - More precisely: there is no fixed way: no twenty steps to realization of a happy life, and therefore no map available.
  - Perhaps the best we can do is describe the orientation, the "pointing towards", looking to a "towards which" [Hanley], even if the object constantly retreats.
  - Listening to Others is the key…
- Experience then, is people. Initially perhaps those who take care of me [Peperzak]?
  - But then most philosophers are mythologists;
  - They describe this life as they are interested in it, or as it

appears interesting to them
- Nietzsche: to see through the singular to the good and beautiful. Yes.
  - Singularity versus individuality:
    - Peperzak: there is no singularity, only individuality; though an individual is still a "type".
  - God is not ever behind, beside, beyond, above, beings: no spatial metaphors can apply: that'd make him finite
  - We need to think more about interiority.
- Can we understand the beginning of experience as the totality?
  - Husserl though gets it right in limiting the purview…

VI. Sixth Session: *Reaching out to the Good (cf. Politeia, 498b-521c): Are we—can we be—content with a transcendentally understood universe (ousia/ ideas)? Or can we (had we better) refrain from transcendence? What is the role of eros, philia, agape, caristas, love, in our attachment to sophia? Marjolein Oele led this session.*
- What might it mean to reach-out-towards the Good?
- The double draw of desire long described and perhaps still understood as:
  - The good versus the polis
    - Is that true? Isn't the dichotomy rather between dedication to the polis and dedication to the intellectual life, and *these* as competing goods?
    - But yet perhaps it is not so easy, as the "good" of the intellectual life is not so clear.
  - How does it work, even if we follow the Greeks: it seems there is an ascent towards the Good (capital "g"?) and then a return;
    - The ascent is sometimes very fast and the descent slow…. Does this tell us anything or is it a mere trope?
  - Is the notion of desire appropriate to describe the obligations/ responsibilities that we, as participant members, have towards the polis?

- The Good: there is no answer to the question of what it is
  - Is it simply a place-holder?
    - Or rather a challenge?
      - Better yet, a locus/non-locus of the pointing towards; a towards which that explains the pointing…
- Towards what end should we contemplate the Good?
  - Example of cultural success: *El Sistema*, Venezuela's music program:
    - Simple, direct focus on the good here and now, with tentacles reaching towards a concrete future.
- *Phaedrus*: is there always a return from transcendence? Vision alone is not enough. Tragedy as anti-philosophy:
  - Does pursuit of the good provoke the return: or if not, is this idolatry of the Good?
  - Socrates' concern with the happiness of the Guardians
    - Role of *prohairesis*: do we choose to engage in thought? In action?

VII. Seventh Session: *Wrapping up: Farewell. Catriona Hanley led this session.*

- At the end, it is always good to return to the beginning. In this case, the very first session of the April 2016 meeting set out three themes to be explored: pedagogy, suffering and experience.
- In the whirlwind of dialogue over the course of three rich and challenging days of philosophical conversation, we came back over and again to those.
- Not to be too fashionably post-modern and self-referential, but: the whole summary of what was said in Chicago constitutes the seventh session.
- In the following pages, we'll hear short pieces from each of the 21 participants in the Chigago symposium. All these pieces were written—and distribute—before that meeting, and set the tone for the free and open discussions we had there.

21 Short Pieces on the Theme: Living with Philosphy

1. Living with Philosophy

§

Adriaan Peperzak

1. The title seems to encourage a reflection about the mutual relation between human *lives* – as lived by you, me, us, and all of them – and *philosophy*, as a practice that we share with other – past, present, and future – philosophers.

2. Starting from my own experience of life in which philosophy has played a big role, I would like to reflect about one element that is recognized as fundamental by all philosophers: *experience*.

3. I have always been irritated by introductions to philosophy that pay much attention to empirical data like the color of this door and the utility of a hammer without revealing or searching for their existential relevance to human *interests* and the *persons* in whose lives such isolated "data" find their splendid, sad, or boring meaning. "Things" or "materials" are not interesting if they are separated from the meaning they receive from their functioning within the *corporeal, affective, exploratory, aesthetic, ethical, political,* or *religious* structures and strata of the persons who integrate them in the experiences of their – neither thingly nor *merely* natural, vegetal, cosmis, or animalic – lives.

4. A confrontation of my *living my life* with my "*doing*" (consuming and digesting, practicing, performing, and teaching) *philosophy* can begin with a comparison between my *experience* of the common adventure of living humanly like (and unlike) all others, and the particular adventure of becoming and being a philosopher who still hopes to become wiser than (s)he is today or yesterday. An accurate *description* and *analysis* of such a confrontation and comparison could fill more than one book; but let's try a first reconnaissance of the double but unified *experience* that has emerged

from living our own lives as humanly well as possible and our specific experiences of *becoming* and (hopefully) *being* capable philosophers. Both tasks are already difficult enough to describe and analyze. However, we must consider them, if we do not want to neglect or falsify the *experienced truth* about our involvement in *living* and *thinking*. Let me therefore postpone for now questions about logical (and methodological) concerns insofar as these can be bracketed (can they?), in order to *first* concentrate our attention on essential "facts" of *life:* your and my conception; living unwillingly within our mother's womb; the frightening shock of birth; being saved from immediate death by mother, father, and family; education by many others, until we became persons who will and think. Even then we were not yet ready to practice philosophy: much *philosophical experience* and many particular relations, revolutions, conversations, and conversions had still to be experienced. But certain seeds or sparks of philosophy must have been operative in our attempts at living well.

5. How should we define "human experience"? What does it and how can it encompass all that may and must interest us because of its belonging to the full humanness of our living, and the human truth of our dedication to a humanly unfolding, but mortal, philosophy.

As an infant, our life began not with interest in hammers or cell phones, but rather as desirous of well-tasting food, hard or soft beddings, handling hands, sounding voices, loving or inspecting eyes that addressed and affected us while encouraging us to react. We had to learn how to focus and distinguish useful from harmful, good from bad, and desirable from undesirable things and persons. Slowly a universe took form whose components showed various forms of meaning: were these faces, words, animals, flowers, and things edible, useful, desirable, handleable, lovable, hateable?

The many ways in which persons, animals, events, smaller or greater dramas, and dreams affected me were received, accepted, or refused in different ways. Nature and culture offered me shifting *place*(s) and gave me *decisive moments*. They suggested responses that could be understood and welcomed, which endeared me to them, or, on the contrary, misinterpreted, which triggered troubling affections in me. But nothing – no person, animal, vegetation, situation, event, or thing – presented itself as isolated from the small and endless, miniscule and cosmic, daemonic, spiritual, and divine universe that – through almost imperceptible or dramatic transformations – would become *my* personal, though universally shared, world.

6. Looking back on my own past from a place with which I have become acquainted at a late stage of my life, I realize more than ever that my first years of life in a tropical climate and a Dutch-colonial culture – among mountains, sawahs, beautiful but incomprehensible men and women etc. – still stretches its influence to a deep layer of my *emotional* and *social* universe. Similarly, my experience of the depressing occupation of The Netherlands by the Nazis from 1940 to 1945 – with its real hunger and freezing cold, its boasting lies in proclamations, its cruel rumors of torture and executions, its anxiety as constant background of arrogantly parading enemies – is still a vivid element of my experience, today when i realize how, in the present world again, similar disasters are organized – and not only far away.

7. In order to describe the *interesting experiences* from which philosophy should start, we must re-evoke and *re-experience* the truly empirical – and thus determining – elements that, as *human* experiences, forbid us to de-humanize the material, natural, vital, ensouled, poetic, beautiful, uplifting, and peaceful manifestations and amazing gifts of good and bad luck that offered solid roots to our philosophical fascination. At the same time, as philosophers, we must dare to confront the awful disasters that, on all levels of human experience, resist our attempts at ignorance or denial.

8. There is no guarantee – neither in our lives, nor in our philosophy – that our experiences of evil can be radically redeemed by nature or history or by the modern and postmodern illusions of human autarchy. There is not even any guarantee for more than a mixture of gratitude and hope. If philosophy is a human – and thus limited – effort of rational or reasonal understanding, then it never will succeed completely. But life has to deal effectively with disasters, to begin (or end) with death. Does philosophical wisdom then also include a (limited?) wisdom about death?

9. Perhaps philosophy cannot solve the most important questions, if we stick to espousing the *perspective* of a panoramic horizon spread out before a lonely ego (cogito) who, as an autarchic (re-)creator, (re)organizes the universe by (re)thinking it. Would another perspective (perhaps from face to face?) offer opportunities for a more appropriate understanding?

Angela and I embrace you,

—Adriaan

2. "Living with Philosophy" (and Phronēsis): A Response to Dr. Peperzak's September 28 Letter

§

Giancarlo Tarantino

In light of some of the questions supported by the title *"Living with Philosophy,"* I am struck by how relevant something like Aristotle's concept of *phronēsis* (wisdom) seems to be here. No doubt there are any number of ways that one could, with the help of this concept, think further about these questions concerning life, living well (or badly), and philosophy. But instead of trying to immediately respond to these questions by giving an "Aristotelian" answer per se, it seems to me that Aristotle's concept of *phronēsis* can also help (me) to reflect on and further determine (by also somewhat altering) the basic question as a question. What exactly am I asking about or desire to know when I consider the relationship between "our lived life" and "(doing) philosophy"?

For me it is all too easy to forget the "with" of the proposed title *"Living with(in) philosophy,"* and thereby immediately interpret the title and its related questions in one of two ways: that is, either in terms of an oppositional relationship (living *versus* philosophy?) or in terms of a methodological relationship according to which philosophy, as "theory," should be "applied" to "life," as "practice" ("applied ethics" or "applied philosophy"?). Without taking the time to spell it out here, I can at least say simply that I am quite dissatisfied with both of these interpretations of the question at issue, although I recognize that there may be some good sense at work in both (e.g., I for one am very happy to say that there is much more to "life" than, or which lies "outside of," the practice of "philosophy." No doubt this at times creates a kind of oppositional situation.).

At any rate, what I like about the proposed title ("*Living with philosophy*") is the way in which the "with" or "within" suggests a much more intimate, and ambiguous, connection between my lived life, and my attempting to practice "philosophy." My mind thus turns to Aristotle's concept of *phronēsis*, which articulates a kind of wisdom of or at work within concrete human living (i.e., whatever is comprised by the whole realm of human cultural life and "*praxis*" – that is to say, our "words and deeds").

My interest in this kind of "reason in action" stems primarily from my search for words in the face of my experience of living in a L'Arche Community together with persons with and without physical and intellectual disabilities. If I can give a quick example that springs to mind: one can find a wisdom at work in the daily life there, e.g., in the way we all eat together – when Catherine, drawing hardly any attention to herself, cleans up the mess Danny made in spilling his coffee and brings him another cup (likely to be spilled again soon enough), she allows him to continue on laughing at someone's joke and be a participant in the conversation without making him feel embarrassed or singling out his predictable clumsiness (not to mention her wisdom of giving someone the chance to be "predictably clumsy" instead of simply doing everything for them in the first place!). There is much more happening in an everyday situation like this than simply "eating" or "talking," and not everyone is capable of doing what Catherine does for Danny (or was it Danny who made Catherine capable of doing that?). But isn't this a wise, reasonable, or understanding response to a very mundane part of "life"? How does Catherine "know how" to do that? What role does or can the more or less specialized discourses of "philosophy" play here, if any? (For what it's worth, both Catherine and Danny live with Down's syndrome, so there is no question here of having "applied" any philosophical "theory" to one's "practice.")

Aristotle seemed to need to distinguish between "*sophia*" and "*phronēsis*" in order to express more precisely what he understood to comprise the basic longing of "*philosophia*." Certainly the modern transformation of "philosophy" into a kind of academic discipline and "science" (in the broad sense) suggests that whatever kind of wisdom Catherine shows in her actions and words, it is not of a properly "philosophical" sort. However, if that is so (and indeed I agree that it is), then the question for me that lies behind the title *"Living with philosophy"* is the following: how and to what extent can academic "philosophy," as a concretely lived practice, cultivate (or corrupt) a *well*-lived life?

Maybe at this point I do now see a way in which a kind of "Aristotelian" response could be helpful. By looking at and describing the habitual practices of contemporary academic philosophy (as Dr. Peperzak points out: reading, discussing, teaching, writing...), insofar as they both further cultivate and grow out of particular kinds of characters, we might at least start to be able to understand the relationship between "philosophy" and "living" – at least insofar as we are focused on the lived life of a particular individual "philosopher." In other words, my question has become: to what extent is our *character* shaped by, and is itself shaping, our praxis of philosophy (for good or ill)?

Appendix: Are Gratitude and Patience Deduced?

The questions and lines of thought that I had been thinking through in light of Dr. Peperzak's letters, as well as the title of our symposium, have somewhat changed course since the actual event took place. In particular, the way that I had been thinking about the relationship of "philosophy" and "living" has been changed, and, one hopes, deepened. During a few of our conversations, Dr. Peperzak used the word "gratitude" to describe an orientation, which thinkers can take towards phenomena, texts, gestures, and words, separate from (prior to?) an explicitly critical-skeptical form of reflection.[145] Was this use of "gratitude" a philosophical one? Is the "gratitude" that inhabits, guides, and accompanies a thinker's path of thinking the result of a conceptually justified grasp of what "must be" the attitude of a philosopher? Does one deduce gratitude and patience? Was the "gratitude" discussed during our philosophizing fundamentally different than that expressed by many people in other words and gestures throughout the

---
145 Hearing about Jeff Courtright's work on "trust" was the specific occasion in which "gratitude" became a somewhat salient topic.

days of the symposium? If not, and if gratitude is a part of good philosophizing, then perhaps its cultivation will be no different from that of any other virtue (intellectual or otherwise).

If this is the case, then we have a clear example of how a habitually well-lived life, culminating in a spirit of gratitude, would necessarily color the thinker's thoughts in the same manner. The gratitude within one's living would generate the gratitude that informs one's philosophizing, and, in turn, such intellectual gratitude would reflect back onto and light up what one encounters in "life." The philosophizing that would take place in the light would be quite different from that done under the harsh light of a spirit of ingratitude and its accompanying affects.

I cannot say that all of this has assuaged that other tension that I feel between the "two lives" described by Aristotle at the end of his *Nicomachean Ethics*, and which, I think, we encountered again on the last day of the symposium while discussing Plato's *Republic* in light of the injustices permeating Chicago today. However, I can say that whether one takes the path of the *"theoretikos"* or the *"politikos,"* a spirit of "gratitude" would be a welcome daimon for a well-lived life – and, I trust, a necessary one.

3. Living with Philosophy

§

Brent Adkins

The phrase "living with philosophy" generates two opposed ideas in me. The first idea arises out of teaching philosophy to non-majors and speaking to colleagues about their disciplines. I tell students that everyone one is a philosopher. It is impossible to live without philosophy. The only real question is, Am I doing philosophy well or poorly? This raises the idea that there is no living *with* philosophy, as if philosophy were something that could be added to living. Life itself is already ineluctably philosophical. I even deploy a version of this view when I talk to colleagues who are not professional philosophers. When they claim, "Chemistry is X" or "Sociology is X," I point out that these are philosophical claims not scientific or sociological claims. Thus, even in disciplines that seek to avoid philosophical entanglements, it is impossible. The only issue is whether one is conscious of his or her philosophical commitments. Whether speaking with students or colleagues, I'm able to draw on a rich tradition of thought. The way that I press students about their philosophical commitments has its origins in Socrates, Plato, and Aristotle. The way that I challenge colleagues about the necessity of philosophy has a much more Hegelian flavor. In the end, though, everyone "lives" with philosophy, because philosophy is inseparable from life. On this view the task of the philosopher is maieutic, helping people bring forth their ideas in a coherent and cogent way.

The second idea that "living with philosophy" generates in me springs initially from the connotations of the construction "living with." While this is no doubt a recent development, "living with" has taken on the valence of struggle. No one has to "live with" fun or happiness or love. No, people "live with" cancer or social anxiety disorder or Hepatitis C. That is, people "live with" unpleasant and often chronic conditions. Now, admittedly, there's something perversely satisfying about thinking of philosophy as chronic disease. It is, as if we philosophers have taken on this additional burden that others are too weak to shoulder, and through our struggle, through our living with philosophy we have managed to persevere, and our perseverance has become a beacon to the rest of the world, those without the fortitude to live with philosophy. It is a heroic and self-serving vision, but it also has its antecedents in the history of philosophy. Socrates and Nietzsche seem to me to be cheerful exponents of this view, while Kierkegaard and Heidegger seem to me rather dour champions of this idea.

The fact we find Socrates at the beginning of both views makes me wonder if this opposition lies at the heart of philosophy itself. I detect here what Derrida would call a "supplemental" logic in the relation between philosophy and life. On the first view, philosophy is essential to life. It fills a lack, in the way that vitamin supplements compensate for deficiencies that compromise individual health. On the second view, philosophy is inessential to life; it is an extra and unnecessary task taken on by the philosopher, in the way that teaching in the summer might provide supplemental income. In both cases philosophy supplements life, but the supplementation occurs in two diametrically opposed ways. Philosophy is undecideable with regard to life. It oscillates between these two determinate positions. Philosophers have tended to focus on one pole of the opposition, but they can never completely eliminate the trace of the other pole.

I find this strangely comforting, at least insofar as it describes my experience "living with philosophy." It's a strange kind of life alternating between confidence and insecurity, between certainty and doubt, between revolution and submission, between creation and destruction. I think this vacillation is not a problem to be solved by philosophy. I think it's what philosophy is. Of course, there's more to the story. We cannot simply remain within this vacillation. We cannot be the "Beautiful Soul" unsullied by the world. We must think. We must write. We must act. When we do, though, the action will be a betrayal of one of the ways of living with philosophy. So we act, but then we are always drawn back to the vacillating nature of philosophy itself. This forces us to reflect on our actions and create anew. These new creations are always provisional, offered in humility. They are revisable. They can even be abandoned, but philosophy itself forces us to continually experiment in life and with life.

Post-Symposium Reflections

What a marvelous event. I have so much gratitude for all those who worked so hard to make the symposium run so smoothly. I would even like to think that they made Saturday's snow squalls possible, since that added the perfect touch to being back in Chicago. After 15 years, and despite the massive changes on and off campus, it almost felt like I never left.

Of course, what brought me and all of us to Chicago was not the hope of a Spring snow but the love we bear for Adriaan Peperzak. His personal and intellectual generosity has left an indelible mark on all of us, and this symposium was an opportunity to not so much repay (how could we?) but to reflect this generosity in thoughtful conversation.

It was marvelous to sit in the same room with so many accomplished thinkers; all graciously sharing how they had transformed what Adriaan had given. Plato's text provided one axis of transformation, while the limits of modernity provided another axis of transformation. In every case, though, an excess remained. Try as we might, we couldn't make our gifts fully present. Whether the topic was love, desire, trust, or the nature of philosophy itself, something always remained unsaid and not merely for lack of time.

I think this excess is precisely the mark that Adriaan has left on all of us. Though we have all tried to make something different with it, it is a gift that remains evergreen. To such a gift I can only respond with gratitude and my own limited attempts to give the same gift to my students. Thank you, Adriaan.

4. "PHILOSOPHY, LOVE, AND INDIVIDUALITY"

§

Nicholas Mowad

Philosophy is a certain kind of intellectual activity but is very different from other kinds, including the otherwise most exalted kinds: the sciences, and law. Philosophy's peculiarity in this respect lies in part in the relation it has to one's own individual life.

Philosophy involves reflection but is distinct from the operations of the understanding characterizing so much intellectual activity, even in what is too often supposed to be "philosophy." The understanding's deficiencies are well-known, e.g. from Hegel's criticisms of Kant and others. In response to these inadequacies, some people hold up as an ideal the notion of pure, raw, unreflective experience, where we are put in touch with reality before reflection covers it over. The practice of philosophy might then involve carefully and patiently uncovering the original experience. But philosophy's uniqueness is most clear in those cases where philosophy does not have to sift through what belongs to an original experience and what does not because what is experienced is of such a character that it throws off any attempt to reduce it to a form digestible by the understanding. Love is the most ready example of this kind of thing which one is *unable* to cover over (even if one wished to do so).

The sciences can treat what they call "love," but there it is misrepresented as a physical event (neurologically as a certain pattern of firing neurons, or biologically as the drive toward or act of reproduction), just as law can misrepresent it as a contract (as the law understands marriage) or the reciprocity of certain rights and duties (as parental and filial ties are understood). Outside of these specialized disciplines, "love" is covered over by the interpretations popular culture offers. To take romantic love as an example, anyone growing up in the late 20th century United States is from early childhood presented with thousands of images and stories of people falling in love in movies, books, television shows, songs, etc. A certain framework begins to take shape in a child's mind that involves things like two people's eyes meeting from across the room, the boy asking the girl out on a date, the two sitting next to each other awkwardly in a movie theatre, the boy walking the girl to her door and kissing her. With this procedure firmly in place, by one's adolescence one experiences the social world through these expectations. In this way, one already attaches a meaning to a word "love" and uses the word correctly before one has ever experienced it firsthand, and this prior acquaintance colors the first experience itself, making it inauthentic.

However, the occulting acculturation one receives both in the high culture of the sciences and law and in the popular culture does not make one insusceptible of the genuine experience of love, which breaks through the medium that the culture creates between a person and his or her beloved. Feeling love involves an involuntary and painful awareness that the ways the culture offers for understanding what is happening are inadequate. The images and concepts which earlier seemed to open up and illuminate the social world suddenly seem small, and irrelevant. But this devaluation of these cultural images and notions is not accomplished once and for all by the first experience of love. After all, in the cases of many phenomena, the ways some parts of the culture offer to understand something can be shown inadequate, but more nuanced and more appropriate ways (as found e.g. in the sciences) can then be found so that one can then confidently maintain that one "understands" the thing experienced. But certain experiences, like love, stubbornly resist such attempts to bring them within the purview of the understanding—and they are characterized by this resistance.

And yet, for all that love does not remain completely opaque, though the only way to begin to get a handle on it is to give up treating it like an object whose contours can be traced by the understanding. It is the anonymity of the understanding which makes it incapable of grasping love. Love touches a person in a way that you might say is *personal* (having to do with the thinker individually, and not *qua* thinker, or *qua* human, male, American, modern, etc.); and, it is something that concerns the person in his or her complete subjectivity. I add the second condition because the feeling of pain from a paper cut concerns me in my individuality (and the general notion of a paper cut does not communicate my feeling of pain, even if it prompts others to recall their own individual feelings of pain from their own paper cuts), but a paper cut (or any similarly private but trivial sensation) concerns not only a small part of my body, but also a small part of my attention and my identity, and so it can be "mastered" by me in a way that the experience of love cannot. So, I can only really begin to describe the experience of love by talking about how it differs from how things are experienced by the understanding (and by corporeal sensation). This description would qualify as philosophy, but not "science" (in the sense of the understanding subsuming things under laws).

That what since Kant we call "the understanding" is concerned with middling objects rather than the highest, and that we stand before this highest "object" alone, as individuals rather than *as human*, or as representatives of this or that institution, is an ancient position, and one which is inseparable from the original and true vocation of philosophy. The right to approach this most dignified object is extended to all, but not without preconditions. Plato wrote: "this power [of knowing, and being educated] is in the soul of each, and [...] the instrument with which each learns—just as the eye is not able to turn toward the light from the dark without the whole body—must be turned around from that which is coming into being together with the whole soul until it is able to endure looking at that which is and the brightest part of that which is."[146]

That is: the practice of philosophy (directing one's eye to the light) is possibly only with the right changes in the *individual* life of the practitioner (the position and orientation of the body). Education for Plato is not putting sight into a blind eye, since the eye already has the ability to see;

---

146 Plato, *Republic* 518c (translated by Bloom, Basic Books 1991).

rather, one must turn the eye (and the person) around toward the proper object. Thus the teacher does not view the student as a patient, a mere recipient of the teacher's knowledge. Rather, the student must be cajoled or incited somehow to turn around on his or her own. Teaching means appealing to the student in the right way to prompt this turning. This appeal must involve something specific to the student, some concern the student already has in his/her benighted state. We have a model for how this appeal is made in how Socrates educates Glaucon: viz., through dialectic. The desires are always for the good, understood more or less adequately. Dialectic can be employed to purify these desires, to get rid of that which makes something ordered toward the good (but is not the good itself) appear to be better than it is, and to properly esteem that in what is desired which is ordered toward the good. Desires are brought around in habits, which need to be maintained with practice. "Knowledge" of the good is different: you can either be turned toward the good, or turned away from it. Whenever you are turned toward the good, it is possible (in one stroke) to turn away from it, or vice versa. Yet knowing the good is not bodily and does not have to be maintained so that it does not slacken as ethical virtues need to be maintained: the conversion happens in an instant.

To have undergone this turning, this conversion, makes one fit to teach and "convert" others. Being fit in this way does not come from some special *knowledge*: one cannot *know* the good, because the good is beyond being, and what is intelligible is intelligible insofar as it *is*. But one must relate to the good somehow, and one does so through a different kind of "desire," love. To love the good is to be drawn to it, subject to it somehow (but not in an utterly passive way, like clay in the hands of a sculptor). In love one is subject to the beloved such that one knows one's identity as being bound up in the beloved.

In the non-philosophical parts of the culture we know generalities through the understanding, and we can fix and know, *master* and *possess* particulars insofar as they can be subsumed under these generalities.[147]

---

147 Hegel, *Enzyklopädie der philosophischen Wissenschaften* Band III §§454-455 (Frankfurt am Main: Suhrkamp Verlag, 1970).

In contrast, love (and in philosophical reflection on love) have the character of what Hegel calls the "concrete universal": the universal is not an abstract "essence," self-identical because removed from the brute existence of the individual, infinitely distant from the individual, yet the latter's only explanation and reality. Rather, the concrete universal is a self-determining universal: realizing its own self (and not merely displaying itself in an image) in the existing individuals.[148] Neither the beloved nor the lover is not an instance of a type, but an irreplaceable individual—and the same is true of the emerging student of philosophy. And the awakening of love in a person (just like the awakening of philosophy) does not require that the person abandon all his/her personal concerns: rather, the spark ignites a powerful flame by kindling the hopes, the ethical character, the commitments already present in the individual.

This certainly does not mean that the opinions of just any person possess philosophical depth, just as the random idiosyncrasies of a person need not be loveable. To be sure, love, and perhaps even philosophy, are in principle within the grasp of each individual (provided the proper commitment and attention are brought to bear). Yet as it happens many people are neither prepared to fall in love nor to be the object of love; and few indeed are prepared to study philosophy. Abstractions like the law may apply to all equally; and the sciences judiciously ignore what stands in the way of a simple but imperious reduction (as e.g. classical economics reduces all human relations to contracts between rationally self-interested individuals, or classical physics reduces all of nature inert matter, responding to being acted upon from outside). Love on the other hand (including the love of wisdom) can only light upon those who are prepared to receive it. The paradox of the intimate relation between the practice of philosophy and an individual's life is that the bare capacity for it is born in each and every human being, but it is the way of the world that the great majority of people are often permanently led astray by distractions (wealth, pleasure, professional success, etc.), and end up closed off to love and philosophy.

---

148 Hegel even calls it "love [*Leibe*]" (*Enzyklopädie der philosophischen Wissenschaften* Band I §159 *Anmerkung*

Appendix

It was a joy to attend this conference with Dr. Peperzak and others of his former students. The daily grind of teaching introductory philosophy classes to (mostly) recalcitrant students can sometimes make me forget why I devoted myself to philosophy in the first place. But trenchant conversations with those who are similarly devoted brings me back quickly and dramatically. Of all the people "in philosophy" I've met, I've known none as devoted to philosophy as Dr. Peperzak and those in his circle. While it seems natural to call someone with a doctorate in chemistry a "chemist," or in history a "historian," I've always thought it to be presumptuous and pompous when philosophy PhDs called themselves "philosophers." I call myself a student of philosophy, but—as I always tell my students—I have known one philosopher: my professor, Adriaan Peperzak.

It was Dr. Peperzak who first put me on the path of studying Hegel and Aristotle, and showed me how to read their works. While Dr. Peperzak and I do not agree on every detail in interpreting Hegel, or even more broadly on Hegel's flexibility and merit, I maintain my position that Hegel still has much to say to us today largely because of the ability to hear what Hegel is really saying, which I learned under Dr. Peperzak's guidance. It is no exaggeration to say that Dr. Peperzak has had a decisive influence on my life: I would not be who I am today if not for my encounter with Dr. Peperzak.

I have the pleasure now of encountering and recognizing Dr. Peperzak's influence and presence when I speak with friends from my time at Loyola, and at the conference speaking with others of his students that I met for the first time. Dr. Peperzak's concern for the singularity of people, his reverence for the philosophical tradition, his horror at suffering and resistance to ways of thinking that cover it up, his unfailing generosity and deep gratitude were all on display at the conference, in himself and in his current and former students. The conference renewed my faith in philosophy by reminding me what it is to participate in a group of friends pursuing wisdom and happiness.

5. Living with Philosophy

§

Alberto Bertozzi

If I understand the proposed theme of our symposium, *Living with Philosophy*, we are here invited not only to think about what it means for a life to be engaged in philosophy as a particular academic discipline, but also to reflect on how the practice of philosophy as something that includes but is not limited to academic activity may contribute to shape a good life. I find the magnitude of the theme rather intimidating. So, instead of dealing with it by addressing directly one of its aspects or elements, I will try to reflect on it obliquely by sharing some of the difficulties and questions I have encountered in my living with philosophy.

From what both Prof. Peperzak and Giancarlo wrote in their contributions, it would appear that to view wisdom as mere analytic intelligence concerned with empirical data and disengaged from (or otherwise engaged with) concrete human living, for the sake of which the data are gathered and intelligence is exercised, means to lose sight of some of the traditional commitments of philosophical activity, most notably the investigation of human experience and some of its fundamental features.

As I reflect on Giancarlo's "quick example," I instinctively sympathize with the idea that wisdom seems to be present in a peculiar yet very real sense in the interaction between Catherine and Danny. But I also ask myself: Is there something that distinguishes the life of someone living with philosophy from the particular manifestation of wisdom at work in that interaction? If there is, what is it? And as I think about prof. Peperzak's reflection on the essential "facts" of human life, in a similar way I wonder what a philosophical reflection on these facts has to offer, if anything, to a life which might be called good. What is the proper work of the philosopher?

I ask these questions because I cannot tell that I find living with philosophy to be something free of struggle. By this I do not mean to say that to live with philosophy requires effort because there are aspects of it which I find particularly unappealing—for example, the difficulty of finding a secure job in the field and the need to "market" oneself in it, long-drawn department meetings, and so on. All these aspects are not very pleasant, but they are not completely unbearable either. In fact, I rather enjoy what I do, but the enjoyment I take in the study of philosophy is often disrupted by a dim awareness that to study philosophy and to live with philosophy may occasionally overlap, but are not quite the same thing. Moreover, I ask those questions, not as one who already possesses a satisfactory answer, but because I sense that my experience of living with philosophy has been that of someone trying to steer his little boat between two equally threatening dangers: that of giving unqualified priority to methodological concerns and academic rigorousness, and that of flirting with the rather popular view according to which philosophy is at best a fine game, less optimistically a superfluous activity, and at worst an excuse to avoid contributing to the betterment of society. (Far from dispelling the uneasiness associated with these twin dangers, the fact that I greatly enjoy studying philosophy often conceals their menacing character, thus making them all the more dangerous.)

I already mentioned that I do not have an adequate answer to the question about the peculiar work of the philosopher, or about the meaning of philosophy; but I do have my preferences, and these usually direct me to one answer (or set of answers) rather than to another. For example, when I consider what should count as wisdom, I prefer a view of philosophy that leaves room for the possibility of finding traces of wisdom in situations like that described by Giancarlo to one that does not. And as I wonder about the relation of philosophy and experience, I prefer to think that to reflect on my personal experience is part of my involvement, or living, with philosophy, not only because lived experience can and has been an object of philosophical inquiry, but, perhaps more importantly, also because my experience can tell me something about what I take philosophy to be and at the same time help me to explain and purify some of my preferences. Or again, when some students and even colleagues from other departments tell me that they cannot take the study of philosophy seriously because philosophical conclusions lack the certainty they are accustomed to reaching in their disciplines (or, as the mantra goes, "because it's just opinions"), I prefer to think that although the presence of certainty may be a sign of wisdom, wisdom (or at least the love of it) is not obliterated by the absence of certainty.

It does not follow from this that my preferences are immutable. Instead, I ask myself how they have come to be my preferences and why they are still changing. I notice that they have been influencing my choices both generally and as regards my living with philosophy, and I cannot help wondering what I have done as a student of philosophy to strengthen and harmonize them (if I found them reasonable), to modify them (if I found them somewhat questionable), or to get rid of them altogether (if I found them unreasonable).

I too wonder whether philosophy can throw some light on the most important questions if it is practiced as some sort of autarchic project or, worse perhaps, as a problem solving technique. Because of this lack of certainty and given the difficulty of our theme, I thought it fit to join the conversation leading up to our April symposium by recognizing the main difficulties I have encountered in my living with philosophy and by briefly touching on a few of the preferences that characterize my understanding of philosophy, along with some of the questions that come to mind as I reflect on those preferences. Prof. Peperzak and Giancarlo prompted this response as they shared some reflections on their life with philosophy. I hope that other responses may also help me to see through some of the difficulties and to make my questions sharper.

Post-Symposium ReflectionChicago, May 2, 2016

"...you are all such beautiful people, every one of you. I love you." It seems fitting that someone who was initiated into a life with philosophy by treading the path to the mysteries of love laid out by Diotima—our teacher, Adriaan T. Peperzak—should end his address to his students with these words.

Whatever else they may be as individuals, ideally students represent a teacher's greatest achievement, his true work of love, for they are generated and nurtured in that same love of beauty and goodness which inspired him. At the same time, they are the expression of the desire for immortality that seems to be essential to all love, for it is through his students that the teacher—a mortal being—tries to perpetuate the beauty and goodness which he was able to appropriate in his work and life with philosophy—the story of his love-of-wisdom.

In this context, I do not take the work of teaching to mean a transfusion of wisdom from one mind or soul into another in the way water is transferred from a full jar to an empty one through a wool thread. With Socrates, one can only wish it were that easy. Instead, here wisdom is the proper name of the beloved, the ever transcending aim of one's love-of-wisdom which constantly challenges this love to improve or purify itself (and which perhaps, precisely for this reason, is not the aim of an intention in any strict sense of the word). And teaching, over and above the acquisition and clarification of necessary information, is a fundamental expression of that love: an attitude, an inspiring testimony, and an invitation to transform oneself in order to become better capable of relating to the beloved in a corresponding manner, or to sharpen the eye of one's soul by becoming accustomed to seeing in a brighter light. For this reason, a life with philosophy contains the realization that one's love-of-wisdom is not immediately attuned to the nature of the beloved, and that if we are to approach the beloved or to be led to it by someone else correctly, we must be willing to refine our love and concede that hardly any declaration of love will do it justice. Thus, it would seem appropriate to look back to the manifestations of our love—that to which we have given birth in beauty—as genuine but not fully successful attempts to live up to the beauty of the beloved.

And if one detected a note of irony in those words ("...you are all such beautiful people...") or in the teary smile which accompanied them on the occasion they were uttered, as well as in the words of approval, encouragement, or criticism that prof. Peperzak regularly offered when he worked as our teacher and dissertation director, I take it that this too was part of that same love. For here irony is not mockery or a sign of superiority; it is rather a reminder that to give birth *in* beauty is not unqualifiedly to give birth *to* beauty: what is generated and nurtured in beauty always seems to point to the possibility of a greater beauty, so that beauty, or goodness, remains as something to be pursued and approximated by means of new births.

Looking back at the years I spent as a student at Loyola, I think I can say that what here I tried, and likely failed, to capture through words was the kind of teaching and approach to philosophy that I experienced from prof. Peperzak. And as I listened to the voices of the ones who took part in the symposium, *Living with Philosophy*, which was held in his honor early in April 2016, they seemed to reveal in their own particular ways the same love that contributed to inspire them. I believe that our little gathering was one more expression of the work of love of our teacher, as well as an occasion that allowed those of us who benefited and were nurtured by that work to come together to thank him for it and to share with him and with each other what we have become in part also because of that love.

6. What Living with Philosophy Means to Me

§

Dr. Jeffrey M. Courtright

Ever since I declared philosophy as my major in college, I always knew the answer to the question "Why are you studying philosophy?" "Because I enjoy it," I would reply. In the past, I would usually add further justification, "I want to do something that excites me, about which I feel passion; something that I can be satisfied practicing for the rest of my life." And until recently, I have stood by this answer. It speaks to my passion and it (sometimes) silenced the naysayers. I am not so sure that I feel the same way now. Upon entering the dreaded job market a few years ago, I came to realize how professionalized the discipline of philosophy had become, how hyper-specialized and narrow the field was (both analytic and continental), and how dreadfully alienating the process of procuring and holding a position as a professor of philosophy could be.

Don't get me wrong. I am grateful for my job and for my chosen field. Little else compares to the achievement of collaborative insight, when thought, speech, and practical interest click together during a rich and stimulating philosophical conversation. The satisfaction and affective affinity between interlocutors when each is pushing the other to new depths of insight is incredibly powerful and important. Additionally, I cherish the enthusiasm and motivation that I feel when I am teaching a philosophical concept, point, or reasoning process to students and I suddenly become aware that the students have been gripped by it, enraptured and enthralled, sensing the relevance and personal import of philosophical ideas for themselves.

Most days, these experiences are enough to convince me that I am at work in the profession that is 'right' and most satisfying for me. Inevitably, however, dark days come, when news of death, destruction, wholly unwarranted violence, wanton cruelty, and degrading suffering, fill the news and occupy my mind and heart. At these times, I feel defeated and useless, confronted by the stark contradiction between my life and the lives of so many others. Does philosophy have anything to say or do in the face of these evils, this depth of suffering? At the end of the day, am I merely spending exorbitant amounts of time reading, studying, and teaching what philosophers have had to say, writing pieces that no members of the public see or read, and engaging in self-gratifying debates about rationally defensible solutions to abstract moral problems with no real intent to translate ideas into concrete practice?

If philosophy is *merely* an exercise in rigorous problem solving, where problems are abstracted from the context of human lives as they are lived, and meaning is limited to what can be confined to logical terms (as with logical positivism and the many variants thereof), then I don't think that philosophy is of much use or "matters" in any real sense. If doing philosophy is *primarily* practiced as a matter of getting Kant or some other thinker 'right,' or a matter of demonstrating how philosopher X is more philosophically profound than philosopher Y, then philosophy doesn't matter in the relevant sense either. On the other hand, if philosophy involves using rigorous modes of questioning and rational methods of inquiry in order to investigate the meaning and significance of contemporary events and perennial issues in a tough and penetrating way, then philosophy *can* be of enormous use and importance to human life. Even better: Philosophy can become an important part of daily practice so that one becomes ever more *thoughtful* about oneself and one's world at the same time that one is better able to take deliberate and justified action against injustice. The figure of Socrates looms large over this understanding of philosophical practice, of course, but I have also found resources and inspiration in the work of Plato and Aristotle, Averroës and Aquinas, Marx and Nietzsche, and in more contemporary times, Simone de Beauvoir, Emmanuel Levinas, and Angela Y. Davis.

Just as these thinkers testified in both words and deed, I am convinced of the necessity of philosophy for *living well* or at least for creating the conditions under which a broader community can flourish.[149]

If someone asks, *What is involved in living with philosophy?* My simplest response is this: Living with philosophy involves *careful thinking* about and *thoughtful care* for what we are doing, what we ought to do, for everyday and exceptional phenomena, and for matters of existential concern.[150] *Careful thought* is thinking that is characterized by the virtues of argumentative rigor, consistency among ideas and beliefs, intellectual clarity and humility, conceptual and descriptive faithfulness to the phenomenon at hand, reflective depth, doxastic awareness, and sound reasoning. *Thoughtful care*, on the other hand, emphasizes the more practical virtues of ethical sensitivity and receptivity, measured discourse, appropriate expression (tone of speech), ethical responsibility and concern, other-directed care, moral awareness, critical consciousness, and mindful practice. Additionally, thoughtful care can also involve certain *affective* traits: what is called 'fellow-feeling', feeling appropriate pain at the suffering of others, feeling pleasure in the flourishing of others, feeling pain or disgust at one's own moral failings, feeling pleasure at the moral good.[151]

Now I understand that this understanding of 'living with philosophy' in the modes of careful thought and thoughtful care is either too narrow or too broad for many philosophers, professional or otherwise. I do not intend to defend it as a comprehensive and complete definition of philosophy as such nor do I think that it is an accurate description of what 'philosophers' actually do in practice. I am well aware that many professional philosophers neither fit my description nor see it as a necessary part of living philosophically. However, I am convinced that something like this

---

[149] Of course, by "living well" I mean more than 'comfortably.' It is not at all evident how one can and should live 'comfortably' in the sense of material wealth and pleasure if that wealth and pleasure is oblivious to the fact of the suffering of others and to the way in which one's comfortable life might be contributing to that suffering.

[150] To clarify. I do think that living with philosophy involves the investigation of the domains of metaphysics, ontology, epistemology, aesthetics, nature, and religion. However, I feel that these areas are part of *careful thinking* about "everyday and exceptional phenomena" and "matters of existential concern".

[151] I am particularly influenced here by my reading of Adriaan Peperzak's *Elements of Ethics* (Stanford: Stanford University Press, 2004).

is an important and necessary part of the philosophical way of life, that it is always important for philosophers to model Hannah Arendt's injunction to always "think what we are doing," and that this conception of the life spent in philosophy has historical precedent in the lives and work of thinkers going all of the way back to Socrates and Confucius. In my mind, just such a conception of philosophical life is taught and embodied by our teacher and mentor Adriaan Peperzak, who remains a model for me not only of how to live that 'life worth living' promised two and a half millennia ago in Athens, but also that "tradition at least as ancient, that does not read right as might and does not reduce every other to the Same,"[152] a tradition that is centered on the virtue of thoughtful care for the neighbor and the stranger.

Post- Symposium Reflection

The April symposium in honor of Adriaan Peperzak was satisfying and invigorating in so many ways that I cannot describe here. It was exhausting, certainly, but also incredibly productive and stimulating. Our daily gatherings were characterized by genuine warmth, friendship, and camaraderie—and it was these features that enabled us to "find a way" through difficult philosophical questions, to be sure, but also to celebrate the person and influence of our beloved teacher and friend. Though the explicit theme of the symposium was "Living with Philosophy," it was also very much a tribute to the formative influence of Adriaan Peperzak on our conception of how best to live with philosophy. Adriaan selected the texts that we read (and re-read) for the symposium—selections from Plato's *Politeia* and *Symposium*—and one of the questions that these readings raise and respond to is: Does the practice of philosophy and its way of raising and addressing core philosophical concerns, *necessarily involve a substantial commitment to the Good*? That is, if I am practicing philosophy properly, if I am "living with philosophy," must my life be oriented toward and committed to the Good in any substantial way?

---

152 Levinas, 'Philosophy and the Idea of the Infinite'. In Adriaan Peperzak, *To the Other: An Introduction to the Philosophy of Emmanuel Levinas* (Lafayette (IN): Purdue University Press, 1993): pp. 105-106.

The contemporary state of our profession, and the expectations and activities involved in the achievement and maintenance of a 'successful' academic career, would seem to indicate that one most certainly does *not* have an orientation toward the good merely by virtue of being a philosopher. Instead, one's standards of goodness are to conform to the standards of professional competence and facility in teaching, university service, and research. There is nothing wrong with professional standards and being technically competent in the methods and influential works that define a specialized domain of discourse. However, if that is an end in itself, severed from its subservience to loftier, higher aims of the Good, the True, and the Beautiful, then perhaps we are no longer practicing philosophy in any way recognizable to many of the great philosophers of the past, or to the great and radical thinkers of our times.

Of course, just because several "great" philosophers might have understood the philosophical life in this way, it does not mean that such a view is justified or 'realistic'. I find such a view tempting, however. Certainly, under the guidance, mentorship, and teaching of Adriaan during my graduate school career, I was convinced that, indeed, just as Plato so beautifully expressed in his *Symposium* and *Politeia*, philosophy and the life of philosophy was by nature directed to the Good and the Beautiful. I felt that the love that drives the pursuit of wisdom is a love that desires the Good and that perhaps might even seek understanding in service to ethical responsibility (as Levinas insists). After I finished my coursework, moved from Chicago, worked as an adjunct, and entered the "job market," I began to lose this sense of the direction of the philosophical life that Peperzak so clearly and lovingly expresses in his teaching and work. I can attest, however, that our conversation over the course of the symposium restored this sense of an orientation toward the good in philosophy. In the work and pleasure of our fellowship and discourse together, guided by the words and presence of Adriaan, I felt that the good at stake in all genuine philosophical thinking and practice was raised and given robust shape. The graciousness of all the participants and of Adriaan himself was a testament to the sense of goodness in philosophical discourse, the beauty in friendship, and the truth in the philosophical way of life. I am not sure that this sense will endure and persist for me as I live with philosophy in the future, but I can hope. Certainly, the words and deeds of Adriaan Peperzak bear witness to the possibility that such a sense can find concrete expression in the life of a philosopher. Thank you, Adriaan.

7. Philosophy as the Practice of Dying: Philosophy, Miscarriage and Inner Life and Death

§

Marjolein Oele

Philosophy, Plato teaches us in the *Phaedo*, is the practice of dying. This has always struck me as a powerful insight that rightfully dethrones with a temporal weight exceeding more than 2000 years pretentious claims that existentialism is the owner and proprietor of dark claims viewing life in the light of suffering and death. Since Plato defines death as the separation of soul from body, the philosophical practice of dying should accordingly aim for separating the soul *as much as possible* from the body, and to make ourselves aim for that which *really* matters – living the life of *kalokagathon* and not let ourselves be swept away by appearances, materialistic desires or bodily ailments.

What would it mean to translate Plato's insights to our current 21st century? And how do Plato's insights relate to the question that Dr. Peperzak has asked us to contemplate: "But life has to deal effectively with disasters, to begin (or end) with death. Does philosophical wisdom then also include a (limited?) wisdom about death?" (# 8, p.4 *Letter* AP).

The wisdom about death that Peperzak asks us to contemplate continues upon Plato's themes in that it wonders whether philosophy can say anything worthwhile about limit experiences that none of us – alive – can ever truly say anything about with certainty. However, such uncertainty has and never will stop philosophy since such uncertainties never radically oppose philosophical practices. In fact, such uncertainties may in fact *stimulate* its practice and propel it forward. For Plato, the uncertainty regarding death surely invites a daring thesis in conjunction with the idea

237

that philosophy itself needs to be defined in regard to this thesis about death. And that thesis itself became part of what me might call the meaning of the Socratic life, namely that the *philosophical life is worth dying for* as it stands up for its ideals. As Peperzak made us see in his phenomenal class on Plato's *Republic*, nothing else than the rise and death of the philosopher in Plato's society stands at the apex of the geometrical triangle that is the composition of Plato's *Republic*.

Is philosophy today wise about disaster and death, and if so, how? Here perhaps Heidegger and Levinas have sharpened our ideas, particularly in pondering *whose* death we are talking about, and contemplating different meanings of death, namely death as the abyss of meaninglessness or death as part of a trajectory of illness and suffering where sometimes the only thing we can do is to bear witness. While I find that Levinas' rebuttal of Heidegger's claim is ultimately convincing in focusing on the death of the other, I also want to push his philosophical focus regarding the death of the other a bit further to contemplate what philosophy might have to say about those extraordinary and painful experiences where the *death of the other happens within me*. Here it is the concrete experience of early miscarriage that I seek to explore, as it is one of those deaths that circles back quickly from the beginning to the end of life and remains astoundingly hidden – both in the phenomenological literature as in life itself. Thus I ask: can philosophy be wise about suffering such an inner death, and if so, how? And can a philosopher who has experienced this inner death directly – I myself as a woman and so many other women like me – become wise with and through it? If philosophy is born out of and responds to our experience, should it not also be able to speak to this phenomenon where both life and death are so intimately connected?

To find words for the experience of miscarriage is difficult. From the beginning, one is at a loss: in a miscarriage, *who* or *what* is one emptied of? Especially in my experience of early miscarriage, the term "who" seems to be too substantial to speak to the amorphous life that is growing within oneself and that is barely a few months old. The same applies to the term "what": does one lose a dream or a reality, a possibility or an actuality, a being whose coming-into-life stopped too early to be yet named and gendered? Also, how to put into words the loss of being pregnant and emerging motherhood that accompanies the loss of such an amorphous being? Finally, the name for the experience itself needs scrutiny, as the term "miscarriage" does disservice in seeing the loss of pregnancy as merely the failing of a logistical, instrumental process such as "carrying" and "transportation," without addressing the holistic and transformative nature of the process of pregnancy and its loss.

If philosophy is to describe miscarriage then, it has to start with an analysis of terms, and rethink its vocabulary. In addition, philosophy would do well to investigate the material circumstances that ground the experience of pregnancy and its loss. *New materialism* – a term connected to the philosophies of Manuel DeLanda and Jane Bennitt for instance – is one of the strains of philosophy that articulates the *immanent unfolding of form and meaning in and through matter*. Accordingly, this kind of philosophy would be well suited to delve into the scientific biomedical literature and address how meaning and form emerge in the complex process that is pregnancy: embryogenesis, maternal physiology and immunology and chorionic/placental development.

By zooming in on the *process* of pregnancy rather than on the agents or "who's" involved (embryo, mother, placenta) we are afforded the possibility to see how not one of the factors involved owns the process but that every aspect participates in a bigger process along which all factors emerge to become what and who they are. Thus, an inquiry into pregnancy and its loss could offer a strong rebuttal of the idea that life is born out of or lived in autarchy. Instead, it would show that every life is fundamentally hosted and enabled by others. In this research, the "face-to-face" perspective promoted by Levinas and Peperzak (# 9, p. 4 *Letter* AP) would thus acquire another, materialistic grounding by investigating the "body-to-body" dimension. Ultimately, such an examination would afford more nuanced tools to grasp the depth and significance of the process of pregnancy and by highlighting its intersecting factors would be better suited to address its devastating loss.

Thus, circling back to Plato's idea of philosophy as practice of dying, my suggestion is that in our own times "living with philosophy" should entail thinking about *concrete experiences of dying in conjunction with experiences of birth*. By following the immanent emergence – and disappearance – of forms and meaning out of this embodied materiality we can come to (re)define what it means to be born, live and die face-to-face. Or perhaps better: it would allow us to (re)define what it means to come-into-being together, co-affected, co-constituted, co-birthed and co-deathed together.

Appendix

The essay I wrote in response to AP's letter focused more than the other contributions on a particular question, namely: "Does philosophical wisdom then also include a (limited?) wisdom about death?" By offering an initial exploration of this question from the perspective of pregnancy and miscarriage, I also sought to answer – albeit implicitly – the overarching question, namely what it means to "live with philosophy." For me, living with philosophy *is personal and embodied,* and for that reason I entrust to philosophy the possibility to carve out an intellectual space for discussing phenomena that deeply shake my existence. Doing so might not necessarily directly relieve suffering but might at least *indirectly* assist by bearing witness and granting more nuanced conceptual tools to grasp the depth and illusiveness of the suffering felt.

Our meeting in Chicago brought me again in direct contact with the "roots" for my current thinking: the person and philosopher Ad Peperzak whose philosophical trust in me has allowed me to become the person and philosopher who I am. The meeting's untraditional format, devoid of static paper presentations and instead dynamically and horizontally centered around themes and texts to which we all contributed, echoed the rhizomatic nature of what may be called the "Peperzak-school-of-philosophy": a philosophy that shuns theoretical, hierarchical and personal "ownership" of philosophy and that deeply cares for the ethical *process* of philosophy as it is lived. His (and now ours) is a participatory form of philosophy that has no beginning nor end, but – much like Diotima's characterization of philosophy as a *daimon*, as in-between – always operates from "the middle", from a certain *milieu*, from which it grows, questions, and inspires.

I feel deeply indebted to these roots that have sustained and inspired me. And participating in the Colloquium allowed me to witness once again all the different directions that such a Peperzakian rhizomatic *milieu* has allowed for. The webbed existence of which we are part evokes nothing but awe, and offers further encouragement to practice the "testimonial attitude" that Gabriel Marcel speaks of so persuasively. My philosophical existence is a gift, made possible to a large extent by Ad Peperzak. If the ultimate gift is a self-gift, then the task remains to pass this gift ever forwards.

In gratitude and love.

8. A Philosophy that Stays with Life?

§

Norman Wirzba

As I have thought about philosophy as a *theoria*, or as a way of seeing reality, I have more and more come to reflect on the *ethos* and *ascesis* that either opens or closes one's point of view. My point is not simply that one's location shapes what one sees (a gardener, for instance, looks at life rather differently than a person who has only ever purchased food in a store), but that the modes of engagement and forms of work we do make possible sensitivities and sensibilities that are crucial for what we take to be the truth of experience (a gardener's experience of impotence in the face of germination and disease, or the humble sense that arises in contexts of serendipity and gratitude for delectable gifts, give to life a different "feel" and resonance).

Some of what I am talking about has been well captured by philosophers like Pierre Hadot, who alert us to the work of philosophy as a spiritual exercise that requires its practitioners to undergo disciplines that train affections as much as they train the mind. Christian thinkers like the Cappadocians and Maximus the Confessor continued this way of thinking by noting that a genuine *theoria* presupposed the purification of the passions that distort our seeing and our engagement with others. Without proper forms of love—love that is learned in the practices of healing, sharing, feeding, companionship, etc.—true insight into the world is impossible because what one sees is determined by what one "wants" and "desires" to see.

I have come to see that the very idea of a *theoria* is laden with difficulties, primarily its temptation to establish *distance* between persons and others. What I mean by this distance or separation is that we remove ourselves from life so as to get a better look at it. Then, to speak and understand what we have seen we then establish abstract forms that fix the meanings of the things seen. Aristotle's doctrine of substance is a perfect example of this. What a thing "is" depends upon it not being confused with something else. Metaphysical work of this sort has the effect of isolating things from another, taking them out of the flow and entanglement that are what I consider to be the hallmarks of a living world. Put differently, philosophical reflection constantly runs the risk of ceasing to be *with* the world it is trying to understand.

If life *is* movement, and if life is its *entanglements* with others in the forms of natality, eating, warmth, breathing, etc., then the effort to theorize from a position of separation is already in some sense a distortion of life. I suspect that part of our difficulty is that we have come to privilege sight and hearing (both senses that entail separation) in the work of philosophizing, without appreciating how touch and taste are the more fundamental senses. These senses make no sense apart from intimacy and interpenetration with others. They presuppose a world in which relationality and dynamic movement are the core and the periphery and everything in between. And they presuppose philosophers who are constantly and necessarily *involved* with others.

I think some of the early Christians, when they began to develop a distinctly Christian metaphysic, understood that discipleship under the inspiration and power of the Holy Spirit entailed their entrance into a corporate life that is always *with* others. To be a person is not to be a self-standing individual but to be one who is constantly facing another and thus always already responsible for their well-being. This is what it means to be a member of the living, moving body called the church. The truth of life can only be understood from out of this communal context or mutual sharing, suffering, and celebrating. Being *as substance* was thus replaced with being *as communion*.

I end with a question: is the good "beyond" being because the language of "being" is too easily divorced from the dynamism and multiple entanglements of life? In other words, is our temptation to succumb to a *theoria* that settles for an abstraction about life (and thereby a suffocating of its movements), and thus a forfeiture of the love or *eros* that leads us more deeply and complexly into the suffering and beauty of life and this world? My claim is that a philosopher committed to staying *with* others and *with* the world will need first to develop the disciplines of love that enable an appropriate sympathy for and embrace of others. It will require a philosophy that is always the exercise in hospitality. No doubt this will require that the forms of philosophizing will need to change. Narrative and drama will become more important because they are forms that better equip us to give expression to our entanglements and movements along with others. And fidelity and trustworthiness will become the essential openings to truth.

9. Living with Philosophy, in Honor of Adriaan Peperzak

§

Justin Nordin

The phrase *living with philosophy* at once brings to mind two essentially related but potentially conflicting aspects of philosophy. First, I believe that all of us in are some way always-already living with philosophy so far as philosophy arises out of important concerns and issues that occur in everyday life. In this sense, the unexamined life is not worth living because to live a human life already demands of us that we critically reflect on the basic values we hold dear and the fundamental commitments that orient our life. We are most truly ourselves, then, when we bring these values and commitments out in the open through philosophical reflection, rather than following to them naively.

It is here, however, that we run into the second sense of *living with*, one that seems to be at odds with the first. Philosophical reflection also indicates a type of radical break with our everyday life. Life, it would seem, does not need philosophical reflection to the extent that philosophical reflection is not necessary for its continuation. For example, a person does not need to engage in philosophical reflection to build a house, perform scientific experiments, run a business, become president, etc. While certain concepts and questions will remain unclear without philosophical reflection, this does not prevent life from continuing on. In this way, philosophy seems to entail a wrenching away of oneself from the world he or she lives in, whereby one can no longer continue on as one had prior to philosophy. Here philosophy takes the form of a burden. One cannot simply engage naively with the world as one used to and as one, perhaps at times, would still like to.

Emmanuel Levinas has, in my opinion, showed that the self who engages in philosophy is already responding to an ethical summons. To engage in philosophical reflection is to enter into discourse with others in the pursuit of truth, which entails that I have *always-already* been called beyond my own limited and self-interested viewpoint by the other to whom I respond. Philosophy thus requires us to welcome the other across the abyss that separates us through language. To speak is precisely to put the world (always experienced from my point of view) in common.

While I gravitate toward Levinas because he traces our "interest" in philosophy back to our concrete, everyday encounters with other people and our sense of being responsible for them, this simply reframes the original tension between *philosophy as something as intrinsic to life* and *philosophy as something at odds with life*. This is because Levinas only shows us how discourse itself is founded on a moral summons directed to me from the other. He does not tell us how to fulfill our responsibilities. At any given time all of us have several, potentially competing responsibilities. For example, my responsibility for my children differs from my responsibility for my wife, and these responsibilities differ from my responsibility for my immediate neighbors, fellow citizens, foreigners, immigrants, refugees, animals, etc. While Levinas shows how all human communities are founded on the demand for hospitality expressed in the face of every other, in reality we must make difficult choices and decide how to best spend our limited time, often at the expense of others for whom I am responsible but unfortunately cannot help. It seems, then, that the priority that Levinas gives to ethics does not serve to solve any of the problems that led to philosophical reflection in the first place—it was not Levinas's intention to do so—but merely reframes them so that we can now understand how they are grounded in our original sense of ethical responsibility. Is philosophy, then, ultimately the last chapter in a great tragedy? If not, from where do we derive hope? Socrates argues that the philosopher has good hope because he has tried to live as good of a life as possible, which he argues entails philosophical reflection. In order for one to live with philosophy, then, one must have faith in the vision of the good/philosophical life that

Socrates seduces us with. That is, one must have faith in the good itself, even if the good remains beyond our reach. Socrates was an optimist, and at times I am seduced by his optimism. However, philosophy also appears to require a degree of pessimism, if only to create a healthy modicum of modesty to combat its hubris. Perhaps it is at this point that philosophy gives way to faith, a faith grounded in a philosophical understanding of its possibility.

Appendix

It was truly a joy to take part in the symposium organized in honor of the retirement of Adriaan Peperzak. I am amazed at how knowledgeable all of Adriaan's former students are and how truly wonderful they are as people. While I had not met most of the participants before the symposium, by its end I felt as if I had known them for years. This is not to say that there were no heated discussions or disagreements among participants. We came to discuss philosophy after all! But even in the midst of intense debate there remained an air of hospitality fitting to the theme of the colloquium and of the man we all came to honor. It became clear to me that it was no accident that all these individuals gravitated toward Adriaan. He is one of those unique philosophers whose philosophy extends far beyond the classroom, conferences, books, or journals, and into every aspect of his life. In a way, to know Adriaan is to already know his philosophy, even if one has never had the pleasure of hearing him lecture on Plato, Plotinus, Bonaventure, Hegel, Levinas, or others. The love and respect directed toward Adriaan from his current and former students gave birth to wonderful and engaging philosophical discussion. While we may have raised more questions than we answered, I can honestly say that the sincere passion for philosophy and love for one another exhibited by each participant reaffirmed my faith in and hope for philosophy despite the reasons I suggested above for doubting it.

10. 'LIVING WITH PHILOSOPHY' AND THE PRACTICE OF TEACHING

§

Rebecca Scott

As I continue to grow in my thinking about the question of what it means to 'live with philosophy,' I have come to be convinced that teaching and learning lie at the heart of what it means to 'live well.' As Levinas teaches us, to be a subject is to be fundamentally in relation to the Other who is my Master, my teacher. As Dr. Peperzak writes, after the "frightening shock of birth," we "learn how to focus and distinguish useful from harmful, good from bad, and desirable from undesirable things and persons" (3). This process by which I am given a meaningful world is one that relies fundamentally on the others who not only "saved [me] from immediate death" (3) but also gave me and continue to give me the gift of meaning. To be a human being who has achieved what Levinas calls 'separation,' the ability to reflect theoretically on the world, thus depends, fundamentally on my being *taught* by the Other.

In our contemporary setting, to 'live with philosophy' or to live a life in which one is recognized as a 'philosopher' by the institutions and discourses that make up 'professional' philosophy, is also, almost always, to be a teacher of others. The fundamental connection between teaching and philosophy has a rich history, going back to Plato whose dialogues are often if not always concerned with teaching and learning. Unfortunately, however, it seems to me that the fundamental relationship between teaching and philosophy is often forgotten or overlooked in our contemporary context. Teaching is so often seen as drudgery that one *must* do in order to do the research that one *wants* to do. And yet, for me, it is in the classroom that 'doing' philosophy or 'living with philosophy' achieves its most meaningful manifestations.

In the speech of Diotima in the *Symposium* to which Dr. Peperzak referred us, we find that our deepest Desire as human beings is to catch a glimpse of the Beautiful (or the Good) itself. But it is what happens *after* we have caught this glimpse that the real work of philosophy begins, or begins again. How do we procreate in Beauty once we have progressed through the stages of love? And what do we do when we descend back down into the cave after having caught sight of the 'Good beyond Being'? To live well as a philosopher is not to remain in view of the truth but to share what we have learned with others.

As Giancarlo points to the practical wisdom that Catherine exhibits in her interaction with Danny, I would like to draw our attention to the hundreds of seemingly mundane decisions that we make each day in the classroom, decisions that for many of us will have a much greater impact in the world than anything that we have written or published. Levinas teaches us of our inevitable and unending responsibility to the Other and nowhere is this more apparent than in the classroom. My mother, who is an elementary education professor and to whom I owe my love and fascination with teaching, has the following quote from Haim Ginott framed on the wall of her office. It reads:

> I've come to a frightening conclusion that I am the decisive element in the classroom. It's my personal approach that creates the climate. It's my daily mood that makes the weather. As a teacher, I possess a tremendous power to make a child's life miserable or joyous. I can be a tool of torture or an instrument of inspiration. I can humiliate or heal. In all situations, it is my response that decides whether a crisis will be escalated or de-escalated and a child humanized or dehumanized.

While as philosophy teachers at colleges and universities, we do not teach children but young adults, our responsibility is no less enormous. As teachers we have to power to uplift or humiliate, encourage or discourage, humanize or dehumanize our students every day.

Derrida, in his essay "A Word of Welcome" in *Adieu to Emmanuel*

Levinas reflects on the theme of teaching in Levinas's work and invites us to read *Totality and Infinity* as "an immense treatise *of hospitality*."[153] The work is a treatise *of* hospitality and not only a treatise *on* hospitality because the work teaches us *about* hospitality by inviting us to hospitably receive its own teaching. To receive the teaching of Levinas's text is to act in the world and to extend the hospitality that we have been offered to others.

In the practice of teaching philosophy, therefore, Levinas's work calls on us to teach in a way that is hospitable to our students. To elaborate on this idea, we might say that the 'home' or 'dwelling' into which we welcome students can be understood as the ongoing conversations that make up the discourses of philosophy. And for Levinas, a conversation is a teaching conversation when it is a 'living breathing discourse,' quoting Plato's *Phaedrus*. That is, the conversation must be one in which the interlocutors are present to each other as unique concrete existents in a face-to-face encounter who, through their ability to offer an 'apology' can open up the plane of question and answer.

In order for the philosophical conversations that happen in our classrooms to become 'living breathing discourses,' we must, therefore, welcome students into the conversation as unique, concrete, irreplaceable existents. As the host who is welcoming students into the world of philosophy, I must, therefore, invite students to enter into the classroom whole--as corporeal, relational, affective beings with hopes, fears, skills, experiences, successes, failures, and so on. As the host, I have to figure out how to make a space within the dwelling of philosophy for each of them. I have to show how their particular concerns, interests, desires, and talents make them excellent and important contributors to the conversations that make up philosophy. It is impossible, of course, for me to satisfy the needs of all my students perfectly, but that is because teaching, like the work of ethics more generally, is structured by what Levinas names Desire. The ethical task is never completed. Rather, as we approach the object of our striving, it always recedes even further from us. Similarly, the practice of teaching is

---

[153] Derrida, Jacques. *Adieu to Emmanuel Levinas*. Stanford: Stanford University Press, 1999. 21.

an ongoing pursuit.

In his references to teaching, Levinas frequently rejects Socratic education, insofar as he sees in it the tendency of 'Western' thought to emphasize the self-sufficiency and autonomy of the subject. That is, he worries that the idea that we already have within us that which we learn obviates the role of the Other as teacher. I would like to end, however, by claiming that Socratic *maieutics* in fact presents us with a model of the teacher-student relationship that can help us to become more hospitable teachers in the way that I believe Levinas's philosophy demands of us.

While Levinas is right to emphasize the fact that to be a subject is to be vulnerable to being taught by the Other, it is also true in practice that our students do not come into our classrooms as blank slates or empty vessels. Rather, our students come into our classes having already been taught by their parents, friends, teachers, various forms of media, and so on. Successful teaching happens when we are able to connect students' pre-existing ways of understanding and relating to the world to the new ways of understanding that we are encouraging them to receive. Socrates, the midwife, is especially good at this practice. He knows who his students are and knows which remedies, which drugs and incantations, are needed to bring about a successful birth. He knows when to bring about and when to relieve pain. He is an expert in practical wisdom, which is precisely the kind of expertise we must develop if we are to be hospitable as we welcome our students into the dwelling of philosophy.

Because so much of my 'life with philosophy' is spent teaching others, for me, to 'live well' involves engaging in the unending task of attempting to meet my responsibilities to my students. In this way, I understand 'living with philosophy' to involve helping others to also 'live well' and to 'live with philosophy.' And as Levinas helps us to realize, my ability to give to others is dependent on my having been the recipient of the generosity of countless others, including my parents, my friends, and of course, my teachers.

11. Living with Philosophy

§

Kristi Sweet

Dear Friends,

The question of "Living with Philosophy" is one that has, of late, preoccupied my thoughts. It is instructive for me already that I pose it principally as a question; it is true that this is what it has become for me, and what I gather, for many of you, it is as well. The theme strikes our ears, it would seem, as one or more of the following questions, "how does one live philosophically?" "What is a philosophical life?" "What is the use or abuse of philosophy for life?" And these questions resonate with us across multiple aspects of our existence: as moral agents, as scholars, as teachers.

The question has taken shape for me more narrowly this way: does philosophy really help us live better lives, be better people? If so, how? I have been loath to announce this worry (a commitment to this idea was one reason I pursued this career—something many of you likely share), but my loneliness in this thought met reprieve when I read that so many of you have concerns that at least circulate in the ether of what has become a doubt for me. Philosophy has a long tradition of both describing a necessary turn that human beings must make toward the good and taking philosophical inquiry itself as one way this turn may be effected. My recent thoughts have become trained on what the nature of this turn is, and how it might be occasioned. Doubts have emerged about the philosophical character of this turn for me, in part, out of the failures I meet in my own person, and in part out of the failure of the discipline as a whole to elevate or distinguish itself professionally. More to the point, it has increasingly come to seem to me that philosophy may provide reflective or abstract flight from our lived experience and from the demands placed upon us by real, living others. It is easier to theorize what we must do, who we must be, and justify what we have done, than to embody the good in our person. Instead of a therapy or maieutic practice, the danger of philosophy is that it presents an escape.

The question of our turning is intimately bound up with the nature of the good. Plato's Euthyphro, for me, is one of the most important texts for teaching on this topic. I take the main thrust of the Euthyphro to be that the good is not self-evident. Euthyphro is chastised not for his particular beliefs, but because he seems not to have thought them through with the care and attention required for a matter with such high stakes. I think the dialogue works as a criticism of Euthyphro only because the matter of what the good may be in this situation is irresolute. The arguments about piety, then, seem not to be so much about piety itself, but about the fact that impetuous Euthyphro has not really devoted the proper care and attention to the matter; he does not seem even to acknowledge that deciding the good in this case is *hard*. In tandem with the Euthyphro, Kierkegaard's discourse on Abraham and Isaac in *Fear and Trembling* speaks with similar force to this same issue. Kierkegaard stands as a bookend to Socrates. Both texts take up characters for whom decisions about the life or death of their most beloved are not clear. What the good is, for both Euthyphro and Abraham, is beyond what can be known. How then, ought they each proceed?

These two texts motivate, I think, with real existential bite what it means that the good is beyond being. We cannot see it, and it does not admit of a knowing. But if this is so, two considerations remain outstanding: how does one comport oneself to that which is beyond what there is? And how might philosophy contribute to cultivating this comportment—either initially in a turn or in instruction? I can see the Socratic method as a proper philosophical way—through dialogue (which is, after all, what comes right before we are released to the good in the *Republic*) Socrates exposes that epistemic certainly about the good is not possible. With this, it is clear that the good is not a matter for *episteme*. And Kierkegaard offers faith; a leap beyond the unknown. These two examples, for me, highlight what we find often in the history of philosophy—shared recognition of something (in the case, that the good is in one way or another beyond being), yet with different approaches about how to deal with this. There is not one voice that speaks across the history of philosophy about what the good is and how we ought to live. Where, then, does this leave us? With whom do we side? And why? There seems, for instance, to be the potential for real danger. If we are wrong about this, it our lives that are at stake.

There is still another worry for me, here, beyond the question of what exactly our comportment toward the good must be and what philosophy's role might be in aiding us in this. This worry is of how the turn itself is effected, and whether or how philosophy may contribute. The late modern thinkers of the will share the insight that the good is beyond being, too: Kant, for whom the good is unconditioned, Fichte, for whom the absoluteness of the will must be posited by us as an act of faith. The primacy of the practical has its fullest iteration in these two philosophers, for whom the good is beyond being, albeit with relation to the modern subject. But does reading Kant's *Groundwork*, does reading Fichte's *Vocation of Man*, both of which are written to bring the reader through a train of thought and leading the reader to the good, actually turn one toward the good? *Can one read at all if one is not already turned*?

This further problem, I think, is the one that ran through our lovely meeting in Baltimore in honor of Adriaan. What struck me then, and more so now, is the concern for education and the risk—even necessity—of violence involved. Philosophers have long employed a discourse of violence to describe what relating to the good involves (Kant too—quite so). It is one thing to enact this violence against one's pathological self in one's own pursuit of being good. What does it look like to aid others in their pursuit? And if they are not yet pursuing it? What does this look like pedagogically?

Thus for me, the theme of "Living with Philosophy" contains mostly questions. I hope that in discussion with all of you, and listening to your thoughts on these questions, we can gain deeper insight on how philosophy might contribute to our pursuit of living well, and especially our pursuit of doing this with others.

12. LIVING-WITH (NOT WITHIN) PHILOSOPHY

§

Karl Clifton-Soderstrom

(I teach philosophy at North Park University. Located on the northside of Chicago. Part of the school's academic vision is to "Make all of Chicago our classroom." I also live 200 feet from the house of my birth.)

Living-with philosophy is multivalent. Let us consider three interpretations.

1. From Home to the World

Living, for us human beings anyway, is always a *living-with*. Life without a "living-with" is perhaps what it means to be a zombie, the living dead. Such a life would be reduced a mere biological functioning.

Living with implies a *cohabitation*. "*co*" meaning together, in combination. Habitation, from the Latin *habitation:* a dwelling. Habitation, of course, has connections to "habit" and its Latin roots*:* to remain, to stay, or even to hold and possess.

Living-with, as cohabitation transforms the empty and open landscapes of the world into habitats from which we dwell. Living-with establishes a sense of place. The desire to find-one's-place in the world is fundamental to human development and cultural creation.

Living-with thus enacts both the cultivation of habits and the building of habitats.

Furthermore, living-with as cohabitation necessitates dwelling together with *an other*. To live with another, one's beloved or friend, is often to be habituated together, to remain together, to find one's place in the world together. And yet, the phenomenon of living-with an other is not fully circumscribed by the movement of dwelling, remaining, or the familiarity of being at-home in the world. The other with whom I dwell draws me out of familiar domestic security. And so while to lack a sense of place is tragic and homelessness is a poverty, merely remaining in one's place is not life's *telos*. As Levinas notes, "The privileged role of the home does not consist in being the end of human activity, but in being its condition, and in this sense its commencement." (TI, 152) If life is a living-with, it is marked by a commencement outward. Something similar may be said of the habits we cultivate. We habituate ourselves so that we may *act from* those habits to effect change in the world.

If we do indeed live-with philosophy, it too entails habitation, habituation, and companionship.

Considering Levinas's claim about the home, we can ask whether to live-with philosophy is to make philosophy our home? Dwelling can be understood as an activity or a location. To live-*within* philosophy would then be to make philosophy the home. To live-with *philosophia*, however, is a practice that habitually leaves the home. Perhaps as professionals, we live *within* the world of philosophy and philosophers, but as persons we live *with philosophia*. Being-within is not the same as Being-with. The risk then for the professional philosopher, or the tenured professor as Kierkegaard would say, is to make philosophy the home to which one retreats from the world, rather than the companion with whom one lives out into the world.

2. From Wilderness to City

In the Old Testament, the author of Proverbs speaks poetically of Wisdom in chapter 8. Wisdom cries from "the highest point along the way, where the paths meet." Such a rich description! In this context, to live with philosophy is to travel along the way with wisdom, to go to where the many paths meet. To remain with (habituate oneself to) philosophy is not to take up residence in a static place, but to walk along the way of wisdom.

The author of Proverbs specifies further. Wisdom resides by the gate, along the path, at the threshold into the city. She has "many doors" and resides where "many paths meet." It is significant to note that wisdom is not the city, nor in the city, but is prior to the place of the city. Wisdom cries out from this liminal space. The author notes that wisdom speaks *understanding* across the threshold. She cries out to the foolish, to those who have lost their way. For to be lost outside the city is to live without place or path. Wisdom speaks across (dia-logos) this emptiness, this open plane without place or path, where the foolish remain.

Plato, in his *Republic*, too speaks of cities and questions the place of philosophy in them. "Is there a place for philosophy in the city?" Is the city where philosophy is found, or is the city what results from practicing philosophy?

When Socrates creates his cities in speech, his first city has no place for philosophy for *eros* is not yet present. It is notable that this first city as self-sufficient, is the cosmos for its simple citizens. It is the only place, and as such is no place. Glaucon's feverish city's *pleonexia* acknowledges that other places are possible, and through its travels wants to bring all goods back into the one city and satisfy all its desires. This sick city too wants to remain the cosmos, by being the center of all places.

In the drama of the *Republic* itself, Socrates and his friends model another kind of polis: one which enacts a shared love of wisdom. Now the paths upon which wisdom dwells are the lines of philosophical conversations around the hearth. Here, it would seem, we have a true living-with philosophy that cultivates the habituation, habitation, and companionship we seek.

It is notable that the dialogue takes place on the far edges of Athens, at the liminal space that is the *Pireaus*. The ports of the Pireaus are indeed the places where nautical paths meet, outside the city, along the way into the city. In both Proverbs and Plato, wisdom cries out from the threshold into the city. Both Proverb's Wisdom and Plato's Socrates warn of living within the city, of habituating oneself to the city and its *pleonexia*, of the city's own hostility toward philosophy. Wisdom cries from the gates into the city! Socrates speaks from the ports! The warning seems the same: If the

257

love of wisdom is not at the threshold *into* the city, it will never arise from within the city itself.

To live-with philosophy is to dwell first in the liminal spaces, at the thresholds and gates or ports into the city. This is where philosophy pitches its tents, builds its hearth, and gathers its friends. To live with philosophy is not to become habituated to a place, but to a path.

3. *From Suffering to Justice*

"When a life is compared to a path, the metaphor simply expresses the universal, that which everyone who is alive has in common by being alive; to that extent they are all walking along the path of life and are all walking along the same path. But when living becomes an earnest matter, then the question becomes: How shall one walk in order to walk the right path on the path of life? ... Worldly wisdom is very willing to deceive again and again answering the question, "Where is the path?" while the difficulty is omitted, that spiritually understand the path is: *how it is walked* ... The path is, how it is walked ... the walking is done in hardship. For that it is not the path that is hard, but that hardship is the path." – *Kierkegaard*, The Gospel of Sufferings

To live with philosophy is to *walk* a path – out of the cave, out of the wilderness between Egypt and Canaan, and into the city. The philosopher does not find wisdom in the city, but walks with wisdom into the city. Thus if the path of wisdom is not begun in the wilderness, nor on the ascent out of the cave, the philosopher will not find wisdom in the city. The philosopher is prepared by walking. And to walk the path of wisdom is difficult.

Socrates seeks to know justice, so that justice may reign in the city. But the paths the dialogues take in the *Republic* are winding. By the middle of the Republic, Socrates wonders whether he has founded the right city in speech. Despite the many paths already taken with his companions, he knows that there still remains a "more difficult path" that must be walked to find true wisdom and the good city. Plato knows that a justice that endures is not found in the bureaucracies of the perfect city, but the perpetual movement in and out of the cave, in the conversations among friends, and in the restless souls seeking truth together. The author of Proverbs too notes that wisdom walks "along the paths of justice."

> *to live with philosophy is to live as a nomad where walking*
> *the path is the dwelling*
> *to walk along philosophy's way is difficult – for difficulty is*
> *the way*
> *to walk along philosophy's way is to walk the path of justice*

As Socrates says in his final philosophical act, before drinking his hemlock, that he must now "transfer his dwelling" and walk the most difficult road.

> *Christ too walked the difficult path*
> *without a place to lay his head*
> *along the path of justice*
> *on the way to the Holy city*
> *where all homecomings will be,*
> *where the dwelling place of God*
> *is among Human Beings*

Final Reflection

> *Living-with philosophy is a cohabitation with wisdom. But is not wisdom homeless? Diotima tells Socrates that the love of it is born of poverty*
> *Is wisdom to be found beyond the here and now?*
> *Proverbs tells the Israelites that wisdom was before the heavens and earth*
> *Though wisdom was before there were cities,*
> *wisdom was always and already a cohabitation – a living-with.*
> *For before the heavens and earth were in place,*
> *before the fields and cities were established,*
> *wisdom lived-with God.*
>
> *Wisdom remains and is habituated to God*
> *a home before there was any place,*
> *a home circumscribed in love,*
> *for to love wisdom is not the same as to love God.*
> *But philosophy is to love that which dwells with God,*
>
> *Philosophy is not the city, philosophy is not God.*
> *Philosophy is life, always walking on the way,*
> *always in lack, always in plenty (with riches beyond silver and gold as Proverbs*

notes)
always meeting friends at the thresholds, ports, tents, and hearths.

For those who find wisdom, find life
and thus to live with philosophy, is to live from life to life
for wisdom lives-with that which is the way,
the truth, and the life

Philosophy live lovingly with wisdom.

<u>Addendum:</u>

Throughout the symposium in honor of our beloved teacher Adriaan Peperzak, his former students, now friends enacted together this love of wisdom described above. This could only result in the way it did from those who were habituated to the shared loved of wisdom. During those three days, there was a palpable sense of *trust* between us all: trust in the wisdom of our teacher, trust in each other as companions along the way, and trust that the age-old questions would continue to inspire us. This trust in the questions and each other as lovers of wisdom is so key to philosophy coming into its own. It is a trust that Dr. Peperzak modeled for us those many years ago when we listened in his classroom as young (naïve?) students. Those classrooms in our youth, and this symposium now in our later years, were not free of contention, or argument, or struggle. Indeed, we learned and practiced together the *eris* of *philosophia*. But those struggles, while deeply personal regarding questions that mattered to us, were not egotistical. The arguments did not sow discord into our concord, but kept alive that desire to understand from each other. From the stories of Dr. Peperzak's moment of awakening to philosophy while reading the *Symposium* in his youth, to the difficult discussions over the nature of the Good, the group enacted its own classic Platonic dialogue. Personally, I left the symposium renewed once again for this long journey along the paths of wisdom, and looking forward to our next homecoming.

13. Living with Philosophy

§

Colin Anderson

The question is the relationship(s) between life and philosophy. And, how we understand *life* and *philosophy* as well as which of the many relationships between the two we are interested in will affect our understanding of the question. There will be a proliferation of possible questions, if we were to follow out each of these conceptions of life and philosophy and explore all of the relations between them. But, perhaps, following out several threads to see where they lead would contribute to thinking the relationship between life and philosophy. These will likely be oblique thoughts, pursuing tangents to the main thrust of the question of living with philosophy, but perhaps they may stumble across something interesting.

Living With Philosophy as therapy

1. One might be tempted to say that all philosophy starts with a diagnosis of life—an identification of the essential problem or ill of the human condition. (Could philosophy arise without such a sense that life is problematic in some fundamental sense?) Philosophy starts always then as a nosology or as diagnostics.
2. Hellenistic and Roman scholasticism would provide the most ready examples, as Hadot, Nussbaum, and Foucault have shown. The Stoics, Epicureans, Cynics, Cyrenaics, and Skeptics all seem to start with the intuition that human life is problematic—that our deepest desires to live well are thwarted both by ourselves and the world. They differentiate in their diagnoses—for the Stoics the problem rests in our being in the grip of our irrational passions which mislead us from a correct estimation of what matters

in our life; for the Epicureans we have given ourselves over to the empty desires of our times which fill our lives with dissatisfaction and turmoils; for the skeptics we have come to believe that being correct about how things really are matters.

3. And each school offers a therapeutics—a discipline and practice that can cure us of our ills and solve the problem of our life. For the Stoics we cultivate *apatheia*, and free ourselves for reason. For the Epicureans we critique our desires and seek to purify those desires for the natural and necessary. The skeptics cultivate equipollence to achieve the *epoche*. And each counsels us to pursue their therapy with concrete practices, exercises, thought-experiments etc.

4. And the same structures might be found in other philosophers. For Heidegger and the existentialists—we are thrown into a world that determines our possibilities and constitutes our very being. The problem of our lives becomes authenticity or freedom –how can we really become the beings that we are. And for Levinas, a different diagnosis—the problem isn't how can we become "real selves"—that's the easy part of existence (at least in T&I). Rather, the problem of existing results from the infinite demands of ethics—how can I be good, rather than how can I be authentic?

5. How far can such a conception be generalized? If these structures are essential to philosophy, then much of what passes for philosophy falls short. Perhaps this is only one conception of philosophy—one more adequate to the existential and practically oriented philosophers and less to the epistemologists, philosophers of science, metaphysicians, etc.

Living With Philosophy as Dis-Ease

1. Sometimes when we use the phrase "living with. . .." we might complete it with a condition or illness, for example, living with depression or diabetes. Is philosophy, then, perhaps something that must be managed in order to be able to live. The skeptics per-

2. The experience is likely familiar. In some ways, philosophy makes life *harder:* The oft-noticed fact that in the history of philosophy marriage was a rarity for philosophers; the Socratic experience that to care about justice or the truth requires a private life; the mysterious *ananke* by which the philosophers are compelled to return to the cave to rule; the voluminous anecdotal evidence of philosophers who are prickly, irritating, obsessive, etc. All of this and more, points to the thought that philosophy makes demands and requires sacrifices.
3. *Theoria* is often at odds or at least in tension with life. (I sometimes joke that many philosophical peculiarities result from ASD—attention *surplus* disorder--a condition most intellectuals are afflicted with that is seen in the obsessive ways in which we seem to relate to some questions, texts, ideas, or issues. To others, intellectuals are curiosities precisely because they devote attention excessively and inordinately.
4. In this sense, we might suggest that philosophy can appear as a sort of dis-ease—a lack of easiness with living. And we might ask, how can we live with philosophy?

Living With Philosophy as community

1. It wouldn't be impossible to hear philosophy as a sort of epexegetic for "living with." *Philosophy* understood as a particular modality of community, as a specific and characteristics inflection of *mit-sein*.
2. The Platonic tradition might see the specifically philosophical mode of *community* as *philia*, perhaps the same understanding of philia as in the apocryphal Aristotelian dicta--"Plato is my friend, but truth is a better friend." But at least philosophy, on this view, only occurs as a shared conversation, as dialogue. Even when we think alone we are "conversing with ourselves," or participating in

a community of thought.

3. Could we imagine Levinas developing a notion of *vivre avec* in opposition to *mitsein* as *vivre de* critiques the "instrumentality" of being-ready-to-hand as a fundamental relation to the world? *Vivre de...* indicates that we are first sustained and nourished by the world before it is present instrumentally. Perhaps there is a glimmer of this in the presence of the "feminine" in the second part of T&I—the source of the *grace* of the welcome in the home—that familiar and familial presence of the home that sustains us prior to the differentiation into social roles and identities.

4. For Aristotle, to "live with" (suzēn) is necessary for friends, though it seems as though he is thinking of "living with" as something like an involvement in shared projects and concerns (mit-sein?) and he seems to be expressing the thought that friendship weakens with distance. But in NE IX he also argues that happiness requires that the good person *sunaisthanesthai,* or "co-perceive" their friends existing which requires shared talk and thought.

5. The question it seems might be, what is the relationship between the "political" nature of human being—the necessity of living in community for human nature—and the universal "stretching towards the truth" of the first sentence of the *Metaphysics?* Strauss seems to see this as a fundamental and irreconcilable tension—the polis as the domain of *doxa* is a fundamental threat to the philosopher whose questions will always be impious. Strauss sees the reference to the polis here narrowly and "literally" as the political community, the city. And yet for Aristotle, the *polis* is only one form of *koinonia.* Heidegger's retrieval of *koinonia* as *mit-sein* seems more fertile than Strauss here, if we are to pose the question of the specifically philosophical mode of living-with: How is philosophy a (highest) form of *living with?*

Peperzakianas: Some Thoughts On Our Philosophical Community

Twice now, through the generosity first of Catriona Hanley and

Loyola College of Baltimore and second of Adriaan and Loyola University of Chicago, I have had the good fortune and pleasure to spend weekends in conversation with a remarkable community of philosophers, all students of Adriaan Peperazak. Some were friends and fellow students during my time studying with Adriaan, some preceded me, and many I have only met due to these occasions.

Although we live in an era of seemingly widespread philosophical scholasticism, our modern individualistic ideology does not sit easily with the thought that we work within "schools" of thought. At most, it seems, we are comfortable either identifying with a tradition ("I work in continental philosophy") or a figure in a tradition ("I'm a Heideggerean") or with an occasional –ism or -ist ("I'm a phenomenologist"). Either, it seems, we recognize a sort of historical dependence or affinity or we recognize a coincidence of dogma. But more generally we are eclectics, mixing and matching influences and interests.

And yet it struck me, both times, that across a wide divergence of individual tastes, interests, and areas of scholarly interests, there existed a certain consistency amongst us. A consistency, I think, in how we think about this peculiar philosophical activity and clearly a result of our years in Adriaan's courses, reading his books and articles, and perhaps most of all his friendship.

I certainly can't speak for others, who might see different consistencies and spaces of agreement, but I might hazard to identify the following orienting points in how I learned to think about philosophy with Adriaan.

1. A certain suspicion of "academic philosophy" as it is currently practiced. The production of scholarly texts, while important, is not the end in itself of philosophy.
2. There are two privileged forms of doing philosophy 1) reading the great texts of philosophy 2) conversing with others about these texts and what they have made possible for thinking.
3. Philosophy is personal in a fundamental sense—its importance is always its importance for the philosopher and philosophers must speak and write about what interests them in life.

4. Philosophical community is a form of friendship arising from shared intellectual interests and existential concerns, congenial orientations and manners, familiarity and kinship in lives.
5. The importance of recognizing gratitude as the "first virtue of philosophers."

I am sure that others would add to or perhaps remove from this list, but around these points, I think there is a distinctive orientation in philosophy, one that I am grateful to have been introduced to by Adriaan and which I am happy to think that I share with others who have participated in these two wonderful philosophical gatherings.

14. Gathering: Living with Philosophy

Jean M. Clifford

<u>April 1-3, 2016 Gathering: Living with Philosophy</u>

After reflecting on the title of our gathering, *Living with Philosophy*, as well as lessons I've learned from Prof. Peperzak, I feel compelled to speak to my experience of learning to include *faith* in my practice of philosophy.

Over this week, I've been teaching the *Euthyphro* to an intro philosophy class. Rereading the dialogue takes me back to my own first philosophy class. I vividly remember reading Plato's *Euthyphro*, struggling with the text, and missing the point almost entirely. In class, however, my instructor made it very clear: we were dealing with a fundamental question that bears on the scope of God's power. The simple question of whether something is good because god loves it really was mind blowing. I remember I was so moved that I called my bother Pat after class to tell him how exciting, amazing, and curious philosophy really was (Pat had been telling me for years that philosophy was interesting, and turns out he was right all along).

This question sat uneasy with me for a very, very long time. In fact, I can point to this moment as the push away from the shores of my family's faith. It's not the case that this experience takes sole responsibility for my course through atheism; I had in fact experienced something of a falling out with my church a couple years prior. At the time, I didn't realize how significant that dismissal was, but it left me looking for a justification that I never found. I think in the *Euthyphro* I found a justification for my own feelings of frustration in lieu of one for my church's actions. I raised up one horn of Euthyphro's dilemma over the other and walked away from that parish.

It was a long journey (though I know others have longer and further divergences from their religion), that began by being asked to reflect upon a metaphysical question. The peak of my atheism was about two years out of undergrad, just before I started at Loyola. I remember it because it was when I finally felt comfortable calling myself an atheist to my religious friends.

The question, "is something good because God loves it" eventually transformed into "what is the Good?" and "what is God?" A darkness settled around my studies; I became convinced that analytic philosophy would never prove God's existence, and science had proven His irrelevance. Continuing to prioritize this way of thinking, I barely knew there was another course of thinking. Possibilities for different philosophical methods were not made clear me.

When I actually started at Loyola, one of my classes that first semester was Metaphysics with Prof. Peperzak. His reading list focused on theological phenomenology, and his lectures on Plato reminded me of why I was first drawn to Plato and ancient philosophy in the first place. That is, I had been fascinated by the Good, the first cause, the prime mover; these *archai* had at first seemed essential to understanding the world but I had slowly moved away from their primacy and focused on the terrible evils in the world. I struggled to find philosophy beautiful while reality seemed so bleak. Yet in Peperzak's classroom, philosophy was beautiful again. Understanding the world, both its beauty and terror, requires meta-consideration. And meta-consideration is best practiced with an awareness and appreciation of our intellectual heritage.

While I have not by any means settled the externalism/internalism debate, I find that the meditation on first principles of being, of understanding, and most significantly, of ethics continues to ground my studies of philosophy and to a great extent my interaction with the world. Recognizing the weight of this question, "what is the Good?" has made me eager to understand others, their philosophical and personal preferences, their assumptions about the world, and their faith in religion, humanity, science, etc.

The most precious lesson I learned from Prof. Peperzak is the role and function that *faith* has in philosophy. While I think that particular faiths can be the subjects of philosophical thinking, what I have in mind is something a bit more abstract – I'm thinking of the structure, or mental capacity, for faith. That capacity which is actualized in Anselm's motto "faith seeking understanding." I think in metaphysics, to really approach the fundamentals Being, we have to follow Bonaventure up his ladder.

In *Journey of the Mind to God*, Bonaventure writes that the ground on which the ladder rests is prayer, and that I must ascend to God from prayer via contemplation of His presence in the world, in myself, in Being in general. This contemplation leads me up the ladder toward illumination and revelation of the mind; however, Bonaventure reveals that "the perfect illumination of our mind" at the summit is not perfect understanding: "when you contemplate these things, take care that you do not think you can understand the incomprehensible."[154] We must instead approach Being, the Good, God with something more fundamental than understanding; with faith. This faith is present at the beginning, when human curiosity leads us to inquiry and investigation, faith that we will find something. First philosophy – whether it is theology, metaphysics, or ethics – requires faith to grasp its *archai*.

I am particularly convinced that this structure – beginning from a place of anticipation (or assumption) and moving through contemplation to end with a new certainty of that with which you began – can be read in the philosophy of Plato, Aristotle, Bonaventure, Hegel, Levinas, and others. I also think this is how we live our lives.[155] It speaks to the fact that, in human learning and development, we cannot begin from nothing; I must start from a place of my singular experience and existence. I depart looking for meaning and find it in what I already had access to.

It's been a privilege reading everyone's' letters and responses. I've

---

[154] Bonaventure. *The Journey of the Mind to God*. Trans. Philotheus Boehner, O.F. M. 1956. Reprint. Ed. Stephen F. Brown. Indianapolis, Indiana: Hackett Publishing Company, Inc., 1993. (6.3, p.34).

[155] Modern psychology would likely calls this confirmation bias – and absolutely it can be problematic. I think even with its problems, it speaks to typical (even automatic?) desire to find and understand patterns and meaning in what we experience. This natural structure and processing of the mind shows itself in our intellectual transformations throughout the history of philosophy.

enjoyed working to get us all together. Looking forward to stimulating conversation over the next few days!

Addendum to April Symposium

Gathered in this atypical fashion, as a conference without prepared presentations, I saw just how truly Professor Peperzak lives philosophy as a way of life. Without formal papers or presentations, without the pomp and circumstance of a standard conference, we were able to take, turn, and transform our discussion according to our collective trains of thought and topics of interest. This unique conference format showed me something unique about professor Peperzak: he is a philosopher and teacher who makes the discipline; he is not made by it. He thinks creatively and intentionally about academic philosophy and how to continue to value and prioritize a dialogic learning and presenting of ideas.

Our conversations over the weekend made me reflect on the origin and necessary conditions for philosophical consideration. Plato tells us this origin is wonder; without wonder, curiosity, amazement, puzzlement, we would lack the reorienting moment that positions us toward the open unknown of our future investigations. Between Plato and Peperzak, I am reminded of the allegory of the cave. The prisoner cannot begin his ascent until he is reoriented towards the unknown, until he turns and faces that which remains concealed from him. But the prisoner does not independently reorient himself. No, the prisoner's reorientation is facilitated by an other, a teacher. Someone breaks the prisoner free, takes his hand, and turns him toward the light. In the same way, our teachers open our mind's eyes and reveal things as interesting, curious, and undisclosed. Prof. Peperzak has been my teacher in just such a way since I enrolled in his class in the fall of 2012. Pulling my clouded mind into the domains of ethics as first philosophy, of theological phenomenology, of the importance of myth and metaphor, and so many others. Now when I descend back into the cave, I see again the same but with new eyes. Having learned from Prof. Peperzak, I return to philosophy with new knowledge and new appreciation of what I am doing and what I am about.

15. REFLECTION ON THE OCCASION OF THE RETIREMENT OF Dr. ADRIAAN PEPERZAK, FRIEND AND TEACHER, AND ONE OF THE MIDWIVES OF THIS COMMENTARY

§

Stacy Bautista

These reflections are based on my experience of philosophizing in the wake of becoming a labor organizer. I have a seven-day per week practice of organizing low-income workers together with others, because more and more of us are not able to make a living, even as government policy consistently gives tax breaks and incentives to the largest corporations (e.g., Mondelez International in Chicago, which is firing hundreds of workers to move to Mexico and exploit workers there), while cutting funds from public education, medical care, and childcare. I help canvass to reach new members weekly, and implement our self-help benefit program to fight for access to basic survival goods, like food and medical care for members who cannot afford it, so that these same members are stable enough that even the poorest workers can lead the broader community in fights against policies that cause poverty - and we do all this without government funding and on a 100% volunteer basis, to maintain our independence to fight for the things our members see they need. That practice gives me a particular perspective on Plato and Socrates that differs from the one I gained through my academic training.

These reflections are based on my experience of philosophizing in the wake of becoming a labor organizer. I am the Administrative Assistant and Education Director for a membership association of low-income service worker families, day-laborers, part-time and seasonal workers and other poor residents of Chicago. We have banded together to create a self-help organization to address survival needs and longer-term solutions to our poverty conditions. As government policies, at every level, give tax breaks and incentives to the largest corporations, basic government services are being cut. We view the creation of organization as absolutely necessary as the $20 an hour jobs that used to define the "middle class" are rapidly going by the wayside.

For example, Illinois, the state I am most familiar with, has a program entitled Economic Development for a Growing Economy (EDGE). In the 2014 fiscal year, Illinois diverted a record $101.7 million in tax revenue from public programs back to the bottom line of business.

EDGE recipients include some of the most profitable companies in the Chicago area – three of which are Abbot Laboratories, Kraft Foods and Mondelez International (which makes Chips Ahoy cookies, Wheat Thins crackers and Oreo Cookies). Abbot qualified for $14.5 million in tax breaks in one division for hiring over 100 workers, while its headquarters eliminated over 1,000 jobs. Kraft Foods, after merging with Heinz, posted $2.7 billion in profits in 2014 and fired 700 workers last summer. Mondelez International, which posted $3.9 billion in profits in 2013, fired 600 workers – the majority of whom earned $25+ per hour.

In the case of Mondelez, those 600 jobs are headed to Salinas Mexico, where factory workers earn between 65-70 pesos a day, $3,25-$3.60 per day in U.S. dollars.

Meanwhile, the city and state are cutting funds from public education, medical care, and childcare.

I lead canvasses to reach new members weekly, and implement our self-help benefit program to fight for access to basic survival needs, like food, medical and dental care for members who cannot afford it, so that these same members are stable enough that even the poorest workers can lead the broader community in fights against policies that cause poverty – and we do all this without government funding and on a 100% volunteer basis, to maintain our independence to fight for the things our members see they need. That practice gives me a particular perspective on Plato and Socrates that differs from the one I gained through my academic training.

Today, I view Socrates through the lens of the collapse of the Athenian empire: Plato depicts a man who is trying to save his city from imperial adventures that have turned other countries against Athens and weakened Athens because its citizens cannot now easily conceive of a life without the spoils of empire - a life based on the robbery and suffering of others. Socrates is seeking students - particularly among the wealthier classes, but Socrates would deal with whoever said they were wise - wise enough, perhaps, to save the city he believes he has a mandate from the gods to serve. Today, American philosophers are faced with the same basic problem: we are living through the collapse of an imperialist nation, and like Socrates, we must act to save our country - through transforming it.

Some may find this a counterintuitive starting point for understanding Socrates, given Socrates's avowal that the philosopher is best-suited to rule because he does not desire to rule, but it need not be such a paradox. Any philosopher today has likely had the experience of being disgusted with a system that gives us a "choice" between a woman who helped start several illegal wars that benefited arms manufacturers while killing millions of civilians and Donald Trump as candidates for the highest office in the land, and where politicians routinely break promises to voters in order to keep promises to wealthy donors - as, for example, when Bill Clinton promised labor not to put NAFTA in, and gained the support of working people for that pledge, but once in office put in NAFTA to assist the largest transnational monopolies, resulting in the devastation of working people in three nations and greater wealth for the wealthiest groupings.

In such a system, a philosopher likely has thought to herself, "If I have to join that to deal politically with the crisis we face, then I would rather not deal politically at all!" But that simply means we must change the system so that we can deal politically with common problems in a way that allows the priorities of those being harmed by the system to become the priorities of political life.

Our chosen text for Sunday's discussion was Plato's Republic, and one question that participants debated was why the philosopher, who successfully ascended to the vision of the good, must return to the cave and the world of shadows. In Republic, the story of the ascent comes out of Socrates's concession to his most headstrong student, Glaucon: when Glaucon is unwilling, due to his youthful passions and aristocratic background, to accept the idea of a city based on securing basic needs for its citizens and living a simple, moderate life, Socrates meets his student where he is. But he injects into the imperial 'city with a fever' - the city prepared for war because, at least initially, it is prepared to take what it desires from others - the story of the formation of the guardians. Socrates's decision to include the guardians subverts the premise of this sick city by elevating to power those who are least likely to permit the fever to last or to catch it themselves because everything in their training and mode of life helps block out the very incentives towards pursuit of personal wealth and sensual enjoyment, which Glaucon so prizes.

The training of the guardians, with gymnastic, and then music, geometry, and then philosophy, follows a dual path: the guardians are warriors, so they must hone their bodies, passions, and minds to deal in making war on behalf of their city, but they also must be trained - mentally, emotionally, and appetitively - to be able to govern society. The process through which children become guardians is a rigorous political-practical training regimen that purges or subordinates too-narrow desires and enjoyments to reason. At each stage, guardian training provides practical experience of their tasks while teaching the guardian-trainees to find satisfaction (happiness) in the good that all the classes of society can enjoy in ways commensurate to their particular function in society. The job of the philosopher-king (or queen) is to render that good available to all through the ordering of society.

This is the context of the ascent to the highest good: whether through the institutional regimen of a society that seeks to produce guardians and eventually philosopher-kings, or through the efforts of individual philosophers in a corrupt city who must undertake a practice of liberation of self and others, those who will govern the city - whichever city it is - must achieve insight into the good. Only through rigorous training for political rule does anyone gain a glimpse of the good - and despite the apparently solitary journey of the escaped slave, access to the highest good does not come outside of a group political practice. Remember that Socrates describes the path of the individual in a corrupt city as beginning in chains, with the person transfixed by lies and distractions - that person must be forced to walk the path of philosophy by someone who frees him and drags him along until the person begins to understand he has been lied to and desire the truth because of the experiences gleaned along this forced path. The guardians and philosopher-kings/queens explicitly train together in all things to achieve this insight. Plato's Seventh Letter, if I recall correctly, corroborates this reading, in that those who have a glimpse of the good have it in the context of intensive philosophical discussion - it appears to them "in a flash" when practicing dialectics with others.

This point leads to the question of what dialectics really is. It is one thing to say it is the art of exposing contradictions through rational argumentation. It is another to experience it as a necessary tool that an organizer must use. Today, I understand Socratic dialectics to be dealing in the art of exposing political contradictions in oneself and in others, and in the city as a whole, which leads then to seeking a reasoned resolution of the contradiction in favor of a better practice not oriented by narrow desires. Dialectics is a process of reasoning and also of training and ordering the desires. From experience, there is very little more difficult than dealing with political contradiction - it requires frankness, but also gauging the person's willingness to struggle with the contradiction, and giving reasons why to continue to practice politically when that may not be personally comfortable because of the person's too-narrow sense of happiness and enjoyment, which excludes others and the collective goal of liberation.

Perhaps that is why highly experienced philosopher-kings, who have achieved the age of fifty, when their ability to carry a charge in the hoplite battle line has declined, are permitted in Republic to "retire" to practice philosophy. Rather than being a retreat into private enjoyment, philosophical dialectic would keep their minds sharp and aid the city by providing leaders capable of just this kind of political engagement, which the elder philosophers, with their much greater experience and fortitude, are better able to do. I offer that as simply a possible reading of an otherwise obscure episode, which puzzled us during our discussion as it seemed so at odds with the refusal to permit philosophers to remain at the summit of the ascent. (On my reading, the entire question would be based on an incorrect understanding of how we access the good, and so point to a possible error in the dialectic - nobody accused Socrates of perfect philosophizing!)

From all of this I take it that there is no true separation of philosophy and (political) practice in Republic, but also that this practice requires the transformation of the practitioner within a collective endeavor to better the politeia. Of note, no other profession offers this insight into the good: the ascent and vision of the good does not take place outside of this context of political-philosophical practice - the descent is simply the continuation of that collective political practice in view of the insight achieved.

But the idea of practicing politics as a group is foreign to the modern American context. The idea of doing it every day is likewise foreign. This conflict between present society and Platonic text leads to the question of what practice we need even to access this part of Socratic and Platonic philosophy.

There are many different human practices, each of which makes certain aspects of experience stand out more or less clearly and sharply. I have been a practicing academic philosopher, teaching Platonic texts to students. But I find that I did not understand what Socrates was describing until I took up a seven day per week practice of working with an association of the lowest-paid workers to unite with more stable workers to fight for policies that would benefit the vast majority of the population. From that experience of gaining insight into the text through a particular political practice, I conclude that to understand what Socrates describes in Republic, you need a practice commensurate with that description. To understand any of Plato's political writing, such as we see it in Republic, Gorgias, Euthydamus, the Socratic dialogues, and Symposium, I believe you need to have a political practice that is based in dealing with others to meet the common needs of the community by organizing to achieve them through governing the 'city'. Likewise, anyone who wants to understand Aristotle's third form of friendship, which is very Platonic and can be used as an aid to understanding Plato, will not really understand that form of friendship unless s/he has a full-time political practice and training with others, as modern friendship is narrowly premised on individual personal likes and dislikes or on simple utility, rather than on pursuit of a good only attainable through a political life.

If there is confusion as to why the philosopher-kings/queens are not described as being allowed to remain in the vision of the good, this confusion I think points all the more urgently to the need for a political practice and experience. Anyone who wants to understand why Socrates and the philosopher kings must "go down" (perform, as it were, the katabasis of the Republic's opening lines) into the masses of poor, oppressed, and ideologically confused, people can only do so by making that journey. A philosopher who wants to understand this point needs to go down to the places where the poor are in their communities and organize to end the poverty that afflicts them. Only then does the need for liberation of the entire community through its political transformation - the end result of the successful philosopher-king's "art" - become clear, evident, and material, as opposed to abstract or doubtful.

I do not say that I believe Socrates understood everything about politics - if he had, he would likely have succeeded and chosen a different way of fighting to save his city. As it was, he failed to do so. But I believe that he understood, as many today are coming to realize, that if you do not deal with the political crisis of your country, it will deal with you. The existing society - then as now - may offer no place for the philosopher-king or modern analogues thereof, but that does not mean that one can abstain from politics or be political only privately. This is a realization that has not come to me through any philosophical text, but only through a reasoned, collective, political practice. If that has made my reading of Republic more relevant to a contemporary situation, then I hope it will inspire action, and I invite anyone who sees value in these reflections or who wants to test them, to join me in organizing and fight for a future of decency and dignity for all.

16. Living with Philosophy in a Dying Empire: Musings on the Meaning of the Pointing Towards

§

Catriona Hanley

My first reaction to the title of our much awaited conversation was in a Nietzschian vein: "living with philosophy" sounds a bit like the language of disease, as in "living with polio", or "living with HIV". Yet while I do feel that philosophy is a burden upon me, I also desire—without ill intent—to impose philosophy on everyone I meet, whereas even in my most frustrated moments, I don't wish my 'flu' on anyone (well, not on *just* anyone). It is not that I want my students, or the clerk in the corner store, or the smarmy politician to share my unhappy lot as a so-called philosopher. It is more that I would like them to take up an obligation that I think is theirs as human beings: in fact I *demand* that they do, and am constantly frustrated that they do not. Then again, I myself consistently fail at my job of living with philosophy. I do it inadequately, but still to the best of my ability, even if I endlessly hide from myself, and trick myself. Is that part of the game? Or is it an attempt to scurry away from the suffocating need to constantly *bloody* philosophize, even as I recognize that no escape is possible…

Well then, is my attitude towards philosophy just wishing that others did it more, and I did so myself in a healthier way? That'd be a bit sad, though consistent with my view that "doing" philosophy is a much richer and more encompassing endeavour than reading and teaching texts.

But let me withdraw, or at least modify the language of disease and the blather about "my unhappy lot". To live with philosophy is to live with faith that there is something, even if that something (coming back to Nietzsche), might be nothing. And that faith is a gift, from wherever it might spring:

it supplies an obligation to keep going despite all the hundreds of reasons to stay in bed with the covers over one's head. Though the gift is often revealed as *giftig*, though this very faith is constantly traduced, though, in other words, living with philosophy carries the double-edged dual nature of *pharmakon*, still somehow, it draws some of us as moths to the light. And Diotima, Adriaan Peperzak's worthy heroine, would not let us stop there.

Here please let me interrupt my solitary musing to enter into dialogue.

Dear Adriaan: I want to thank you for your provocative letter, in which you asked us, your students-- many now grown and flown from the nest, others still lingering on a nearby branch, or a few trees over—to identify the most urgent questions that occupy our thoughts.

Your question is ever that of Plato, or rather that inevitable re-gathering of Plato's most central and mysterious thought: the epikeina tēs ousias. And though I have spent many of my intellectual years so far on that concern, and though in my youth that question filled my heart, my mind, my thoughts, it has since faded. It has not disappeared, but it has faded. My own approach to the question was primarily through Aristotle, the positing of a necessity rather than the admiration of the glow on the horizon, and perhaps that is still the case. But now (I hesitate to reveal) the necessity for the Necessity has also grown dimmer. It is not Heidegger who has taken me here: I think it is living here in this land of dying empire. I'm losing perspective.

Studying with you, being awakened to a new way of thinking[156] through your inspiring lectures that often left me weak in the knees and giddy with intellectual excitement… reading Levinas with you, absorbing your Platonic Levinas unconsciously through the strange process of translating your articles about him, I yearned to find a way to think. The effort of translation I call strange, because in translating words and sentences I elided the mere content of the words, so concentrated as I was on form in the effort to transmit their meaning….

The same is true of editing work. I hope you won't object to my saying that as your first graduate student assistant in your time at Loyola Chicago, there was a lot of translating in my editing. Nor will you mind, j'espère, my telling you what a joy and privilege

---

[156] Not entirely new! I'd come from doing my Master's degree at the Université de Montréal, with my thesis written under the wonderful and kind direction of M. Bertrand Rioux. On the first day of class, you had all students write down their philosophical experience and education: reading mine quickly, you called me back. In perhaps the most wonderful and fortuitous coincidence of my life, it turned out that not only had you two been to school together at the Sorbonne, but that you'd been good friends, both students of Paul Ricoeur. My conversation with you turned out to be a wonderful deepening of my discussion with Rioux, starting from common ground and going far beyond.

it was to do that work, often through a nuit blanche.[157] Of course, as your student, my editing had little to do with challenging the content of your thought (though you often complimented me by requesting critique), and much more to do with seeking clarification, looking for an explanation. Or perhaps, like all my seeking and learning together with you, I was attempting a description of the meaning of the pointing towards-- that same pointing toward, that for the sake of which, you were and are still always pointing towards.

And all the time, I kept my eye on that glow on the horizon, and the excitement of learning from you how to be more attuned to it, how to (almost) sense it: the beauty of that seeking without the possibility of finding. In my Aristotelian understanding of Levinas, of Christianity, I found it embodied. I discovered the groundlessness of ontology, and with Tom Sheehan explored the Heideggerian understanding of the temporality of it. The my quest for the eternal was no longer in any <u>beyond this</u>, but entirely <u>within this</u>. My grasp of your Plato was the paradox of Plato pointing to the immanence by way of transcendence, this an imminance that transcends immanence. A todi ti, a this here now before me that is infused with the transcendent—and yes, the lovely impossibility of capturing it in any trap of human poiesis. Glimpses only, and those rare and few... unless we adopt the poet's stance. Just a pointing towards.

But we are philosophers, not poets, not Jungian psychologists, not astrologers— and also not theologians. We do not countenance notions of fate and destiny, the non-coincidence of serendipity, or the fairy tale stories of the true divine life behind the curtain of mortality. We are much too sophisticated to believe in on-call divine intervention in the trivial matters of our everyday life.

Still, perhaps I have returned, once again, to a more cynical positioning of myself vis-à-vis the universe. I may have come back to a greater, more mature, but more bitter Aristotelian understanding: events on earth unfold in accordance with the principles of nature. It is true that the story, in its fascinating details, changes every year. And when the paradigm changes, even more vistas open up for discovery and questioning. It is amazing—again, what a gift that there is no end to this puzzle, physical or spiritual.

This 21st century has so far been tragic, and the tragedy continues daily. Of course life has always been a vale of tears for the many and a festival for the few. So we live now, at the festival. But after the horrors of the 20th Century—those you lived through yourself, Dr. Peperzak, can you help me with these questions?

---

157 Do you remember? This was before email attachments, so you'd finish writing a page and hand it to me, and I'd put red ink all over it, and hand it to your great assistant Beth. Then she'd type it up and give it to you, and you'd send it back to me, then me back to you. All done in person and on foot! What a rich conversation that was for me.

How can philosophy help guide us through this often-horrendous task of being human in a world of uncertainty and terror? How can we negotiate straits of hypocrisy, inadequacy, ignorance, refusal to look, to see, even when directly confronted nose-to-nose with the problem? How can I reconcile my existence with the death of millions? Or does me asking this question already condemn me?

Can I permit myself retreat to the tower so long as I desire a better world? Can I ignore the fact that the ivory that built the tower was ripped from the tusks of elephants?

How can philosophy help us come to greater awareness of the singularity of our own individual existences—without being sickened by the thought?

But if I really and truly had only one question to ask, it'd be something impossible like this. This glimpse of the glow at the edge of the horizon, this felt necessity that the whole amazing structure somehow makes sense: this universal pointing towards something other, eventually to some epikeina tēs ousias... *what can you tell me about it? How can I maintain or revive any trust/hope in its presence? I hear your answer, of course: faith, hope, and above all, gratitude. That is a very hard path to follow. But, you will reply, it has always been hard, no less for those in 399 BCE than for those in 2016.*

As you enter into another phase of your life (the life of the retiree, the life you quite rightly refused when you came to Chicago from Nijmegen), how can we continue to be with you, learn from you, and even perhaps to teach and inspire you? How can we keep you aware that your former students are still and ever your students? And how to assure that the conversation we are having will continue through your retirement, and even after your death, in case you predecease us?

Finally, a last analogy about living with philosophy: Imagine the ski hill. Downhill skiers are in line for the chairlift. As the queue narrows, single skiers are paired up casually with duos and trios: it is a four-person lift, and the lift operator is working to reach maximum efficiency. Skiers get ready for the chairlift, pairing up, those in front move forward and catch their chair, and then you move into place. You get to the demarcated spot-- with your companions or alone, and wait for the chair to come beneath and sweep you up the mountain.

Appendix: After the Event: Still Living with Philosophy

The April 2016 union/reunion of students who wrote or are writing their doctoral dissertations under the careful and loving guidance of Adriaan Peperzak could be described as: *joyful, fruitful, inspiring, extremely difficult, deeply enjoyable, exhaustion, revelatory, intellectually challenging, emotionally fraught, spiritually piercing, beautiful,* but also *irritating* and *frustrating.* But in describing how twenty people *did philosophy together* over the course of a weekend, these words work better as adverbs.

Our *way* of doing philosophy together was through an unstructured dialogue that lasted three days, engaging in a conversation that shifted easily between consideration of nihilism in one moment, and religious conviction in the next, and with everything in between. We all spoke, and we all listened; our teacher/mentor guided us very little, trusting us, and releasing us to think beyond his teaching, and even against it. We each spoke freely from our hearts and minds of our truths and worries, formed by long years of philosophical inquiry, study, commitment and doubt.

There was a moment on the Saturday afternoon, a kind of epiphany, when we were all suddenly conscious of the fact *this was working*—that the theory that Adriaan had been presenting us with over the years though his lectures, his critiques, his books, his one-on-one discussions—was being practically enacted *by us*. It is impossible to describe the joy that seemed suddenly to bond us deeply or a shared, secret thrill, that worked its way through our conversation, even when it became contentious. And it suddenly seemed so evident that dedication to a life of healthy spiritual quest-- searching for some kind of truth through conversation and action, even through our own flawed lives, even despite our inauthenticities and self-deceptions, our betrayals and defeats-- that <u>this</u>, this dedication, was the default position of the group.

How deeply satisfying to witness the words of one's mentor finding life and truth in fact and practice. Adriaan: damn it, you were right all along!

> *Living with philosophy after the high: it took courage to come up on the ski-lift, but now you have to go back down. Find a path that meanders through the snow and the rocks, between the trees, or through the jungle, across the ocean, though it may well be a straight, precipitous downward run. It might be treacherous, might be painful. There is nothing to be done but maintain embers of hope until you reach the bottom. Then, on a good day, even if the lift is no longer running, you'll find the energy to climb back up. It will so often feel like a burden, sometimes too heavy to bear. But shining through the dread will be the feeling of sunshine*

on your face: there will be the joy of climbing, and the prospective thrill of flying down the mountain again.

This is Sisyphus as mortal, Sisyphus transfigured: no longer shaking his fist at the absurdity of it all, but embracing the contradiction between his life of struggle and the overwhelming passage of time. I doubt that philosophy alone can get us to this place, but I retain hope that though dialogical engagement we might at least keep pointing towards the Good, and enacting it when we can. In short: let's keep speaking the truth, and calling out lies.

Adriaan, and all my wonderful, thoughtful, engaging symposiasts, to all those bearing hope: thank you for helping us get a bit closer. This with love.

17. LIVING WITH(IN) PHILOSOPHY.

§

Greg Clark

Philosophy is larger than an individual life; it spans cultures and centuries. But I want to consider the experiences that provoke my own philosophical thinking, framed as moments (Platonic and / or Hegelian) in a narrative.

Living without Philosophy. (Inside the Cave / Immediacy)

I was born and raised in a conservative religious context. When Isaiah 40:4 said that in God's kingdom,

"*Every valley will be lifted up, and every mountain and hill will be lowered; the rough ground will become level, and the mountain ridges made a plain*" we knew the text was describing our flat plains of our central Illinois home, and that we would dwell in the house of the Lord forever. Philosophy was nowhere to be seen or heard nor its absence felt.

But all was not well. Small towns are only a semblance of community. The cornfields that seemed to stand for the simple, natural values of rural peoples actually function as plantations to feed urban dwellers. And friends sometimes drink too much and die in automobile accidents. We are not made to dwell forever. Absence can be felt after all.

<u>Living within Philosophy. (Journey out of the Cave / Reflection)</u>

I went away to college and started a new life in the big city of Chicago. Now the tree in the courtyard below my dorm window was all the "nature" I could see, my community of friends was prearranged to last only four years, and I had no love-life.

But I discovered philosophy. It seemed like a vast meticulously furnished building. One could live many lives and not have visited all the rooms. Here, in this room one can read Whitehead on nature, across the hall Thomas on wisdom, on the next floor, Plato on love. Here, it seemed to me, are the texts, the arguments, the language that not only expressed but founded culture. Thus, culture might also be corrected or strengthened by critiquing or retrieving texts, arguments, or language. "Modernism" named a problem; but did the solution lie with the Greeks? The Medievals? Or the Post-moderns? I chose to work on the post-moderns: "Heidegger could be corrected yet, if I could just clarify how Levinas uses Bergson to do the job!"

But all was not well. My mastery of the languages, texts, and arguments were insufficient to create a paradigm shift in the literature. Students at my small liberal arts college weren't excited to exchange their life-goals for a life of scholarship. Most telling, I wondered more at philosophies than at my own lived-experience.

Philosophizing within Life. (Return / Mediation)

Of course, I had not discovered philosophy; I had been taught it. I had often wondered at my teachers: What kind of lives do these people lead, these thinkers with the keys to wisdom? For the most part, I could not get close enough to tell.

If philosophy were adequately represented in the picture above, perhaps the question is irrelevant to philosophy. But certain texts won't let philosophy or philosophy teachers off the hook. As Plato writes in his Seventh Letter: Philosophy "does not admit of exposition like other branches of knowledge; but after much converse about the matter itself and a life lived together, suddenly a light, as it were, is kindled in one soul by a flame that leaps to it from another, and thereafter sustains itself."

What if philosophy in practice cannot be separated from the Academy or the Lyceum, the community of Epicureans, the monastic schools, the salons of Paris, etc.? What if it requires a teacher with the personality of a Socrates? What if philosophy is not the rooms of the building but the life that made those rooms? What if tracing the arguments through the literature shows that tracing arguments, while necessary, is not sufficient to the philosophical life? What if you found a teacher and a community of students who embodied this ancient practice? What is a wanna-be philosopher to do?

I have returned to those experiences I'd had in central Illinois. (Most summers I also return to the place.) I speak Midwestern fluently. Death, divorce, the many faces of the natural world, and the disconnect between urban and rural populations, these are more than sufficient to spur philosophical reflection. And these are not foreign to students. The problem of the one and the many, the mystery of wooshing up and of fading away, foundations of good and of evil are all ready to present themselves. No paradigm shifts are necessary to claim success. Our lives are our texts.

18. "Living With Philosophy" or "Philosophical Living"? Personal Reflections on What it Means to Be a Philosopher

§

Corinne M. Painter

The first weekend in April of this year, I had the honor and pleasure of participating in a Philosophical Symposium, entitled "Living With Philosophy," which was organized in order celebrate the work, teaching, and life of one of my most treasured teachers, Adriaan Peperzak, who retired at the end of 2015. And I did so with several other students of Peperzak, who studied with him either before I arrived at Loyola University, alongside me, or after I left. Though many of those who participated in what I can only describe as a beautiful meeting of compassionate, passionate, reflectively engaged persons who are oriented towards discovering and living according to truth and justice were already dear friends, after this meeting, despite the fact that prior to the Symposium I had only met some of the meeting participants once or twice, and some not at all, because of our weekend together, I believe that a philosophical friendship and discussion, and of Peperzak's genuinely philosophical character, which is at one and the same time, nurturing and challenging. Indeed, Peperzak's deep care and concern for his students, old and new, which he generously and consistently demonstrates, is moving in a way that words cannot capture adequately.

The reflections that follow, while certainly inspired by the various sets of very thoughtful and engaging written reflections and questions of other participants, which I read and reread with great interest, are informed by the provocative discussions within which we engaged during our weekend Symposium. So, too, do my reflections represent a sort of sequel to the reflections that I wrote seven years ago for the 80th birthday gathering for Peperzak,[158] which Cartiona Hanley so generously organized in May of 2009 at Loyola in Baltimore.

Tellingly, those reflections, which offered remarks about the importance of socratic questioning in education, remain, for me, a fundamental ingredient of my sense of what it means to be a philosopher in the most authentic way. For in those reflections, I acknowledged that Pepezak is one of the greatest influences in my life, but not only because he taught me how to skillfully and thoughtfully read and interpret major philosophical thinkers, from Plato to the present, but also because he taught me through his written work, his teaching, and indeed his very person, all of which reveal his Socratic character, what it means to *live a philosophical life*. To be sure, I remain humbled and shaped by Peperzak's constant and steadfast theoretical and lived ethical commitment to the pursuit of truth, wisdom, and goodness, which, as I wrote seven years ago, he exhibits quite clearly and consistently – and I would add, lovingly – to his students, not just in the classroom, but in various ways and in many contexts.

While my previous reflections focused on our responsibilities as teachers of philosophy, particularly as teachers of undergraduate students, the brief, informal remarks[159] that follow focus on being a philosopher more broadly construed and on how this manifests itself in our lives generally, but especially socially and politically.[160] In this connection, Peperzak's claim that "philosophy is a way of becoming true that does not stand on its own, independent of how the philosopher *exists* and is *related to other persons and things*" (55, emphasis his)[161] and that "truth does not deliver

---

158 These earlier reflections also appear in this *Collection*.
159 These reflections are intentionally not written in an argumentative fashion, as I hope for them to have a noticeably informal, personal character.
160 The use of the term "political" here is not meant to refer to engagement in professional politics (whatever that is). Rather, I use it as a way of pointing to a link that I believe exists between authentic philosophy and working to bring about justice, which will hopefully become apparent very shortly.
161 Peperzak Adriaan. (1986). *System and History in Philosophy: On the Unity of Thought and Time, Text and Explanation, Solitude and Dialogue, Rhetoric and Truth in the Practice of Philosophy and its History*. New York: State University of New York Press. Further references to this author will refer to this text

itself to an abstract, uprooted thought... but makes way for itself at the most genuine and truest level, where the meaning of life is realized" (ibid.) – which I also quoted in my earlier reflections – still provides the foundation for the conception of philosophy that strikes an illuminating chord for me. For I believe that genuine philosophical engagement – or, more simply, philosophical living – is necessarily and intimately connected to actively working to change the social and political realities that structure our knowledge about and ways of organizing our communities, our collective lives, and our world, which, together, constitute the only "site" where the meaning of life is crafted.

It is in this spirit that I also believe that both (so-called) theoretical philosophy, including engaging in scholarly work or research, as well as the work of teaching philosophy, at the undergraduate or the graduate level, is most authentic when it is *recognizably* connected to what I just referred to as the "active work" of philosophers, who are driven to respond to justice concerns of the polis, since this seems to be the most genuine manner of pursuing truth, wisdom and goodness in a humble and honest way, as, I believe, both our ultimate teacher, Socrates, did, and Peperzak still does.

Moreover, I believe that both Socrates and Peperzsak understood, appreciated, and incorporated into how they conducted their lives that, as Peperzak thoughtfully put this, the questions with which philosophical reflection and life confront us, which are certainly not confined, for example, to abstract metaphysical questions but include at the most fundamental level ethical, religious, social, and political questions, "are just too difficult" (Peperzak, 71) to answer once and for all, since "they go beyond the boundaries of our capacity for insight" (ibid.). Interestingly, this extremely humble, Socratic acknowledgment suggests, amongst other things, that what it means to be an *authentic* philosopher in contrast to merely a *professional* philosopher is not determined on the basis of external standards of the profession,[162] or, even, by whether crafty or sophisticated philosophical

---
and shall be cited by author's last name, followed by the appropriate page number(s).
162 For example, whether she has a position at a well-reputed institution, whether she is recognized by other philosophers, or how much she has published and in what venues.

jargon is used in her work,[163] but, rather, on the basis of (1) whether she accepts the public, social, and urgent nature of the challenge that the work of true philosophy offers, and is inspired rather than discouraged by its necessarily limited and perspectival, though richly informed, extremely careful and thoughtful analysis, and (2) whether she willingly and actively pursues justice, truth, and goodness in the face of this challenge, not just in her teaching and in her scholarly work, but also in who and how she lives, and for the sake of all those for whom justice and goodness is at stake.[164]

In any event, during the course of our weekend Symposium, which, again, I am truly honored to have participated in, many of Peperzak's students, following his lead, spoke of themes related to questions concerning our responsibility as philosophers to our students, to our colleagues, to our neighbors, both known and unknown, friend or foe, and to the world generally. And although there were many contexts and foci that guided our various conversations, including the meaning and possibility of autonomy, the nature and possibility of trust, and the necessary and important role of perspective and experience with respect to the philosophical life, Plato's thought constantly provided a framework for our examinations. This was no doubt most obvious when we explicitly discussed Diotima's speech about *Eros*, about which many questions were raised by our Symposium participants. Amongst the many thought-provoking questions that were raised about Diotima's speech, one such question pondered whether we are always-already lovers in some sense and whether Diotima was intimating that our "natural love" ought to be trained, via her "ladder," so that we love and are loved by Beauty itself, that is so say, by what is pure, untainted and uncompromised by falsity or impurity, divine, infinitely generous, and good, since this is the only "reality"[165] that is worthy of guiding not just our

---

163 I have the impression that it is common practice for professional philosophers (and academics in general) to intentionally speak and write in ways that are unduly inaccessible and obfuscating, where the thought is that greater inaccessibility signals more valuable philosophical thinking. This is likely motivated, at least in part, by expectations and norms of the profession; nevertheless, it saddens me that many philosophers seem to simply go along with this praxis with little to no objection, as I think this suggests a sort of arrogance and high-mindedness.

164 Perhaps we could say that in seeking to bring about justice, true philosophers engage in something like "revolutionary midwifery," just as Socrates did well over 2,000 years ago.

165 I use this term fully aware that it is inappropriate. However, as most of us, I assume, admit, this is a failure of language that cannot be traversed. I am also compelled to admit that I hesitate to capitalize

sight – e.g., our theoretical gazing – but our very life, insofar as being in touch with Beauty itself allows us to "give birth not to images or copies of virtue, but to true virtue, *virtue itself*" (212a1-2, emphasis mine).

Although Diotima's speech is beautiful (pardon the pun!) and moving, at the same time, its meaning is not transparent, at least not to me, and I suspect that it is not meant to be. There may also be multiple interpretations of her speech that can be reasonably defended; indeed, I think we must accept this possibility if we acknowledge our fallibility and fragility as knowers.[166] Nevertheless, I believe that whatever else may be (legitimately) taken from Ditoma's speech, one insight that may – and dare I say, "should" – be collected from her speech is the idea that there is a necessary link between living philosophically and living beautifully, authentically, humbly, and virtuously in *this world*, which is messy and complicated and full of injustice. Perhaps in a world within which images or copies of virtue are sufficient, it would be appropriate to speak of the "idea of virtue" or a true understanding of virtue (or something akin to this). But, tellingly, Diotima does not speak of this; instead, she speaks of the philosopher as the one who, being in touch with Beauty itself through love, gives birth to "virtue itself."

Importantly, giving birth is not only a signal or expression of generosity, creation, and the beyondness of the singular individual, it also signals messiness, suffering, and interdependency, at the very least. No less importantly, in this general context, "virtue itself" points to or, more simply, means: *a life that is lived excellently*. Thus, paradoxically, the genuine philosopher who loves wisdom, truth, justice, and the good,[167] cannot be who she is by spending her time alone contemplating the so-called

---

the terms "wisdom," "truth," "justice," "the good," and similar terms, since I do not want to unduly reify them.
166 To admit our fallibility as knowers is not tantamount to claiming that every position, claim or belief is as reasonable as another; rather, this admission is linked to respecting the claim (offered earlier) that, unless we are full of hubris, the questions that philosophy asks are too difficult for us to believe that we can answer once and for all with adequacy, given the limited nature of our capacity for insight or thinking. However, it is important to note that this position is consistent with recognizing that there are standards of reason that allow us to make judgments about and critical comparisons of the reasonability of interpretations of texts, experiences, and etc.
167 Recall the admission offered in a previous endnote within which I explained my hesitancy to capitalize the terms "wisdom, "truth," "justice, "the good," and similar terms.

eternal truths – assuming this would be possible for humans – because she necessarily exhibits virtue – i.e., lives excellently – in the only life that she knows she's been given without her having chosen it. Just as the philosopher is utterly uninterested in and unmoved by self-indulgent pleasures of the material world that would stroke her ego (to use modern psychological terminology), such as honor, reputation, or material wealth, she responds to the gift of life willingly – and not begrudgingly – by living responsibly for the sake of justice, goodness and truth for all those who have a stake in these. And although this may be done in different ways, by engaging in different journeys, what seems to be incompatible with the philosophical life, at least to me, is a life that does not attempt to bring about justice, not just in the classroom, while teaching (pliable or unpliable) students about various theories of justice, or even in scholarly work, by reflecting on and writing about justice issues.

Instead, I submit that the genuine philosopher must live for the sake of bringing justice about in the world, which requires more than theoretical knowledge of justice and related ideals (however incomplete that may be), but a *character that is called and moved to act in the world,* wherer this call is borne of the sense of "homelessness," "dis-ease," and "discontent" – themes that were also discussed during our Symposium – that she experiences due to the needless suffering and injustice that continues, unabashed, to permeate the world – a world for which the philosopher feels responsible in some sense, as Socrates quite clearly did. *For what else could giving birth to "virtue itself" mean?* Indeed, doesn't it make sense to believe that Plato gave us the image of Socrates that he did in his dialogues in order to help us figure out how such a life might be lived?

In the sprit of humility and honesty, I want to close these admittedly very personal remarks with a confession. Although I wholeheartedly believe the reflections I just penned about what it means to live philosophically, I admit that I struggle each and every day to live this way. To be sure, living philosophically commands me in a way that is always present, guiding my reflections, my decisions, and my life, but as a fragile, finite being, at the same time, I also realize that I cannot bring about justice in this world alone; nor can I live without taking missteps in my journey, or without failing to complete some of my projects.

So, in the face of this almost paralyzing realization – almost, but not quite, thankfully – and mindful of not wanting to be guilty of the indefensible human exceptionalism that so many cling to today, I choose to spend my philosophical life energy fighting for the justice of non-human animals, who comprise some of the most oppressed and abused beings in our world today, and who, not incidentally, in the early Books of Plato's *Republic*, Socrates suggests should not be eaten, since eating non-human animals is not part of the just polis.[168]

---

[168] For this, see section 371e–373e of Book II of Plato's *Republic* (any translation). Also, see: Painter, Corinne. (Fall 2013). "The Vegetarian Polis: Just Diet in Plato's Republic and in Ours." *The Oxford Journal of Animal Ethics*, Vol. 3, No. 2: pp. 121-132. See also: Dombrowski, Daniel. (1984a). *The Philosophy of Vegetarianism*. Amherst: University of Massachusetts Press, and Dombrowski, Daniel. (1984b). Was Plato a Vegetarian? *Apeiron*, 18 (1): pp. 1–9 (both of which are referred to in my 2013 essay).

19. Living with Philosophy

§

Laurel Madison

This past April I had the great honor of attending Adriaan Peperzak's Chicago Symposium, which focused on the questions of how philosophy is expressed and experienced within our lives and how it impacts our teaching and guiding of others. In addition to providing a forum for lively and provocative discussions, it was also, at the same time, a celebration of Dr. Peperzak's career as a teacher, mentor, and friend to a large and diverse group of students who have become, over the years, a true family.

My responses to the questions posed at the symposium are in many ways very different from my fellow colleagues and friends as a result of the different turns my life has taken since I finished my graduate work. Due to family obligations and a shifting of priorities, I did not, in the end, pursue a full-time career in philosophy. While I continue to teach philosophy on a consistent part-time basis with an eye to cultivating an appreciation of and desire to contemplate the great ideas of the greatest thinkers, my primary expression and experience of philosophy is to be found within my home.

As a homeschooling mother of six, my focus is now on the formation of my own children and the cultivation of their experience and pursuit of the Good, the True, and the Beautiful. This focus guides and inspires every subject they study, from math to literature to music, and permeates the culture of our household. Unbeknownst to me at the time, the generous guidance that I received from Dr. Peperzak during my years as a graduate student would become the impetus and model for our home education, an education whose focus is not only intellectual, but moral and spiritual as well.

It was from Dr. Peperzak that I first came to see philosophy as a way of life and one that exists far beyond the walls of academia. And while I may no longer be pursuing the traditional academic dream. For me, philosophy has rather become something lived with and among my children whose formation it is my privilege to oversee.

20. Living with Philosophy

§

Ryan Madison

The April 2016 symposium in honor of Adriaan Peperzak was a joyous event and a great blessing for all of us. I can never adequately thank Adriaan for all he has done for me and for the discipline of philosophy, and this sentiment is clearly felt by all who were present. No professor is more dedicated to his students or displays such genuine concern for their personal good than Adriaan, and only this can explain why so many travelled so far to be present. While no gesture of ours can adequately signify this deep gratitude, we hope it went some way toward expressing our true thoughts.

The institutional practice of philosophy in today's academy, in spite of its frequent criticisms of modern thought, continues to be dominated by one of modernity's most compelling and powerful "imaginaries," the philosopher as heroic thinker. This model, so evident in Descartes, portrays the philosopher as an isolated individual beset by a myriad of obstacles such as opinion, prejudice, tradition, and passion, all of which threaten to submerge the philosopher's self in an unreflective and undifferentiated sea of un-thinking. The heroism of the philosopher consists in overcoming these threats, asserting the "I," and constituting his or her unique selfhood through a grand act of thought and self-consciousness. This grand act of thinking, in order to remain its heroic self, must continually renew itself in the face of opposition and threats.

Of course, this is merely an "imaginary," for if philosophy is truly a tradition then each person must be initiated into this practice by others. But the model of self-assertion, which continues to inform so much of philosophy, often prevents one from recognizing it as a human and ethical practice that takes place within a community and presupposes a shared way of life. An exclusive emphasis upon the active, self-assertive thinker obscures the role of passivity and receptivity, viewing these as weaknesses, deficits, and the absence of power. Yet the fact that philosophers are humans who belong to communities and traditions should not be interpreted as a sign of impotence. As Aristotle remarks, the foundation of human communities, and particularly communities of philosophers, is friendship, which is the love without which, he goes on to say, no one would want to live. This is a strikingly different vision of philosophy than the one to which many of us have grown accustomed. It requires certain virtues such as trust, piety, humility, and, most of all, gratitude for all the goods one has received.

I am grateful to have learned the true meaning of philosophy and friendship from Adriaan, and for all that he has so graciously bestowed upon us.

21. LIVING THROUGH PHILOSOPHY

§

Aron Reppmann

We have been invited to testify to our experience of "living with philosophy." Adriaan, you call us to "a reflection about the mutual relation between human *lives* . . . and *philosophy*." This is in no way surprising: although this call to reflect on the intersection of philosophy and living comes at a specific occasion, the same appeal has been the persistent theme (sometimes explicitly posed, other times just beneath the surface) of all our encounters with you. Therefore these reflections occasioned by your official retirement signal not an end, but a continuation.

Following the lead of several of our friends – and also following Plato's example that philosophical writing should handle others' ideas with some recognizable playfulness – I would like to alter the terms of the discussion, shifting my meditation to the theme of "living *through* philosophy." I offer this revised theme not because it is inherently better than the original suggestion! In fact, I will point out a few rather troubling interpretations that it suggests; but I believe that these degraded forms of "living through philosophy" not only mark besetting dangers but also point the way toward a more wholesome response.

One way of interpreting "living through philosophy" is: "I am a professor; I make my living through philosophy." This is, of course, a highly privileged occupation, and all the more so as increasing numbers of our fellow philosophers are unable to earn their livelihood by studying, teaching, and serving within a stable and supportive academic community; for the time being, I myself am a survivor of institutional austerities, as the number of positions in my own department is half what it was just a couple of years ago. I am deeply grateful that I am one of the fortunate ones. But I am also uncomfortably aware that this privileged position can be a compromising one as well: I (indirectly, but surely) demand fees from students for the instruction that I offer them; I actively recruit students to take more than the required set of philosophy courses, to join me in making philosophy a specialized concern; and I even suggest (promise?) that applying themselves to the study of philosophy will contribute to their worldly success – higher scores on the Law School Admissions Test, positions of professional and societal leadership in their mature years, and so on. Based on that description, Socrates might reasonably label me a sophist, not a philosopher. Making one's living through philosophy threatens to denature philosophy itself.

Another way of interpreting "living through philosophy" is that we are perpetually enduring the long march of philosophy's history: not only are we "living through" the particular complex of challenges and possibilities presented by the current moment in philosophy's history; we also, as historically oriented philosophers, find ourselves constantly rehearsing, "living through," our schooled memory of how we arrived at this current moment.[169] This, too, is a gift, a privilege, not to be completely hemmed in by the assumptions and prejudices of one's own time and culture, but instead to daily subject those assumptions and prejudices to the relatively more immortal, ennobling vision of the greats whose literary remains weigh down the shelves in my office and whose peculiar ways of encountering the world in speech have taken hold of my consciousness so that I cannot resist giving abstruse interpretations of even the most inane examples of popular culture. (Ask my students, some of whom make a sort of parlor game out of introducing me to an artifact of contemporary pop culture – a song, a video, a t-shirt slogan – and challenging me, "What would Plato (or Bonaventure or Descartes or Nietzsche) say about that?"

---

169 Adriaan, although the phrase "philosophy as schooled memory" is borrowed from another of my philosophical forebears, I use it here as a reference to the sensitive, demanding hermeneutic of the history of philosophy that I encountered in the first work of yours that I ever read, *System and History in Philosophy*. (On "schooled memory," see Calvin Seerveld, "Philosophy as schooled memory," in Craig Bartholomew, ed., *In the Fields of the Lord: A Calvin Seerveld Reader* [Piquant, 2000].)

I always take the bait.) But here, too, lurks a temptation to decadence: sometimes I wonder whether my commitment to channeling the insights of the great ones makes me something like the hapless rhapsode of Plato's *Ion*, impressively conducting divine insights but never having a thought for myself. (And yes, I just did it again right there, ducking behind the mask of a Platonic dialogue to make my point for me.)

This leads to yet one more interpretation of "living through philosophy:" philosophy as a potential substitute for actually living, a vicarious form of existence that puts on a philosophical mask rather than authentically living one's own life. But as risky a choice as the *theōrētikos bios* is, as much is at stake in immersing my own immediate concerns in the bracing waters of philosophical exercise, I believe that this is actually the only way to transcend the besetting problems of all the degraded forms of "living through philosophy." Every life involves a choice of life, a commitment and a risk, whether it is recognized or not; as Socrates says, "Whether one falls into a little pool or into the middle of the biggest sea, one nevertheless swims all the same" (*Republic* 453d).

Adriaan, the philosophizing life, as you have lived it and invited us to join you in it, offers no once-for-all, foolproof solution for the risks it requires; in fact, the very promise of the philosophical life is that its theoretical acuteness helps us to keep the practical risks in view, to constantly remind us that we actually are swimming rather than already arrived at the isles of the blessed. As Catriona summarized our discussion of "reaching out to the Good" during our Chicago colloquium in April 2016: "The Good is not a solution, answer, *telos,* but a (persistent) *challenge.*" The Good, which is beyond being (*epekeina tēs ousias*), calls forth our "beyonding" (*epektasis*), as Gregory of Nyssa calls it in his *Life of Moses* (yet another book, Adriaan, that I have come to cherish through your pointing it out to me): "Since those who know what is good by nature desire participation in it, and since this good has no limit, the participant's desire itself necessarily has no stopping place but stretches out with the limitless. … The perfection of human nature consists perhaps in its very growth in goodness" (I.7, I.10).

How do we know that in "living through philosophy" we are actually devoting ourselves to pursuing the Good, rather than becoming self-absorbed in sophistic careerism, cast adrift on the high seas of history, or hiding our true lives behind the obfuscations of theoretical masks? We know it because the Good reveals itself as ever more wondrous, and because we desire it more and more, even as that increasing desire shows us ever more clearly how far we fall short of attaining it.

There are no permanent philosophical achievements, and there are no truly retired philosophers. As you lay down the formal obligations of university teaching, Adriaan, may you never be without philosophical friends. In that friendship, we know ourselves to be akin (*oikeioi*) to one another because together we belong to the Good for which we are striving.

Conclusion

§

Giancarlo Tarantino

It was a pleasure to help with the Chicago conference with Jean Clifford, Justin Nordin, and Randy Newman, together with Dr. Peperzak. It was also a little unpredictable: I don't think any of us really knew how the conference would go once we decided to forgo the usual practice of reading papers in favor of trying to foster live conversations. Academics are occasionally allergic to trying new things. But Dr. Peperzak's own commitment to discerning the authentic from the dull, and to "faithful creativity" in the praxis of philosophy, encouraged us to write, think, and respond to one another in our own ways throughout the months leading up to the symposium. As the written responses from former students came in, and then as the symposium itself finally got underway, it was truly delightful to see that so many of his students embodied that same orientation toward creative, authentic, and friendly dialogue (as this publication attests). In that context, if "*theoria*" includes also "dialogue," then I can almost grasp why Aristotle said that it was the most pleasurable activity.

NOT THE LAST WORD

CONCLUDING TOASTS
§

A Toast from Norman Wirzba to Adriaan Peperzak

It has been such a delight to be at this symposium with Adriaan and all of you, his former students. I've been thinking to myself how jealous I was of all of you: you actually got to have *classes* with Adriaan!* The benefit I had with Adriaan was that I got to have him tell me how my dissertation was wrong and ill conceived, and how I could make it a better dissertation. But you all got to sit at his feet, and listen to a mind so alive and so in love with beauty, and with truth, and with goodness. I was telling a young colleague here how fortunate she is to have had a teacher like Adriaan; to have a teacher with that kind of wisdom and that kind of patience, and a fundamental courtesy to listen is simply beautiful! I have been in teaching a long time, and there are not many teachers like you Adriaan, there are simply not. So let's raise a glass to you Adriaan.

Bless you sir for all of your work.

*Norman's was the first doctoral dissertation that Adriaan directed upon coming to Loyola University Maryland in 1995. He had completed all his PhD coursework before Peperzak arrived.

A Toast from Adriaan Peperzak to his Students

I am so grateful for all of you that you have all come, and that you have shown who you are by your remarks, and by your eyes, and by your faces and their expressions. I believe you when you say you are happy. And I hope this happiness will grow, and chase away all the unhappy experiences that you have had to go through, and still will have to go through. I am so proud of you! I almost cry: I'm so emotional, to see how you have grown into your own lives, and into your own teaching, and I have great hope for your pupils.

I think the greatest thing a philosopher can reach in this world is not to get good reviews: that is not so important (only when you are young is it important to make a career). But when you are old, you look about your writings and you say: "How did I dare to publish that? It is really not good enough! I would like to still publish a *better* version of that piece." But really, in those moments, that feeling is because you remain fond of those original things that inspired you. You want to return again to the inspiration that was there when you first made them.

Yesterday I talked about my first experience of the *Symposium* and of Diotima who was the prophetess who announced the lifelong love of wisdom. I am sure you have had similar experiences, and similar incentives to continue to unfold your inspirations. And so I hope for you that the inspiration never quits you, and that the inspiration is more important than the logic (which is necessary of course so they say). But I am sure that you will make it, for you are all such beautiful people, every one of you. I love you.

NOT THE LAST WORD
§

Catriona Hanley

There isn't one. Not here. *Logos,* the beginning, is enacted in all we humanly do. It guides us in our reaching for the infinite, in glimpsing signs of the mystery we call divinity. Through our conversations here we continued the human attempt to make the light visible. May we learn to listen to what is spoken. May we tread softly on the earth. May we meet again soon in thoughts and words.

Adriaan Peperzak

Isn't it wonderful that these messages can be *re-generated* in faithful but never identical modes of life and thought by anyone who knows how to transform them into new possibilities of promise and gratitude?!

CONTRIBUTORS

§

Adriaan Peperzak*: Professor Emeritus, Loyola University Chicago
Brent Adkins*: Professor of Philosophy, Roanoke College
Colin Anderson*: Associate Professor of Philosophy, Hiram College
Stacy Bautista: MidWest Workers Association, Chicago
Alberto Bertozzi: Assistant Professor of Philosophy, Loyola University Chicago
Greg Clark*: Professor of Philosophy, North Park University
Jean Clifford: Graduate Student (PhD), Loyola University Chicago
Karl Clifton-Soderstrom: Professor of Philosophy, North Park University
Jeff Courtright: Assistant Professor of Philosophy, Mississippi University for Women
Catriona Hanley*: Associate Professor, Loyola University Maryland; Director of Peace and Justice Studies (Loyola University Maryland)
Laurel Madison: Instructor, Saint Louis University
Ryan Madison*: Associate Director of the Notre Dame Center for Ethics and Culture; Instructor of Philosophy, Notre Dame University
Nicholas Mowad: Professor of Philosophy, Chandler-Gilbert Community College
Justin Nordin: Graduate Student (PhD), Loyola University Chicago
Marjolein Oele*: Associate Professor of Philosophy, University of San Francisco
Corinne Painter*: Professor of Philosophy, Washtenaw Community College
Aron Reppman*: Professor of Philosophy, Trinity Christian College
Rebecca Scott: Graduate Student (PhD), Loyola University Chicago
Kristi Sweet*: Associate Professor, Texas A&M University
Giancarlo Tarantino: Graduate Student (PhD), Loyola University Chicago
Norman Wirzba*: Professor of Theology, Ecology, and Agrarian Studies, Duke Divinity School

* *Indicates participation in both symposia.*

ADRIAAN PEPERZAK BIOGRAPHY
§

Adriaan Theodoor Peperzak was born in Malang (Java, Indonesia). He studied philosophy and theology in The Netherlands, continuing his philosophical studies in Louvain (Belgium), where he obtained his licentiate degree from the Higher Institute of Philosophy with a thesis on G.W.F. Hegel. He continued studies at the University of Paris (Sorbonne), and took his PhD, writing on the young Hegel, under the direction of Paul Ricoeur, with J. Wahl and J. Hyppolite as readers.

For much of his career, Peperzak taught at Nijmegen university, coming to the States only in 1991, when he was invited to take the special chair, the Arthur J. Schmitt chair in the department of philosophy at Loyola University Chicago.

Besides Dutch, Adriaan Peperzak speaks and writes English, French, German, Spanish, and Italian; he also reads Portuguese, as well as ancient Greek, Latin.

<u>*Dr. Peperzak's book publications include:*</u>

Le jeune Hegel et la vision morale du monde, deuxième édition corrigée et augmentée. La Haye: M. Nijhoff, 1969; XV + 264 pp.

Gronden en Grenzen; Wijsgerige en teologische overdenkingen. Haarlem: Gottmer, 1967; 273 pp. (*Grounds and Bounds*)

Der heutige Mensch und die Heilsfrage: eine philosophische Hinführung. Freiburg: Herder, 1972; 244 pp.

Vrijheid: Inleiding in de wijsgerige antropologie I. Bilthoven:

Ambo, 1972; 92 pp. (*Freedom: Introduction to a Philosophical Anthropology I*); 1973; 1975.

Weefsels. Een inleiding in het Filosoferen. Bilthoven: Ambo, 1974 (*Textures: an Introduction to Philosophical Thought*), 234 pp.

U en ik: Inleiding in de wijsgerige antropologie II. Bilthoven: Ambo, 1976; 104 pp. (*You and I: Introduction to a Philosophical Anthropology II*).

System and History in Philosophy. Albany: SUNY Press, 1986; 172 pp.

Philosophy and Politics. A Commentary on the Preface of Hegel's Philosophy of Right (International Archives of the History of Ideas n. 113). Dordrecht/Boston/Lancaster: M. Nijhoff, 1987; X + 144 pp.

Selbsterkenntnis des Absoluten. Grundlinien der Hegelschen Philosophie des Geistes (Spekulation und Erfahrung II, 6). Stuttgart: Frommann-Holzboog, 1987; 181 pp. (*Self-Knowledge of the Absolute*).

E. Levinas & A. Peperzak, *Etica come filosofia prima* (a cura di Fabio Ciaramelli). Milano: Guerini, 1989, 185 pp.

Zoeken naar zin. Kampen: Kok, 1990; 131 pp. (*Searching for Meaning*).

Hegels praktische Philosophie. Ein Kommentar zur enzyklopädischen Darstellung der menschlichen Freiheit und ihrer objektiven Verwirklichung (Spekulation und Erfahrung II 19). Stuttgart: Frommann-Holzboog, 1991; 372 pp. (*Hegel's Practical Philosophy*).

Tussen filosofie en theologie. Kampen: Kok, 1991; 192 pp. (*Between Philosophy and Theology*).

Filosofie als Wetenschap; Introduction, translation and commentary of G.W.F. Hegel *Encyclopedia* §§ 1-37. Kampen: Kok-Agora, 1991; 166 pp. (*Philosophy as Science*).

To The Other. An Introduction to the Philosophy of Emmanuel Levinas (Purdue Series in the History of Philosophy). West Lafayette: Purdue UP, January 1993; 247 pp.

Ethics as First Philosophy. The Significance of Emmanuel Levinas for Philosophy, Literature and Religion (ed. and with an introduction by Adriaan T. Peperzak). New York & London: Routledge, 1995; 251 pp.

Adriaan Peperzak, Simon Critchley, Robert Bernasconi (eds.), *Basic Philosophical Writings of Emmanuel Levinas*. Bloomington: Indiana University Press, 1996, sv + 201 pp.

Platonic Transformations. With and After Hegel, Heidegger, and Levinas. Lanham: Rowman and Littlefield, 1997, xiv + 265 pp.

Beyond. The Philosophy of Emmanuel Levinas. Evanston: Northwestern UP, 1997, xviii + 248 pp.

Before Ethics. Atlantic Highlands: Humanities Press, 1997/Amherst: Prometheus Press, 1998, 145 pp.

Reason in Faith: On the Relevance of Christian Spirituality for Philosophy. New York: Paulist Press, 1999, xi + 152 pp.

Modern Freedom: Hegel's Legal, Moral, and Political Philosophy. Dordrecht-Boston: Kluwer, 2001, xxvi + 675 pp.

Het Menselijk Gelaat. Essays van Emmanuel Levinas; new introduction, new translation, and new notes to essays of Emmanuel Levinas, Amsterdam: Ambo Anthos, 2003. (*The Human Face*).

The Quest for Meaning. Friends of Wisdom from Plato to Levinas. New York: Fordham University Press, 2003, x + 240 pp.

Elements of Ethics. Palo Alto: Stanford University Press, 2004, xiv + 283 pp.

Philosophy between Faith and Theology. Addresses to Catholic Intellectuals. Notre Dame: Notre Dame University Press, 2005, xiv + 216pp.

Thinking. From Solitude to Dialogue and Contemplation. New York: Fordham University Press, 2006, 178 pp.

Apprentice House Press
Loyola University Maryland

Apprentice House is the country's only campus-based, student-staffed book publishing company. Directed by professors and industry professionals, it is a nonprofit activity of the Communication Department at Loyola University Maryland.

Using state-of-the-art technology and an experiential learning model of education, Apprentice House publishes books in untraditional ways. This dual responsibility as publishers and educators creates an unprecedented collaborative environment among faculty and students, while teaching tomorrow's editors, designers, and marketers.

Outside of class, progress on book projects is carried forth by the AH Book Publishing Club, a co-curricular campus organization supported by Loyola University Maryland's Office of Student Activities.

Eclectic and provocative, Apprentice House titles intend to entertain as well as spark dialogue on a variety of topics. Financial contributions to sustain the press's work are welcomed. Contributions are tax deductible to the fullest extent allowed by the IRS.

To learn more about Apprentice House books or to obtain submission guidelines, please visit www.apprenticehouse.com.

Apprentice House
Communication Department
Loyola University Maryland
4501 N. Charles Street
Baltimore, MD 21210
Ph: 410-617-5265 • Fax: 410-617-2198
info@apprenticehouse.com • www.apprenticehouse.com

www.ingramcontent.com/pod-product-compliance
Lightning Source LLC
Chambersburg PA
CBHW021143160426
43194CB00007B/672